THE CAMBRIDGE BIBLE COMMENTARY

NEW ENGLISH BIBLE

GENERAL EDITORS

P. R. ACKROYD, A. R. C. LEANEY,
J. W. PACKER

2 SAMUEL

THE SECOND BOOK OF
SAMUEL

COMMENTARY BY

PETER R. ACKROYD

Samuel Davidson Professor of Old Testament Studies
University of London, King's College

CAMBRIDGE UNIVERSITY PRESS

CAMBRIDGE

LONDON · NEW YORK · MELBOURNE

Published by the Syndics of the Cambridge University Press
The Pitt Building, Trumpington Street, Cambridge CB2 1RP
Bentley House, 200 Euston Road, London NW1 2DB
32 East 57th Street, New York, NY 10022, USA
296 Beaconsfield Parade, Middle Park, Melbourne 3206, Australia

First published 1977

Printed in Great Britain at the
University Press, Cambridge

Library of Congress cataloguing in publication data
Bible.   O.T.   2 Samuel.   English.   New English.   1977.
The second book of Samuel.
(The Cambridge Bible commentary, New English Bible)
Bibliography: p.
Includes index.
1. Bible.   O.T.   2 Samuel–Commentaries.
I. Ackroyd, Peter R. II. Title. III. Series.

BS1325.3.A33   222'.44'06   76–58074
ISBN 0 521 08633 7 hard covers
ISBN 0 521 09754 1 paperback

GENERAL EDITORS' PREFACE

The aim of this series is to provide the text of the New English Bible closely linked to a commentary in which the results of modern scholarship are made available to the general reader. Teachers and young people have been especially kept in mind. The commentators have been asked to assume no specialized theological knowledge, and no knowledge of Greek and Hebrew. Bare references to other literature and multiple references to other parts of the Bible have been avoided. Actual quotations have been given as often as possible.

The completion of the New Testament part of the series in 1967 provided the basis upon which the production of the much larger Old Testament and Apocrypha series could be undertaken. With the publication of this volume and its companion (*Haggai, Zechariah, Malachi*) and the last two (*Genesis*; *1 and 2 Esdras*) in the near future, the whole series is complete. The welcome accorded to the series in its earlier stages was an encouragement to the editors to follow the same general pattern throughout, and an attempt has been made to take account of criticisms which have been offered. The Old Testament volumes have included the full footnotes provided by the translators, since these are essential for the understanding of the text.

Within the severe limits imposed by the size and scope of the series, each commentator has attempted to set out the main findings of recent biblical scholarship and to describe the historical background to the text.

The main theological issues have also been critically discussed.

Much attention has been given to the form of the volumes. The aim is to produce books each of which will be read consecutively from first to last page. The introductory material leads naturally into the text, which itself leads into the alternating sections of the commentary.

The series is accompanied by three volumes of a more general character. *Understanding the Old Testament* sets out to provide the larger historical and archaeological background, to say something about the life and thought of the people of the Old Testament, and to answer the question 'Why should we study the Old Testament?' *The Making of the Old Testament* is concerned with the formation of the books of the Old Testament and Apocrypha in the context of the ancient Near Eastern world, and with the ways in which these books have come down to us in the life of the Jewish and Christian communities. *Old Testament Illustrations* contains maps, diagrams and photographs with an explanatory text. These three volumes are designed to provide material helpful to the understanding of the individual books and their commentaries, but they are also prepared so as to be of use quite independently.

With the completion of this project, there are many whom the General Editors wish to thank. The contributors who have produced their manuscripts and cooperated willingly in revisions suggested to them must clearly be mentioned first. With them we thank the succession of members of the staff of the Cambridge University Press, but above all Mr Michael H. Black, now Publisher at the Press, who has joined so fully in the planning and development of the series and who has been present at all the editorial meetings from the initiation of the project to its conclusion.

P. R. A.
A. R. C. L.
J. W. P.

EDITOR'S PREFACE

The commentary in this volume forms a sequel to that already published on the First Book of Samuel; inevitably much of what is said here is only fully intelligible when it is seen in relation to what precedes in that book, and also to what follows in the First Book of Kings. At many points the reader will find it useful to refer to the fuller discussions of historical, literary and religious questions which may be found in larger books such as those listed at the end of this volume (p. 240) or conveniently in the general volumes noted on p. vi to accompany this series of commentaries.

The interval of six years which has elapsed between the appearance of the commentary on 1 Samuel and the present volume on 2 Samuel is much longer than was planned. I must plead the pressure of other work, not least that involved in the editorial work of the whole series.

I wish to express my thanks to those who have given me help in the preparation of the commentary, and especially to my colleagues as General Editors of the series, Professor Emeritus A. R. C. Leaney, and Canon J. W. Packer; to Miss Fiona Malcolm; and to the staff of the Cambridge University Press.

P. R. A.

CONTENTS

LIST OF MAPS AND PLAN

The maps and plan are only approximate and the precise identification of places is often uncertain

x

THE FOOTNOTES TO THE
N.E.B. TEXT

The footnotes to the N.E.B. text are designed to help the reader either to understand particular points of detail – the meaning of a name, the presence of a play upon words – or to give information about the actual text. Where the Hebrew text appears to be erroneous, or there is doubt about its precise meaning, it may be necessary to turn to manuscripts which offer a different wording, or to ancient translations of the text which may suggest a better reading, or to offer a new explanation based upon conjecture. In such cases, the footnotes supply very briefly an indication of the evidence, and whether the solution proposed is one that is regarded as possible or as probable. Various abbreviations are used in the footnotes:

(1) Some abbreviations are simply of terms used in explaining a point: *ch(s).*, chapter(s); *cp.*, compare; *lit.*, literally; *mng.*, meaning; *MS(S).*, manuscript(s), i.e. Hebrew manuscript(s), unless otherwise stated; *om.*, omit(s); *or*, indicating an alternative interpretation; *poss.*, possible; *prob.*, probable; *rdg.*, reading; *Vs(s).*, version(s).

(2) Other abbreviations indicate sources of information from which better interpretations or readings may be obtained.

Aq.   Aquila, a Greek translator of the Old Testament (perhaps about A.D. 130) characterized by great literalness.

Aram.   Aramaic – may refer to the text in this language (used in parts of Ezra and Daniel), or to the meaning of an Aramaic word. Aramaic belongs to the same language family as Hebrew, and is known from about 1000 B.C. over a wide area of the Middle East, including Palestine.

Heb.   Hebrew – may refer to the Hebrew text or may indicate the literal meaning of the Hebrew word.

Josephus   Flavius Josephus (A.D. 37/8–about 100), author of the *Jewish Antiquities*, a survey of the whole history of his people, directed partly at least to a non-Jewish audience, and of various other works, notably one on the *Jewish War* (that of A.D. 66–73) and a defence of Judaism (*Against Apion*).

Luc. Sept.   Lucian's recension of the Septuagint, an important edition made in Antioch in Syria about the end of the third century A.D.

Pesh.   Peshitta or Peshitto, the Syriac version of the Old Testament. Syriac is the name given chiefly to a form of Eastern Aramaic used by the Christian community. The translation varies in quality, and is at many points influenced by the Septuagint or the Targums.

Sam.   Samaritan Pentateuch – the form of the first five books of the Old Testament as used by the Samaritan community. It is written in Hebrew in a special form of the Old Hebrew script, and preserves an important form of the text, somewhat influenced by Samaritan ideas.

Scroll(s)   Scroll(s), commonly called the Dead Sea Scrolls, found at or near Qumran from 1947 onwards. These important manuscripts shed light on the state of the Hebrew text as it was developing in the last centuries B.C. and the first century A.D.

Sept.   Septuagint (meaning 'seventy'; often abbreviated as the Roman numeral LXX), the name given to the main Greek version of the Old Testament. According to tradition, the Pentateuch was translated in Egypt in the third century B.C. by 70 (or 72) translators, six from each tribe, but the precise nature of its origin and development is not fully known. It was intended to provide Greek-speaking Jews with a convenient translation. Subsequently it came to be much revered by the Christian community.

Symm.   Symmachus, another Greek translator of the Old Testament (beginning of the third century A.D.), who tried to combine literalness with good style. Both Lucian and Jerome viewed his version with favour.

Targ.   Targum, a name given to various Aramaic versions of the Old Testament, produced over a long period and eventually standardized, for the use of Aramaic-speaking Jews.

Theod.   Theodotion, the author of a revision of the Septuagint (probably second century A.D.), very dependent on the Hebrew text.

Vulg.   Vulgate, the most important Latin version of the Old Testament, produced by Jerome about A.D. 400, and the text most used throughout the Middle Ages in western Christianity.

[. . .]   In the text itself square brackets are used to indicate probably late additions to the Hebrew text.

(Fuller discussion of a number of these points may be found in *The Making of the Old Testament* in this series.)

THE SECOND BOOK OF
SAMUEL

✳ ✳ ✳ ✳ ✳ ✳ ✳ ✳ ✳ ✳ ✳ ✳ ✳

WHAT THE BOOK IS ABOUT

This book continues the story begun in the First Book of
Samuel, showing how, after the death of Saul, David came to
be king over all Israel. It recounts some of David's achievements as king and traces the process by which eventually
Solomon became David's successor. This theme forms the
subject of the opening of the First Book of Kings (1 Kings 1–2),
but the preparation for these events is found here. In the First
Book of Samuel, it is the figure of Samuel which dominates
the events; even after his death (1 Sam. 25: 1), he continues to
reveal God's will to Israel. Yet in fact Samuel recedes into the
background once David appears: the true king has now been
designated and Samuel's work is virtually complete. It was
nevertheless with a quite proper instinct that the two books
came to bear the name of Samuel, for thus it is made clear that
to the author the story the books tell reveals the working out
of a divine purpose, and Samuel fittingly represents the
declaring of that purpose.

The last chapters of the book (chapters 21–4) may be seen
as a kind of appendix to the main narratives.

THE DIVIDED 'BOOK' OF SAMUEL

In reality, the two books are one. At an early date the large
work was divided, and similar divisions have been made in
other Old Testament books. Thus, the 'book' of Kings has
been divided into two, and the writings of the author we
conveniently call 'the Chronicler' have been divided into four

– 1 and 2 Chronicles, Ezra and Nehemiah. So too the first four (or perhaps five) books of the Old Testament should be regarded as a continuous work divided into smaller, more convenient, units – Genesis, Exodus, etc. The divisions may have been made partly on the basis of length: the two books of Samuel are more or less the same length. But it is clear that considerations of content have also played a part, and the division at the death of Saul marks off the period of Samuel and Saul from that of David, established as king. The division of the commentary on these books into two volumes is dictated by the demands of space; but much that appears in this volume necessarily assumes that the First Book of Samuel has been read.

THE LARGER WORK TO WHICH THE BOOK OF SAMUEL BELONGS

The division of the 'book' of Samuel into two parts was not first made in the original Hebrew text, but in the later translation of it into Greek. Translations of Old Testament books were made for the use of Greek-speaking Jews, particularly in Egypt but also elsewhere in the Mediterranean area, from about the third century B.C. At that time, the conquests of Alexander the Great, which took place in the period 333–323 B.C., had resulted in the spread of Greek language and culture in the Near East, and Greek became the common language employed for diplomatic and commercial purposes over a very wide area. The Greek translation of the Old Testament is very important because it provides evidence of a sometimes rather different Hebrew text, and helps in our understanding of the way in which the books were handed down. It is often known as the Septuagint, 'the translation made by the Seventy', from a story told in a writing called the Letter of Aristeas. This tells how representatives of all the tribes of Israel (actually seventy-two rather than seventy, six from each tribe) translated the Law – the first five books of the Old Testament – in Alexandria. It is a legend, but no doubt contains some elements of history. The name Septuagint came to be used for the whole Greek translation; it is abbreviated in N.E.B. as Sept., but often by the Roman numeral LXX.

In the Septuagint, the two books of Samuel are divided, but they are called the first two books of Kingdoms (Reigns), and the two books of Kings which follow are called the third and fourth books of Kingdoms. These Greek names are very appropriate, and they also show clearly that the division between Samuel and Kings is artificial. The death of David, the central figure of 2 Samuel, is in fact described in the opening of 1 Kings, because it there paves the way for Solomon's reign and the building of the temple in Jerusalem. Originally all four books belong together. But we may go further. The book of Ruth, which in the English Bible stands between Judges and 1 Samuel, appears in a different place in the Hebrew Old Testament, in a group of five books known as the five 'Scrolls', the Megilloth; the others are the Song of Songs, Lamentations, Ecclesiastes and Esther. The division between 1 Samuel and Judges is artificial, and Judges is also closely linked with Joshua. We are really dealing with the parts of a much longer work which extends from Joshua to 2 Kings. In the Hebrew Bible these books are given a special title: the Former Prophets. This distinguishes them from a second group of books: the Latter Prophets. The names indicate the position of the books in the Old Testament; the first group is made up of what we often call the 'history books' (though not including Ruth, Chronicles, Ezra, Nehemiah, Esther); the second group has what we call the books of prophecy (Isaiah to Malachi, but omitting Lamentations and Daniel).

The book of Deuteronomy is also closely connected with this large work covering the period from the conquest of Canaan in about 1200 B.C. to the exile in Babylon in the sixth century B.C. So it is sometimes called the 'Deuteronomic History'; this is a modern title, indicating the nature and purpose of the work in its final form. To understand this, we must look a little more closely at how these books came into being.

HOW DID THE BOOK COME TO BE WRITTEN?

The answer to this question is complex. We know nothing directly concerning those who were responsible. The most we can hope to do is begin from the book as we have it and see what we may deduce about the time when it reached this form, the kind of concerns and interests of the final author(s), and then work back by careful examination of the contents of the book to see what lies behind it.

The first part of the discussion clearly turns on the probability that this book is part of the much larger work mentioned above, covering the whole period from the conquest to the exile. Since the last recorded event in 2 Kings is the release of the captive king of Judah, Jehoiachin, from prison, in 561 B.C., we may say that the final form of the work cannot be earlier than this. Whatever the earlier stages, the last author(s) were working when the northern and southern kingdoms of Israel and Judah had fallen, the one to Assyria in 722 B.C., the other to Babylon in 587 B.C. Part of the population was in exile in Babylonia, part in Palestine, and some scattered elsewhere, in the neighbouring lands, and in Egypt. We know very little indeed about their condition, but we can appreciate that at such a moment of depression and doubt about the future, the writing of a history from the conquest to the exile would be of considerable importance. It might help in answering two questions: What went wrong that the great hopes of the conquest and Davidic periods should come to nothing? How, if there is a time of restoration, can the people so organize their life that the future will be better? The whole work – Deuteronomy to 2 Kings – appears to be concerned with this, and answers the questions in terms of God's promise, his giving of the land of Canaan, his care for his people, and the disobedience of leaders and people to his demands, their turning away to other forms of worship, their failure to conform to certain standards of justice and right. It should not surprise us to find, in the Second Book of Samuel, some passages in which the emphasis rests on this final consideration of the meaning of judgement and the nature of hope.

But it is not likely that the book was first written at that late date. The later interpreters or editors made use of much already existing material, though it is not easy for us to discover now just what they had at their disposal. There are several possibilities. (1) We could suppose that the final authors made use of a great mass of early material, stories, poems, annals (that is, lists of officials, names and the like), and that they built this up into its present complex form. (2) There may have existed already one or more accounts of the period and they may have dovetailed these together, fitting them into a sequence in somewhat the way that in the second century A.D. a Christian named Tatian made up a Gospel harmony, using pieces of the four gospels to create a unified narrative. (3) We might picture the process more in terms of the gathering of stories around certain great figures of the past – stories associated with Samuel, others with Saul, with Jonathan, with David.

Probably we should not assume that any one such approach will solve all the problems; we are dealing with a work whose beginnings lie back in the eleventh to tenth centuries B.C. in the lives of Samuel, Saul and David; its final form was reached 400 to 500 years later, and the process is almost certainly much too complicated to be unravelled from the information available to us.

In the last century and more, the literary study of the books of the Old Testament has been actively pursued. Although there is no complete agreement about the answers to many of the questions which have to be asked, it is most often believed that in the books with which the Old Testament begins – Genesis to Numbers – two or perhaps three early accounts covering the first stages of the people's life have been woven together. Some scholars believe that these accounts can be traced also in Joshua, Judges and Samuel (perhaps even in Kings). Others would lay greater stress on the gathering of traditions around the heroes, and in the Second Book of Samuel these centre on David. It would be natural enough if in the period of David and Solomon, when the kingdom was at the height of its new-found prosperity and unity, an attempt should have been made to set out the story of how this had been achieved, to endeavour to trace the hand of God at work in the events and in the people involved in them. Other such accounts may have been developed later, within the life of both the northern kingdom of Israel and the southern kingdom of Judah. Eventually all this different material, or selections from it, has been welded together to form books something like those which we now have. But it is likely that the process was accompanied by much addition of other material, and revision of emphasis. For in the ancient world, where everything was done by hand, a rewriting of a book may well mark a re-presentation of its material, suited to a new situation, offering a new insight into men's thinking. If we read sensitively, we may detect some of these levels in the material, and gain a deeper understanding of how men lived and thought, not just in the period which is being described, but also when these stories were being retold and reinterpreted.

THE PURPOSE OF THE BOOK

Why are books written? Clearly the question may be differently answered for each book we consider and for each of the stages through which a book may have passed. For an ancient book, we may recognize the possibility that it was produced to offer an explanation – what led up to the rule of David and Solomon could be related by a professional scribe, working at the court, whose business was to record events from day to day and perhaps also to glorify the ruler under whom he worked. His interpretation of the story would be determined in part by this aim. A book may be written for the sheer joy of telling a story. But though this could be a factor in the preservation of many ancient traditions in Israel, the books which we have in the Old Testament must all be regarded as religious books in the sense that they offer an interpretation in religious terms of what they relate. This does not make them any the less artistic as stories.

If we ask what the purpose is of the Second Book of Samuel, then clearly we can give only a partial answer. Its purpose can only be fully understood when it is seen as part of the larger work to which it belongs. But within that larger purpose, we can see some of the particular interests which are developed. The author(s) set(s) out to tell us how David, designated as king and acknowledged as such already in stories in 1 Samuel, actually took over full control of both the southern and northern areas. The capture of Jerusalem, till then remaining in Jebusite hands, provided a political capital and a new and eventually great religious centre (chapter 5). Other stories indicate the extension of the power of David into surrounding areas. The theme of the Davidic dynasty is expounded (chapter 7), and stories of David and his sons enable us to see how Solomon is shown as the true successor to David. This introduces the story of the building of the Jerusalem temple which is a major theme in 1 Kings. The full centrality of that temple was to be established only in the seventh century under King Josiah (2 Kings 22–3), but as the new home of the Ark (2 Sam. 6) Jerusalem became a focal point of religious sentiment already in David's reign. Thus the story of the establishing of the true sanctuary is developed after Shiloh has ceased to be regarded as acceptable. The theme of the priesthood is also taken further. The survivor of the Eli line, Abiathar, is active under David, but was to suffer an eclipse at the accession of Solomon. It is the new and unexplained figure of Zadok who takes his place, and so the lasting priestly line at Jerusalem is established.

7

Kingship, holy place, priesthood – three themes which were eventually to be of fundamental importance in Old Testament thought – were linked together in 1 Samuel; here they become explicit in David, Jerusalem, and Zadok. The other great line of religious influence which is linked with Samuel is the prophetic movement; this too is developed in 2 Samuel. The figures of Nathan (chapters 7 and 12) and Gad (chapter 24) express the idea of a prophetic succession, standing alongside kings and priests, involved in events but critical of them. This movement was to flower in the eighth century B.C. into one of the richest movements the world has ever known, in the great figures of Amos and Hosea and Isaiah and in their successors over the centuries that followed. Such a flowering cannot be understood without a recognition of where the roots lie; this book provides us with some further indications of what prophecy was to be.

HISTORY AND INTERPRETATION

The book as we have it has a long history; we may detect in it some traces of how its content has been affected by the particular interpretations, the particular purposes, of those who were responsible for transmitting and shaping the material. How far does it represent what actually happened, and how clearly can we describe the people involved?

A little earlier the point was stressed that the books of the Old Testament as we have them are all religious books. So we may properly recognize at the outset that the authors at the various stages of the book's composition were not setting out to write history as a modern historian might attempt to do it. They are offering stories and traditions about the past of their own people, and offering them in such a way as to tell us what they believed that past experience to mean. They provide us with a great deal of important information. But where a modern historian offers his interpretation of the past, he is also concerned with sifting the information and assessing its historical value. If he has two accounts of the same event, or two estimates of the same person, he will show why he believes certain elements in these to be reliable, or more reliable, while other elements may be shown to be due to misunderstanding or propaganda or bias. The ancient writer is more likely to set down both accounts, side by side or in an interwoven form; or he may use only one account because it offers what fits best with his own understanding of the past.

An example will illustrate what can happen. For some parts of the books of Samuel we have a parallel account in 1 Chronicles. It is clear that the author of that much later work (probably in the fourth century B.C.) knew the material of the books of Samuel, though we cannot be sure whether he used the books more or less as we know them or whether he was working with a somewhat different 'edition'. We notice that in 1 Chronicles a great deal of what is in the books of Samuel does not appear. For example, 1 Chron. 19: 1–20: 3 uses the same story of David's war against the Ammonites as is found in 2 Sam. 10–12; but whereas in the earlier work there is woven into this story that of David's adultery with Bathsheba, the wife of Uriah the Hittite, in the later work this is entirely absent. In 2 Sam. 12 the stories are shown to lead to the birth of Solomon; for the Chronicler, the succession of Solomon, the designated temple-builder, needed no such explanation. In addition, all the narratives in 2 Sam. 9 and 13–20 are without parallel in 1 Chronicles, and we may observe that some of these too, like the story of Bathsheba, shed rather discreditable light on David whom the Chronicler idealizes to a much greater extent than does the author of 1 and 2 Samuel. Again, because of an even greater concern with the temple, the Chronicler (1 Chron. 21: 1–22: 1) takes the story of the census and plague and weaves it into the temple story; he believed that the temple was built on the threshing-floor bought from Araunah (1 Chronicles has Ornan) at the checking of the plague. In 2 Sam. 24 it is not linked with the remaining David stories, except with 2 Sam. 21: 1–14.

We do not have the same precise evidence when we try to get behind the narratives in the books of Samuel, for we do not possess an earlier form of these narratives with which we can make a comparison. But from the present form which they have, from the selection of events which they offer, from the pictures they present of the various great personages, we may readily recognize that here is an interpretation based on a particular handling of the material. One example may illustrate this. The section 2 Sam. 9–20 (together with 1 Kings 1–2) is often thought to be a single coherent narrative. It used to be called the 'Court narrative' because of its stories about the court of David; more recently it has been termed the 'Succession narrative', because of the way the moves towards Solomon's accession are presented. It has been thought to be early, nearly contemporary with the events it describes, and hence perhaps the earliest surviving 'historical' writing; while this is possible, the arguments are not conclusive; nor is it really clear that it ever formed a separate document. We may observe links back into the preceding chapters and note the presence of many different elements, now woven together with great skill. The story of David's kindness to a lame son of Jonathan is interwoven with that of Absalom's rebellion. That of David and Bathsheba is set in the context of the war against Ammon. A long section deals with the causes and outcome of Absalom's rebellion against his father. Other troubles of David's reign are briefly related. We may see that, diverse as they are, these stories are handled so as to be in some measure subordinate to a main theme: where is true kingship, and who is to be the true successor? The setting aside of any last claim for the house of Saul, and the gradual elimination of sons of David, paves the way for Solomon's succession. But behind the present ordering of the material, we may detect problems regarding the order of events, and it seems clear that we have both a selection of material and a skilful ordering of it. In chapters 21–4 there are some further passages associated with David, now only loosely attached to the main narratives. We have seen that the Chronicler built one of these into his account for a specific purpose; he also used some of the lists of heroes' names (in a more complete form) in a different manner. This illustrates the point that interpretation is more important than the mere telling of a story, exciting and significant though the various story elements are in themselves.

The evaluation of the actual people involved is also difficult. The central figure of David, as is clear also from the many stories in 1 Sam. 16–30, was too great to leave only one impression; he was a hero around whom later tradition was to gather. We may detect the various elements, but not write a straight biography. Of the many other characters who appear, we can do no more than try to understand their words and actions; we must set them in the context of the period in which they are described, and endeavour to depict that period on the basis of a careful sorting of the information provided by the biblical material and by such non-biblical sources as are available.

The non-biblical sources are, as so often, somewhat elusive. Some of them are described more fully in *The Making of the Old Testament*. We do not have any documents which mention by name any of the people known to us in 1 and 2 Samuel. We have some knowledge of the kings of Phoenicia, among whom must rank Hiram of Tyre who had close relations with David and Solomon, and established trade relationships with them (2 Sam. 5: 11; 1 Kings 5).

The Jewish historian Josephus, in his account of this period, makes use of the biblical material and of evidence from Phoenician records. These indicate a king of Tyre named Abibaal who was succeeded by Hiram. The name Hiram may be a shortened form of Ahiram (= 'my kinsman (i.e. my god) is exalted'). Fuller documentary evidence exists for the line of kings at Byblos, a very important coastal city; here we find a ruler named Ahiram in about 1000 B.C. whose name appears inscribed on a great stone sarcophagus, itself probably about 200 years older.

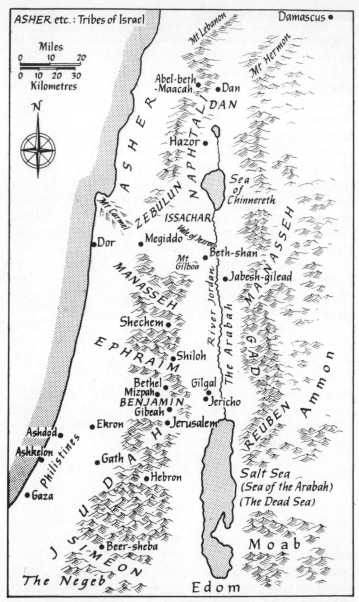

1. The land in the period covered by 2 Samuel (showing approximate areas of tribal settlement)

The general background to this period is one of weakness in Egypt and in the north-eastern and Mesopotamian areas; it was therefore a time during which Palestine was free of external pressures. Already by the time of Solomon, Egyptian pressure began to be felt again as Egypt gave support to opponents of Solomon, and after his death Shishak of Egypt marched through Palestine, claiming that the land was really his (cp. 1 Kings 14: 25f.). The route described in Shishak's own account of the march on an inscription at Karnak indicates that not only Judah – as the Old Testament account suggests – but also the northern kingdom of Israel was affected by Egyptian policy; more than fifty places in Israel are mentioned, including Beth-shan and Megiddo, and about one hundred in Judah. The dates of Shishak's reign, about 935–914 B.C., the dates given in 1 and 2 Kings (often problematic to interpret and correlate), and some other indications, enable us to place David's reign from about 1000 to 960 B.C. and Solomon's 960–922 B.C. But these dates are only very approximate.

If external pressures were less severe during David's reign, there were great internal difficulties and much of the narrative of 2 Samuel is concerned with these. The Philistine threat, drawn out so clearly in the fate of Saul, is overcome and the Philistines contained in the coastal area. Military successes were also achieved by David over other neighbouring areas, but at home there were divisions, rival claimants to the throne, and many uncertainties.

The general historical outline of the period is clear enough. We shall see some of the historical problems as we read through the book. But how far can we know the detail of the events? Here we have to weigh two opposing factors. On the one hand, we must give proper recognition to the fact that ancient traditions are likely to contain more of actual historical content than was once believed. Stories such as those told by Homer in the *Iliad* contain much more of accurate detail about the period of the Trojan wars than was at one time thought; archaeological discovery has made this clear. Ancient peoples clearly preserved much sound tradition about their own past. On the other hand, we have to recognize that such popular tradition, handed down over centuries, imparts its own twist to the material. It selects, it interprets, it transfers tales told about one area to another or from one person to another; stories gather around particularly notable personalities. These two points, the one more positive and the other more negative, have to be carefully balanced.

Even where the time lapse between events and written records is likely to be much shorter – as may be true of parts of the David story – we must recognize that selection and interpretation play an important part in producing what is only one way of describing what happened. This means that in the end we find greater interest in discussing how the story is interpreted than merely in trying to discover what happened. The two cannot be fully separated; but since we are studying a book which offers a religious interpretation of a period, we should be doing its authors less than justice if we did not take full account of what they thought the events meant.

Any attempt at writing a consecutive story of the period covered by this book comes up against the problems raised by the variety of its material. Here we have one interpretation of the way the different elements may be related; the Chronicler, as we have seen, provides an alternative selection and assessment. Josephus, the Jewish historian, in his *Antiquities* (v. 10. 1–vi. 14. 9) follows the Samuel order, but offers some dovetailing and reconciling of points of difference, utilizing also some material from the Chronicler's narrative. He omits the psalms in chapters 22 and 23, but includes a short statement on David's composing of psalms (cp. 23: 1 and the Qumran text quoted in the note on that verse) and making of musical instruments (perhaps based on Amos 6: 5). Later writers up to our own time, with greater or less skill, have made further attempts at ordering and explaining; it is proper that this should be done, but the tentative nature of the results must be kept in mind.

THE SECOND BOOK OF SAMUEL AS A
THEOLOGICAL WORK

By a theological work we mean one which sets out to tell us
something of what its author believes about God and about
the way in which he acts in relation to men. Men's ideas of
God do not stand still. We must therefore look at what is said
in the light of the way in which beliefs and practices in Israel's
religion changed over the years. We must ask: what did men
believe at the time about which we are reading? and further:
what did those who told the stories believe? In any period the
attempt at saying something about God is beset with difficulties, for what may be termed the 'otherness' of God makes
all our human language less than adequate. Those who come
after us will be critical of the ways in which we express
ourselves, and we are right to be critical of what has been said
in the past. But we may hope that those who read the theological books of our time will be fair and will try to understand what we were endeavouring to say. So, if we are to be
just to this biblical book, we must attempt to see what was
really being said, and even where we can see it to be quite
inadequate by later standards, we must see what truth it
contains. For the Christian reader of the Old Testament, there
is always the temptation to dismiss its ideas about God as out
of date, as inadequate in comparison with Christian thought
at its best. For the Jewish reader, for whom the Old Testament
is his Bible, the same difficulty is present; he is aware of the
differences of level within the Old Testament and aware too of
the ways in which the understanding of God has developed in
the course of later Jewish history. Martin Buber, the great
Jewish philosopher and theologian of this century, has
confessed his total inability to accept that God could have
commanded the murder of Agag by Samuel (1 Sam. 15:
10–33): 'I could never believe', he wrote, 'that that was a
message from God...it was Samuel who did not understand
God.' A similar comment might be made on the grim story

of Saul's descendants in 2 Sam. 21: 1–14. But we must still ask how far, even with such misunderstanding, there is true insight.

Whatever particular view we take, whether or not we accept a religious interpretation of life, we are still bound to ask questions about meaning. When we consider the world as we know it, we cannot help asking how it is to be understood, what purpose, if any, lies behind it. Whether we use theological language in trying to answer such questions, whether we express our understanding by speaking about God and his purpose or prefer to use philosophical terms of one kind or another, we still have to take seriously what men have said in the past, because it is from them that our ideas derive. The religious tradition which stems from the Bible has been and still is one of the most powerful factors in creating our present-day ways of thinking. A deeper insight into its meaning is part of our equipping ourselves for more adequate thinking and living today.

THE TEXT OF THE BOOK AND ITS INTERPRETATION

The Old Testament was originally written in Hebrew, with only some quite short sections, mainly in Ezra and Daniel, in Aramaic, another language of the Semitic group. Any ancient language presents problems of understanding, and this is particularly true of Hebrew for which we have only a rather limited amount of material. Furthermore – and this is true of all ancient texts which have been frequently copied – there are many points at which the text as we have it may have become corrupt as a result of mistakes made by the scribes. A letter may be misread – and the Hebrew alphabet is such that confusion of letters is rather easy; the manuscript may be accidentally damaged and the next copyist may quite sensibly try to write what he thinks ought to be there. Sometimes, quite understandably, a scribe may have altered the wording to avoid something which he felt to be theologically difficult

or perhaps offensive. An example of this is to be seen in
2 Sam. 12: 14. Here the N.E.B. rightly renders: 'you have
shown your contempt for the LORD', but adds a footnote to
point out that the Hebrew text has 'the enemies of the LORD'.
The words 'the enemies of' represent an addition by a pious
scribe who felt that the text was theologically undesirable.

Reference has already been made (p. 2) to the Greek
translation of the Hebrew text. There are other ancient translations too – into Aramaic and Syriac, both Semitic languages;
and into Latin. The great scholar Jerome in the late fourth
century A.D. produced a revised Latin version which came to
be known as the Vulgate, that is the 'common', or generally
accepted, translation. This was used throughout the Middle
Ages and has been particularly revered in the Roman Catholic
community. In various ways these translations help us, not
only to understand the Hebrew text, but also to see that
different forms of the text were once in existence.

All the great Hebrew manuscripts are rather late, from about
the ninth century A.D. onwards. But in 1947 and the years that
followed, discoveries of manuscripts and fragments were made
in the region near the Dead Sea. These are often called the
'Dead Sea Scrolls', or, from the name of the centre of the
community from which many of them stemmed, the 'Qumran
Scrolls'. Some of these are very old indeed, perhaps of the
third century B.C., and certainly of the last two centuries B.C.
and the first century A.D. Some important small fragments of
the books of Samuel were discovered among them. These
reveal a form of text which at some points is closer to the
Septuagint, the Greek translation, though at other points the
text is different from both the standard Hebrew text and the
Greek. Some of these points appear in footnotes to the N.E.B.
text. (A note on the abbreviations used in these footnotes
appears on pp. xi–xii.) Since at certain points the differences
affect our understanding of the text, we shall have to comment
on them. But it is important to realize that though some of the
differences are just points where one text or another clearly

has a form due to a mistake in copying, most of them show different ways in which the material could be understood. If we want to get a full picture of the way in which the material of the books was understood, then we must take account of even quite small differences which lift a curtain on some point in the handing down and interpreting of it. The study of the text, a highly technical aspect of biblical study, is not to be separated from the study of its interpretation. The modern commentator builds upon the work of his predecessors, and among them are those who, in the biblical period itself and after, were responsible for copying and presenting the text.

✳　✳　✳　✳　✳　✳　✳　✳　✳　✳　✳　✳　✳

David's rule at Hebron

THE NEWS OF SAUL'S DEATH

1 WHEN DAVID RETURNED from his victory over
2 the Amalekites, he spent two days in Ziklag. And on the third day after Saul's death a man came from the army with his clothes rent and dust on his head. When he came into David's presence he fell to the ground in
3 obeisance, and David asked him where he had come from. He answered, 'I have escaped from the army of Israel.'
4 And David said to him, 'What news? Tell me.' 'The army has been driven from the field,' he answered, 'and many have fallen in battle. Saul and Jonathan his son are
5 dead.' David said to the young man who brought the news, 'How do you know that Saul and Jonathan are
6 dead?' The man answered, 'It so happened that I was on Mount Gilboa and saw Saul leaning on his spear with the
7 chariots and horsemen closing in upon him. He turned

18

round and, seeing me, called to me. I said, "What is it,
sir?" He asked who I was, and I said, "An Amalekite." 8
Then he said to me, "Come and stand over me and dis- 9
patch me. I still live, but the throes of death have seized
me." So I stood over him and gave him the death-blow; 10
for I knew that, broken as he was, he could not live. Then
I took the crown from his head and the armlet from his
arm, and I have brought them here to you, sir.' At that 11
David caught at his clothes and rent them, and so did all
the men with him. They beat their breasts and wept, 12
because Saul and Jonathan his son and the people of the
LORD, the house of Israel, had fallen in battle; and they
fasted till evening. David said to the young man who 13
brought the news, 'Where do you come from?', and he
answered, 'I am the son of an alien, an Amalekite.'
'How is it', said David, 'that you were not afraid to 14
raise your hand to slay the LORD's anointed?' And he 15
summoned one of his own young men and ordered
him to fall upon the man. So the young man struck him
down and killed him; and David said, 'Your blood be 16
on your own head; for out of your own mouth you
condemned yourself when you said, "I killed the LORD's
anointed."'

* The preceding chapter, 1 Sam. 31, relates how Saul and his
sons fell in battle at Mount Gilboa (see map, p. 12). The present
narrative provides a different view of that event, concentrating
on the theme of Saul's death and also laying emphasis on that
of Jonathan which is not singled out in 1 Sam. 31: 2. This
provides a preface for the lament over Saul and Jonathan in
1: 17–27.

There are significant differences in detail between the two

accounts. In 1 Sam. 31, Saul's armour-bearer is called upon to kill him; his unwillingness and hence Saul's suicide are stressed. Here an Amalekite is willing to carry out Saul's last wish. Saul's battle against the Amalekites in 1 Sam. 15 is depicted as a major moment of his failure as king, so there is poetic justice in his meeting his death at the hands of an Amalekite. The compiler here uses an alternative tradition, no doubt because he sees it as an apt pointer to divine judgement on Saul.

1. The N.E.B. has transferred the reference to Saul's death to verse 2. The text actually begins: 'Now after Saul's death ...' This is the dividing line between the period of David as the designated king and David acknowledged openly, in due course by all Israel. *victory over the Amalekites:* the story is told in 1 Sam. 30, and both that story and the reminder here may be seen as pointing to David's proper defeat of a people which became a symbol of those opposed to God's will (cp. Exod. 17: 16 'the LORD is at war with Amalek generation after generation'). David's victory may be contrasted with Saul's in view of the latter's disobedience (1 Sam. 15). *Ziklag:* the city, known as a Judaean royal possession, from which David operated his raids (cp. 1 Sam. 27: 6; map, p. 29).

2. *his clothes rent and dust on his head:* signs of mourning and distress at the disaster to Israel (cp. verse 11). *obeisance:* simply showing respect or actually acknowledging David's kingship.

4. *'The army has been driven from the field':* the text is perhaps not quite complete and appears to mean rather 'the people fled from the battle'. *Saul and Jonathan...are dead:* this is the crucial statement, even more stressed in the Hebrew: 'even Saul and Jonathan...' The narrator's skill is seen in the way in which we are gradually led into the heart of the matter. A similar skill is shown in the comparable narrative of 1 Sam. 4: 12–17.

5. *'How do you know...?'* It is a common device of Hebrew narrative style for a question to lead the responder into committing himself to a statement which will bring judgement

upon him. A significant example is in chapter 12 where David
unwittingly judges himself for Uriah's death.

6. *It so happened:* the chances of battle brought him near to
Saul, but what appears as chance may be viewed also as the
result of the divine will to bring judgement upon Saul.
chariots and horsemen: in 1 Sam. 31: 3 Saul is hard pressed by
archers.

8. *"An Amalekite":* the narrator underlines the point
already made. Saul will accept the inevitability of judgement
at the hands of such an appropriate instrument of divine
action.

9. *I still live...:* the meaning is not entirely clear, and the
word rendered *throes of death* only occurs here. It might mean
'dizziness' or 'terror'. Perhaps we should understand Saul's
words as meaning: 'Though I am still in fact fully alive, I
know myself already in the realm of death'; he belongs
already in the alien realm of Sheol, the abode of the shadowy
dead (cp. on 1 Sam. 28: 8).

10. *broken as he was:* a free rendering of a phrase which
means literally 'after he had fallen', possibly a gloss to har-
monize this account with 1 Sam. 31: 4 ('he...fell on it', i.e.
his sword). *the crown...the armlet:* evidently symbols of royal
status, brought to David as a sign that the kingdom now
passes to him. The word for crown (*nēzer*) indicates consecra-
tion, being used also for the symbol on the high priest's
turban (Exod. 29: 6).

11f. The actions performed by David and his followers are
signs of mourning and distress (cp. verse 2). *beat their breasts:*
the word so rendered may denote wailing or some other
indication of distress. In a small number of instances, the
N.E.B. renders as here, assuming that it is this particular
action which is meant. Certainly it is proper to recognize the
unrestrained response of the ancient Israelite to death and
disaster. For a comparable description, cp. the wailing at the
child's death in Mark 5: 38. *the people of the LORD:* the text
underlines the nature of the disaster by this description of the

dead as belonging to God's own chosen people. The Septuagint has an alternative 'Judah' for *the LORD*; this would
describe the people as belonging to the two communities of
Judah and Israel, but it is perhaps more likely that the second
phrase 'even *the house of Israel*' is an addition.

The response of David to Saul's death and to the disaster to
Israel must be seen first as a proper reaction to death and
disaster; it is also of a piece with David's attitude to Saul which
is made even plainer in verses 13–16. That David was to gain
by Saul's death is for the moment irrelevant.

13. Again we may note a characteristic of Hebrew narrative style. The previous verse has indicated what went on all
day. Now we move back to the original scene and hear its
immediate sequel. *son of an alien, an Amalekite:* again his origin
is stressed, but with a significant addition. *alien* (Hebrew *gēr*)
is a technical term for one who, though a foreigner, has taken
up residence in the Israelite community and has therefore
acquired certain rights to protection. The point is brought out
in Exod. 12: 43–9 in the rules for the Passover: a foreigner as
such is excluded, but an alien 'living with you' (*gēr*) is to take
part, alien and native-born being treated alike. This makes the
killing of Saul even more an act of impiety.

14. *the LORD's anointed:* David reveres Saul as divinely
chosen, as is made clear in the narratives of his sparing Saul's
life in 1 Sam. 24 and 26. David will not act so as to anticipate
even what he knows to be God's will for him. The same spirit
of acceptance appears clearly in other incidents in this book
(cp. e.g. on Absalom's rebellion, and especially 15: 25f.).

16. *you condemned yourself:* literally 'your own mouth
answered you' or 'testified against you'. This is law-court
language. The Amalekite has declared his own guilt as if in a
legal case. Even Saul's request to him to kill him could not
excuse his impious action (cp. the attitude of the armour-
bearer in 1 Sam. 31: 4). *

LAMENT FOR SAUL AND JONATHAN

David made this lament over Saul and Jonathan his 17
son; and he ordered that this dirge over them should be 18
taught to the people of Judah. It was written down and
may be found in the Book of Jashar:[a]

O prince[b] of Israel, laid low[c] in death! 19
  How are the men of war fallen!

Tell it not in Gath, 20
proclaim it not in the streets of Ashkelon,
  lest the Philistine women rejoice,
  lest the daughters of the uncircumcised exult.

Hills of Gilboa, let no dew or rain fall on you, 21
  no showers on the uplands![d]
For there the shields of the warriors lie tarnished,
  and the shield of Saul, no longer bright with oil.
The bow of Jonathan never held back 22
from the breast of the foeman, from the blood of the slain;
the sword of Saul never returned
  empty to the scabbard.

Delightful and dearly loved were Saul and Jonathan; 23
  in life, in death, they were not parted.
They were swifter than eagles,
  stronger than lions.

Weep for Saul, O daughters of Israel! 24

[a] *Or* the Book of the Upright.
[b] *Lit.* gazelle.
[c] *Lit.* on your back.
[d] showers on the uplands: *prob. rdg.; Heb.* fields of offerings.

who clothed you in scarlet and rich embroideries,
who spangled your dress with jewels of gold.

25 How are the men of war fallen, fallen on the field!
O Jonathan, laid low[a] in death!

26 I grieve for you, Jonathan my brother;
dear and delightful you were to me;
your love for me was wonderful,
surpassing the love of women.

27 Fallen, fallen are the men of war;
and their armour left on the field.

✶ A great moment in Israel's history is marked by a commemorative poem. This clearly takes a positive view of
the greatness of Saul whose heroism appears in a number
of narratives in 1 Samuel, though it is there obscured by
the emphasis on David. Equally the heroism of Jonathan,
described especially in 1 Sam. 14, is made plain. Thus we get a
fuller insight into a moment of Israel's development and a
better estimate of the achievements of Saul than the main narratives provide.

The poem is a superb work of art, its structure skilfully
developed. In this it may be compared with the Song of
Deborah in Judg. 5; it is quite unlike the short lament on
Abner in 3: 33f. The text (verse 17) implies that it was com-
posed by David himself as do the personal references of verse
26. Similar ascriptions of authorship are made in other instances, e.g. in chapters 22 and 23: 1–7. But it is equally
possible that it is a poem celebrating the event and pointing to
the meaning of this calamity and its relationship to the accession of David.

17. *lament:* or 'dirge' as in Amos 5: 1 where a lament is
sung by the prophet at the downfall of 'virgin Israel'. It is a

[a] *Lit.* on your back.

formal utterance, expressive of distress and grief. The collection of poems in the book of Lamentations applies the form to the downfall of Jerusalem.

18. This is a very obscure verse. It begins with the words 'and he said' which should lead immediately into verse 19. There appear then to be two parenthetic notes. The second is clear: *It was written down . . . in the Book of Jashar.* A similar note appears at Josh. 10: 13 with reference to a short poem, and the Septuagint has a similar note to the poem at 1 Kings 8: 12f. *Jashar*, rendered in the N.E.B. footnote as 'Upright', may be seen as a title of God or as a title of Israel: a similar title 'Jeshurun' is used in Deut. 32: 15 where it parallels the name Jacob. The collection would thus be of poems concerned with Israel's life or with God's actions for Israel. The first note is obscure. *this dirge over them:* the Hebrew text has a single word 'bow', and the N.E.B. rendering is based on an ingenious but unprovable supposition. It is that the heading, literally 'dirge – on the two of them – this', was abbreviated by the initial letters (*q-sh-h*) of the three words of that heading to give the letters of the word for 'bow'. Ingenious as this is, it would seem much more probable that the word 'bow' is accidentally misplaced, and belongs in verse 22. We should then read: *he ordered that* (it) *should be taught . . .*

19. *O prince:* a very small alteration could give 'Alas for . . .', well paralleled in *How . . .* The rendering *prince*, rather than the literal 'beauty', brings out the sense and is a better parallel to *men of war* or 'heroes'. The word can also mean 'gazelle' (see N.E.B. footnote), appropriate to the hills of the next phrase (cp. below). Since Hebrew poetry depends much on the parallelism of its units of verse, we may often detect meanings and structure by seeing the relationship between one clause and another. *laid low in death:* the N.E.B. footnote's literal rendering 'on your back' is quite possible; but the term used often means 'high places', and it seems not improbable that the text here is intended to refer to the heights upon which the disastrous battle occurred. The opening of the

lament is an utterance of the distress felt at what has happened.

20. The poet skilfully moves the scene to suggest the Philistine reaction to Saul's death; a prose equivalent to this may be observed in the narrative of 1 Sam. 31: 9 which tells of the 'good news' being taken to the Philistine land; the same word is used, here rendered *proclaim*, but better 'do not tell the good news'. As often in the Old Testament, *Philistine* and *uncircumcised* are used as equivalent terms; they stand for the alien outside world, and hence the term Philistine has come to be used of those hostile to what is good and beautiful. *Gath* and *Ashkelon*, two of the Philistine cities, here stand for all Philistia (see map, p. 29).

21. Again the scene shifts, and the battlefield at Gilboa is to respond to the disaster. The prophets often express divine judgement in terms of withdrawal of *dew* and *rain* (e.g. in Hag. 1: 10); thus the land itself is to mourn the loss of the heroes. *no showers on the uplands:* a very obscure phrase. Analogies in Canaanite texts suggest 'upsurgings of the deep' (cp. the Revised Standard Version), i.e. the waters under the earth are not to flow out, to bring fertility. Other possible meanings are 'fields of the heights' or 'O treacherous fields', both neat parallels to the first line of the verse. *tarnished:* may be understood literally, parallel to the picture of Saul's shield no longer polished; but the word also means 'defiled', and both phrases may suggest the defilement of alien contact and of death. *no longer bright with oil:* or, more literally, 'not anointed with oil', i.e. either 'not ritually prepared for battle' or 'now with no anointing', God's favour being withdrawn (cp. 1 Sam. 28). Again we may observe that the narrative of 1 Sam. 31: 10 depicts Saul's armour as put into the temple of the goddess Ashtoreth, dedicated to the glory of a deity particularly abhorrent to Israel.

22. The armour theme of verse 21*b* leads us into the heroism of Saul and Jonathan. The N.E.B. has rearranged the lines of this verse and has thus obscured the true poetic structure which is beautifully balanced:

> 'from the blood of the slain,
> > from the fat of the foeman,
> > the bow of Jonathan never held back,
> > > the sword of Saul did not return empty.'

The N.E.B. *breast* is a simple paraphrase of the literal 'fat', i.e. flesh.

23. Heroism, brought out in verse 22, is further expressed here, with a deep expression of loyalty and affection, and a vivid comparison with *eagles* and *lions. in life, in death:* a poetic way of saying 'perpetually'.

24. The summons to lament provides a balancing theme to the prohibition of Philistine rejoicing in verse 20. The theme of spoils of war brought back to the women is used in an ironical manner in Judg. 5: 28–30, where the mother of Sisera and her attendant princesses wait for the spoils to be brought on his return – ironical, because we, the readers, know that Sisera is dead. *rich embroideries:* not certain. A small change would give 'in linen'.

25. *How are the men of war fallen:* there is no regular refrain in this poem, though such refrains are known in Hebrew poetry (cp. Pss. 42–43 and 107 for good examples); but there is an echoing use of words. Here, and again in verse 27, these words are picked up from verse 19, but extended here by a further idea: *fallen on the field,* a free rendering of words meaning 'in the midst of battle'. The following line too echoes the first part of verse 19 (see note there on the rendering), though an attractive emendation would give 'at your (Jonathan's) death I am broken-hearted'.

26. *I grieve:* the same expression in 24: 14 is rendered 'I am in a desperate plight'. It is a common phrase in psalms of lament (cp. note on 24: 14). The love of Jonathan for David is an important theme in 1 Samuel, and it will be picked up again in David's concern for his family in chapter 9. Cp. especially 1 Sam. 18: 1–4, and the narratives of chapters 19 and 20. In these narratives, and especially in 1 Sam. 23: 17, this theme is

brought into relation with the recognition of David as the true successor. This point is not made here, but we may observe how skilfully the poem, as now placed, provides also a preface to the establishment of David's kingship in 2: 1–4*a*.

27. The final note of the lament echoes its opening and the theme of verse 21*b*; the latter half of the verse reads literally: 'and the equipment of war is lost'. ✵

DAVID, KING IN HEBRON

2 After this David inquired of the LORD, 'Shall I go up into one of the cities of Judah?' The LORD answered, 'Go.' David asked, 'To which city?', and the answer
2 came, 'To Hebron.' So David went to Hebron with his two wives, Ahinoam of Jezreel and Abigail widow of
3 Nabal of Carmel. David also brought the men who had joined him, with their families, and they settled in the
4*a* city*a* of Hebron. The men of Judah came, and there they anointed David king over the house of Judah.

✵ The first stage of David's assumption of the kingship is at the ancient centre of Hebron in Judah. That it remained a focal point may be seen from its place in the rebellion of Absalom (15: 7–12). David is now recognized as king of Judah.

1. *After this:* a loose link phrase. No dating is given. *David inquired of the LORD:* the technique is more fully set out in the narrative of 1 Sam. 23: 1–13. In all probability, only answers 'yes' and 'no' were given by the particular mechanism, perhaps Urim and Thummim, of which the nature and meaning are not known; they were apparently objects put in the ephod worn by the priest (cp. on 1 Sam. 14: 18). David's first question gets a positive answer 'Go'. The second is probably abbreviated; David would ask 'Shall I go up to Hebron?'

[*a*] *Prob. rdg.; Heb.* cities.

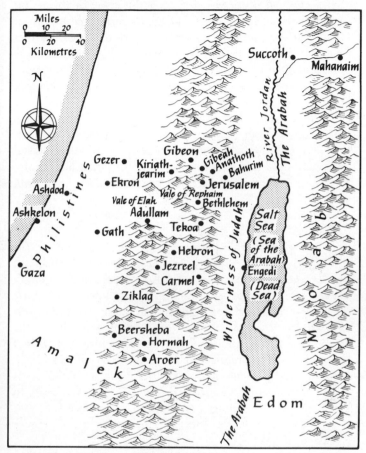

2. David at Hebron and Jerusalem (2 Sam. 2–5) and events during
Absalom's rebellion (2 Sam. 13–19)

Hebron was an obvious choice (cp. map above); it had been a
significant royal city (cp. Josh. 10: 3), conquered by Caleb
(Josh. 15: 13). It is connected with Abraham in Genesis (e.g.
13: 18), and still today revered as the traditional burial-place
of Sarah (Gen. 23) and Abraham (Gen. 25: 9f.).

2. *his two wives:* the story of Abigail is given in 1 Sam. 25; she had been the wife of Nabal, an important personage of Carmel in the south. Ahinoam came from Jezreel, another important place in the south (cp. map, p. 29). These marriages represented useful alliances for David in the southern area.

3. *they settled in the city of Hebron:* as the N.E.B. footnote indicates, the text has the plural 'cities'. According to Judg. 1: 10, Hebron had formerly been called Kiriath-arba, which means 'city of four (quarters)'; the plural may indicate the four divisions of the one city (as there were also 'quarters' in Jerusalem; cp. e.g. 2 Kings 22: 14). Or the plural might refer to smaller townships dependent on Hebron (cp. e.g. Josh. 15: 45).

4a. *they anointed David:* for such anointing, cp. that of Saul by Samuel in 1 Sam. 10: 1. The N.E.B. rendering may be right in suggesting that the anointing was carried out by *The men of Judah,* i.e. the leading men from the whole area. But the text could equally mean: 'he was anointed', literally 'they', those whose proper function it was, whether prophets or priests, 'anointed him'. Such anointing with oil was evidently understood as a sign of divine favour; hence the king is 'the LORD's anointed' (cp. 1: 14), a term which was later to be used technically for a future chosen ruler (Messiah, Hebrew *māshīaḥ,* anointed one, translated into Greek as *christos,* the Christ, the anointed one). The story appears to know nothing of Samuel's anointing of David (1 Sam. 16: 1–13); the later Chronicler supplies the cross-reference (1 Chron. 11: 3). ✶

THE DEVOTION OF THE MEN OF JABESH-GILEAD

4b Word came to David that the men of Jabesh-gilead
5 had buried Saul, and he sent them this message: 'The
  LORD bless you because you kept faith with Saul your
6 lord and buried him. For this may the LORD keep faith

and truth with you, and I for my part will show you favour too, because you have done this. Be strong, be 7 valiant, now that Saul your lord is dead, and the people of Judah have anointed me to be king over them.'

* A theme from Saul's reign is used to point forward to David's wider acceptance as king.

4*b*. The information given here is related more fully in 1 Sam. 31: 11–13. The background to this action by the men of Jabesh-Gilead is to be found in 1 Sam. 11: 1–11 which tells how Saul was inspired to rescue the besieged population of this city (map, p. 12). Proper burial was regarded as a matter of great importance; the fate of not being buried is a common prophetic judgement theme (cp. e.g. Jer. 8: 2). It would appear from the description of the fate of the dead ruler described in Isa. 14 that the ancient Israelites believed that the unburied could not share in the proper state of the dead (cp. especially verses 18–20).

5. *you kept faith:* loyalty (Hebrew *ḥesed*), an important concept both in human relationships and between man and God. As verse 6 makes plain, the blessing of God will be expressed in such loyalty on his part.

6f. *I...will show you favour too:* David promises special kindness, the promotion of well-being, to the men of Jabesh-Gilead. They are invited to continue to show military valour and to recognize that the loyalty they have shown to Saul who is now dead may appropriately be transferred to David, *anointed...king* over Judah. The real point of David's message is unspoken; it may be inferred from what has been said. This is a common characteristic of Hebrew speech; the perceptive hearer can pick up what is meant. A good example is the conversation between Abraham and the Hittites at Hebron in Gen. 23. *

THE TWO KINGDOMS UNDER ISHBOSHETH AND DAVID

8 Meanwhile Saul's commander-in-chief, Abner son of Ner, had taken Saul's son Ishbosheth,[a] brought him
9 across the Jordan to Mahanaim, and made him king over Gilead, the Asherites, Jezreel, Ephraim, and Ben-
10 jamin, and all Israel. Ishbosheth was forty years old when he became king over Israel, and he reigned two years.
11 The tribe of Judah, however, followed David. David's rule over Judah in Hebron lasted seven years and a half.

✲ These verses set the scene for the conflict narratives which follow to the end of chapter 4 and to which 5: 1–5 marks both the climax and the link to David's rule in Jerusalem. It becomes evident that there was considerable influence remaining in the Saul family.

8. *Abner son of Ner:* described as *Saul's commander-in-chief.* It is natural to find the military leader taking the initiative in setting up a surviving son of Saul as king in his place, and it becomes evident that Abner really holds the power. *Ishbosheth:* not a real name at all but an artificial construction in which the second part *bōsheth* is the Hebrew word for 'a shameful thing'. As the N.E.B. footnote shows, this son is differently named elsewhere. 'Eshbaal' in 1 Chron. 8: 33 represents a more original form in which the word *ba'al* (husband or lord) is used as a divine title. Its use for the Canaanite deity, Hadad, resulted in its coming to be regarded as an improper title for Israel's God (cp. the change of title demanded in Hos. 2: 16). Eshbaal signifies 'Baal (God) is'; Ishbosheth would mean 'man of shame'. The other alternative 'Ishyo' (1 Sam. 14: 49) means 'man of God (Yahweh)', using a short form of the

[a] Ishyo *in 1 Sam. 14: 49;* Eshbaal *in 1 Chron. 8: 33.*

divine name, common in proper names (cp. Jonathan).
Mahanaim: see map, p. 29. The fact that this centre is east of
Jordan suggests that Philistine pressure was strong (cp. 1 Sam.
31: 7).

9. The area claimed for Ishbosheth is large; his actual control may well have been less, especially if Philistine pressure
was strong. The claim serves to point forward to the transfer
of allegiance of *all Israel* to David. For *Asherites* the text has
'Ashurites' (cp. Gen. 25: 3), probably an error: possibly
'Geshurites' (in Transjordan; cp. Josh. 12: 5).

10*a*. The chronology is uncertain; 1 Sam. 13: 1f. has no
sure information about Saul. *forty years old* looks suspiciously
like a conventional figure, and the *two years* of rule hardly fits
with 3: 1 (but cp. note on that verse).

10*b*–11. The reiteration of David's *rule over Judah* emphasizes the conflict. The period of that rule may have been added
here from 5: 5. *

WAR BETWEEN THE TWO KINGDOMS

Abner son of Ner, with the troops of Saul's son Ish- 12
bosheth, marched out from Mahanaim to Gibeon, and 13
Joab son of Zeruiah marched out with David's troops
from Hebron.[a] They met at the pool of Gibeon and took
up their positions one on one side of the pool and the
other on the other side. Abner said to Joab, 'Let the 14
young men come forward and join in single combat
before us.' Joab answered, 'Yes, let them.' So they came 15
up, one by one, and took their places, twelve for Benjamin and for Ishbosheth and twelve from David's men.
Each man seized his opponent by the head and thrust his 16
sword into his side; and thus they fell together. That is

[a] from Hebron: *so Sept.; Heb. om.*

why that place, which lies in Gibeon, was called the Field of Blades.

17 There ensued a fierce battle that day, and Abner and the
18 men of Israel were defeated by David's troops. All three sons of Zeruiah were there, Joab, Abishai and Asahel.
19 Asahel, who was swift as a gazelle on the plains, ran straight after Abner, swerving neither to right nor left in
20 his pursuit. Abner turned and asked, 'Is it you, Asahel?'
21 Asahel answered, 'It is.' Abner said, 'Turn aside to right or left, tackle one of the young men and win his belt for yourself.' But Asahel would not abandon the pursuit.
22 Abner again urged him to give it up. 'Why should I kill you?' he said. 'How could I look Joab your brother
23 in the face?' When he still refused to turn aside, Abner struck him in the belly with a back-thrust of his spear*a* so that the spear came out behind him, and he fell dead in his tracks. All who came to the place where Asahel lay
24 dead stopped there. But Joab and Abishai kept up the pursuit of Abner, until, at sunset, they reached the hill of Ammah, opposite Giah on the road leading to the pastures of Gibeon.

25 The Benjamites rallied to Abner and, forming themselves into a single company, took up their stand on the
26 top of the hill of Ammah.*b* Abner called to Joab, 'Must the slaughter go on for ever? Can you not see that it will be all the more bitter in the end? Will you never recall
27 the people from the pursuit of their kinsmen?' Joab answered, 'As God lives, if you had not spoken, the people would not have given up the pursuit till morn-

[*a*] a back-thrust of his spear: *prob. rdg.; Heb. obscure.*
[*b*] the hill of Ammah: *prob. rdg., cp. verse 24; Heb.* a single hill.

ing.' Then Joab sounded the trumpet, and all the people 28
abandoned the pursuit of the men of Israel and the fighting ceased. Abner and his men moved along the Arabah 29
all that night, crossed the Jordan and went on all the
morning till they reached Mahanaim. When Joab re- 30
turned from the pursuit of Abner, he assembled his troops
and found that, besides Ashahel, nineteen of David's
men were missing. David's forces had routed the Ben- 31
jamites and the followers of Abner, killing three hundred
and sixty of them. They took up Asahel and buried him 32
in his father's tomb at Bethlehem. Joab and his men
marched all night, and as day broke they reached Hebron.

The war between the houses of Saul and David was long **3**
drawn out, David growing steadily stronger while the
house of Saul became weaker and weaker.

✳ The first stage in the relationship between the two kingdoms is described in terms of warfare. Two incidents –
presented as belonging to one moment of conflict but probably originally quite separate – illustrate this. The first is a
stylized picture of single combat, which serves also to explain
a place-name (verses 12–16). The second is a battle-story, but
concentrates on the death of Asahel and on the recognition of
kinship between the two sides (verses 17–32). This latter is the
more important, for it points forward both to the fate of
Abner (3: 22–39) and also to the recognition of unity under
David (5: 1–3).

12. *Gibeon:* an important town (cp. Josh. 9: 17 and especially
1 Kings 3: 4 where it is described as 'chief hill-shrine'), commonly though not certainly identified with el-Jib, about 6
miles (9½ km) north of Jerusalem (see map, p. 29). It lies in the
area which in later years was to be border territory between
Judah and Israel, so that a meeting between the opposing

forces here suggests that the territorial demarcations were already clear. David's forces are apparently advancing into Benjamite territory.

13. *the pool of Gibeon:* a feature of the excavations at el-Jib was the discovery of a great artificial entrance to the water supply, a huge open structure with steps running spirally down its sides to a tunnel leading to the spring. A similar construction has been found at Megiddo. This would give access to the spring from within the city in times of siege. But this cannot be the pool – as is sometimes supposed – for that must rather be the open water at the spring, outside the city. It is referred to also in Jer. 41: 12 where the Hebrew actually mentions 'great waters', suggesting the abundance of the water-supply at this point.

14. *join in single combat:* this is clearly the sense of the passage, though actually the word used often means 'play', and is used of the blinded Samson fighting 'to make sport' for the Philistines (Judg. 16: 25). It is something like jousting in mediaeval times, but here it is in earnest. Single-combat fighting is found elsewhere in the ancient Near East. A picture in relief from Tell Ḥalaf in northern Mesopotamia shows two men fighting; each grasps the hair of the other with his left hand while thrusting his sword into his opponent. The story of Sinuhe the Egyptian traveller (set in the early second millennium B.C.) vividly relates such a combat (cp. *Ancient Near Eastern Texts relating to the Old Testament* (see p. 240), pp. 18–22), not unlike that of David and Goliath in 1 Sam. 17 (cp. on 1 Sam. 17: 4).

15. *twelve for Benjamin:* it now appears that this is really a contest between Benjamites and Judaean supporters of David (cp. also verse 25). Perhaps this confirms the impression that verse 9 exaggerates the extent of Ishbosheth's control.

16. The stylized character of this little narrative is evident in the picture of all twenty-four men falling dead at one and the same moment. It is linked to a particular place-name, *the Field of Blades;* the early translations provide alternatives

which suggest 'Field of sides' (the word for 'blade' and the word for *side* used in the description of the fighting are very similar). We may see here what is technically called an aetiological expression, i.e. a story told to explain a place-name or a custom (an example may be seen in 1 Sam. 7: 12 explaining Eben-ezer); probably it is a popular explanation, in which a story has been attached to a particular place-name which may well have an entirely different origin. The word translated *Blades* may in fact mean 'flints' as in Josh. 5: 2. It is important to recognize that such an aetiology attaches a story, which may be quite independent, to a particular place. The recognition of this stresses the difficulty of discussing the historicity of what is here related. That there was war between David and Ishbosheth is likely enough; what we cannot expect to know is to what extent particular incidents have a precise historical basis.

17. *a fierce battle:* at this point the real battle narrative begins, but it is not fully related. We are provided simply with the setting for the death of Asahel.

18. *sons of Zeruiah:* a significant trio, two of whom appear in 1 Sam. 26: 6. Joab was David's army commander (cp. verse 13 and 8: 16) and is prominent in a whole series of narratives; Abishai appears as a hero, leader of the 'thirty' (23: 18) and Asahel as a member of that group (23: 24). Here it is his speed as a runner that is brought out, as he pursues Abner. According to 1 Chron. 2: 16, Zeruiah was David's sister; her husband was already dead (cp. 2 Sam. 2: 32). *gazelle on the plains:* better 'in the open country'.

21. *win his belt:* an evident mark of military prowess (cp. 18: 11). The achievements of David's heroes in chapter 23 are reckoned in some cases in terms of the number of their victims. The appeal by Abner to Asahel to desist from pursuing him is best explained in relation to what follows. Abner is to be the instrument in bringing over all Israel to David: his involvement with Asahel is, however, to be the cause of his death (cp. 3: 17–27).

37

23. *a back-thrust of his spear:* if this is the correct rendering, it gives a vivid picture. Abner presumably allows Asahel to get very close and suddenly drives his spear backwards into his pursuer's body. But the Hebrew is obscure; possibly a word has been copied in erroneously from the next line where it is correctly rendered *behind him.* If so, the text could read simply: 'he struck him with his spear'. *All who came to the place...:* the implication of this, in the light of verse 24, is that all except Asahel's brothers were too afraid to go further.

24. The localities mentioned presumably lie east of Gibeon. *Ammah* means 'cubit'.

25. The second part of the incident begins here, with the fugitive Benjamites grouped around Abner to defend themselves.

26. *Must the slaughter go on for ever?:* literally and picturesquely 'must the sword devour for ever?' Civil war, as many in the contemporary world know, is even more bitter than international, for the aftermath is suspicion and hatred which may last for generations. The appeal and the response by Joab suggest a mood of reconciliation; but Joab was not to forgive his brother's death.

27. *As God lives:* the normal oath form uses the divine name Yahweh, 'as the LORD lives' (so the Septuagint). *the people would not have given up...:* a possible alternative is: 'the people would have given up *from* the morning', i.e. a prolonged pursuit was not in question.

28. *the trumpet:* strictly 'the ram's horn', used to summon to battle or to worship (e.g. Ps. 150: 3).

29. *the Arabah:* the deep valley through which the Jordan flows. *all the morning:* a word of uncertain meaning, here understood to denote the first 'division' of the day. An alternative is to suggest that 'division' means 'cleft', i.e. 'all through the ravine'.

30f. The losses are assessed and the success of David's troops underlined. A slightly different sentence division would give better sense: *...found that...nineteen of David's men were missing*. But *Asahel and David's forces had routed...*

3 : 1. This is a summarizing verse, making it clear that the foregoing narratives serve as illustrations. That *the war...was long drawn out* appears to envisage a much longer period than the two-year reign of Ishbosheth noted in 2: 10. Or is this statement perhaps intended to underline the whole conflict between the royal *houses of Saul and David*? If so, we may see this not simply as a summary of this particular section, but as a resumptive statement referring back to the whole period from the beginnings of David's claims to power right through to the eventual establishment of his sole rule. *

DAVID AT HEBRON

Sons were born to David at Hebron. His eldest was 2[a] Amnon, whose mother was Ahinoam of Jezreel; his 3 second Chileab, whose mother was Abigail widow of Nabal of Carmel; the third Absalom, whose mother was Maacah daughter of Talmai king of Geshur; the fourth 4 Adonijah, whose mother was Haggith; the fifth Shephatiah, whose mother was Abital; and the sixth Ithream, 5 whose mother was David's wife Eglah. These were all born to David at Hebron.

* A short inserted piece of information concerning David's family, supplemented in 5: 13-16 by a further statement on wives and sons in Jerusalem. Three of the sons mentioned here are of significance in the subsequent narratives: the others are not mentioned again. Amnon, the *eldest*, provides the first cause of Absalom's (verse 3) eventual rebellion against David (cp. chapter 13); Absalom was evidently a favourite, but caused most grief to his father (cp. 13: 1 - 19: 8); Adonijah

[a] *Verses 2-5: cp. 1 Chron. 3: 1-4.*

(verse 4), presumably eventually the eldest surviving son, claimed the succession for himself as David was dying (cp. 1 Kings 1–2). We may note too the importance of Absalom's mother's family: *Talmai king of Geshur* was an Aramaean ruler (see map, p. 85; cp. 15: 8). David's policy of establishing alliances by marriage is here being continued. Absalom took refuge with his grandfather at the time of David's displeasure after the murder of Amnon (13: 37–9). ✶

ABNER AND DAVID

6 As the war between the houses of Saul and David went on, Abner made his position gradually stronger in 7 the house of Saul. Now Saul had had a concubine named Rizpah daughter of Aiah. Ishbosheth asked Abner, 'Why have you slept with my father's concubine?' 8 Abner was very angry at this and exclaimed, 'Am I a baboon in the pay of Judah?[a] Up to now I have been loyal to the house of your father Saul, to his brothers and friends, and I have not betrayed you into David's hands; yet you choose this moment to charge me with disloyalty 9 over this woman. But now, so help me God, I will do all I can to bring about what the LORD swore to do for 10 David: I will set to work to bring down the house of Saul and to put David on the throne over Israel and 11 Judah from Dan to Beersheba.' Ishbosheth could not say 12 another word; he was too much afraid of Abner. Then Abner, seeking to make friends where he could, instead of going to David himself sent envoys with this message: 'Let us come to terms, and I will do all I can to bring the 13 whole of Israel over to you.' David sent answer: 'Good,

[a] *Lit.* Am I a dog's head which belongs to Judah?

I will come to terms with you, but on this one condition, that you do not come into my presence without bringing Saul's daughter Michal to me.' David also sent messengers 14 to Saul's son Ishbosheth with the demand: 'Hand over to me my wife Michal to whom I was betrothed at the price of a hundred Philistine foreskins.' Thereupon 15 Ishbosheth sent and took her away from her husband, Paltiel son of Laish. Paltiel followed her as far as Bahurim, 16 weeping all the way, until Abner ordered him to go back home, and he went.

Abner now approached the elders of Israel and said, 17 'For some time past you have wanted David for your king; now is the time to act, for this is the word of the 18 LORD about David: "By the hand of my servant David I will deliver my people Israel from the Philistines and from all their enemies."' Abner spoke also to the Benjamites 19 and then went on to report to David at Hebron all that the Israelites and the Benjamites had agreed. When 20 Abner was admitted to David's presence, there were twenty men with him and David gave a feast for them all. Then Abner said to David, 'I shall now go and bring 21 the whole of Israel over to your majesty, and they shall make a covenant with you. Then you will be king over a realm after your own heart.' David dismissed Abner, granting him safe conduct.

* The next stage in David's rise to power rests in Abner's hands. In three vivid scenes we are shown his quarrel with Ishbosheth (verses 6–11), his negotiations with David, involving also the restoration of Michal (verses 12–16), and the establishing of a firm basis for the allegiance of all Israel to David (verses 17–21). Into this the compiler has welded various elements that are not all of one piece, but the result is a skilfully constructed whole.

6. *Abner made his position gradually stronger:* the impression that Ishbosheth was little more than a puppet ruler, controlled by Abner, becomes clearer (cp. on 2: 8).

7. *Rizpah daughter of Aiah:* though a *concubine*, a secondary wife, Rizpah appears as a remarkable heroine in another incident (21: 1–14). Her significance here rests in the fact that the wives and concubines of a dead ruler belonged to his successor (cp. on 16: 21f.): to take one of them (as some Greek texts actually state here), or to claim one (cp. 1 Kings 2: 13–25 for a claim by Adonijah, David's son), is to claim the kingship. We have no means of deciding whether the accusation against Abner was a true one, or whether it was perhaps contrived by opponents at court who resented his power. Abner's denial (verse 8) equally gives us no clue.

8. *Am I a baboon...?* This rendering supposes that 'head of a dog' denotes 'dog-faced baboon', an interpretation given by the Greek translator Symmachus (cp. p. xii). The literal translation of the text appears in the N.E.B. footnote, and the use of the word 'dog' suggests the sense: to term oneself a dog was to demean oneself (cp. 16: 9). The reference to Judah is textually uncertain and probably not original. *friends:* this could be a singular form, i.e. 'his Friend', Saul's special associate, known as the 'King's Friend' (cp. on 15: 37). Saul's household would then be described in terms of *his brothers*, i.e. his whole kin, and of this special officer, whose position is not entirely clear but who was evidently felt to belong very closely indeed with the person of the king.

9f. Abner's declaration here seems somewhat strange. That he should threaten Ishbosheth with the risks which would attend his withdrawal of support is natural enough; but one would hardly expect a declaration not only of the total reversal of his policy, but also of his conviction of God's purpose to establish David as king. Here we may see how the narrator is developing the story so as to bring out its signifi-

cance in relation to the eventual total acknowledgement of
David in a unified kingdom, anticipated in the earlier narratives in 1 Samuel and reaching its climax in the succeeding
chapters (cp. especially chapter 7). We are being invited to
read not a simple story of double-dealing by Abner but a
working-out of divine purpose, the meaning of which is being
unfolded, though we, the readers, know where it must end.
from Dan to Beersheba: a common way of describing the whole
land by its extreme points (cp. map, p. 12).

11. The weakness of Ishbosheth is again brought out; as the
narrative is presented this comes as a comment on the statement just made that all Israel would eventually acknowledge
David.

12. The second stage of the narrative begins with the negotiations by *envoys*. The direct approach to David comes only
in the third stage. *seeking to make friends where he could:* an
emended text, literally: 'thinking "To whom can I be pleas-
ing?"' The Hebrew text is uncertain, and it begins the words
of Abner to David twice: 'To whom (belongs the) land?'
'Make a treaty...' The first phrase could be due to erroneous
copying, or it could conceal a rhetorical question, inviting
David to acknowledge his divinely appointed right to the
whole land; less probably it could indicate Abner's own claim
to control the northern area.

13. The agreement introduces the condition that *Saul's
daughter Michal*, David's first wife (cp. 1 Sam. 18: 20-9),
would be restored to him. Undoubtedly this demand is linked
to David's desire to claim to be legitimate successor to Saul,
and perhaps also to an endeavour to win over to himself the
affection centred on the house of Saul. A son to David and
Michal could combine in one ruler the two rival lines. A link
is provided in this way back to the beginning of the story of
David in 1 Samuel; it also points forward to the failure of this
endeavour narrated in 6: 20-3.

14f. An alternative account of the demand for Michal is
interwoven with the Abner theme: in this David makes a

direct demand to Ishbosheth, who is depicted as too weak to resist what can only be a move to supplant him. *betrothed*: a word used in reference to the paying of the bride-price. *Paltiel*: cp. 1 Sam. 25: 44, where the name appears in the shortened form Palti.

16. Here the Abner story is resumed, with the sad picture of the loving second husband driven off. Political manoeuvre has no place for private affection. *Bahurim*: see map, p. 29.

17f. In the third stage of the narrative, wider aspects of the transfer of allegiance to David are developed. *the elders of Israel*: leaders of the tribes, portrayed as themselves already acknowledging David as king, and now provided with the occasion for action. David is the chosen deliverer of all Israel (cp. David's taunting words to the Philistine in 1 Sam. 17: 45–7).

19. An approach to Benjamin represents the drawing over of the allegiance of Saul's own tribe, clearly important for David's full power. The negotiations with David become full and open.

21. *king over a realm after your own heart*: the N.E.B. does not quite convey the sense of the text which is 'king over all that your heart desires'. The granting of a *safe conduct*, literally 'in peace, safety', provides a link to the next narrative. ✳

THE DEATH OF ABNER

22 David's men and Joab returned from a raid bringing a great deal of plunder with them, and by this time Abner, after his dismissal, was no longer with David in Hebron.

23 So when Joab and his raiding party arrived, they were greeted with the news that Abner son of Ner had been with the king and had departed under safe conduct.

24 Joab went in to the king and said, 'What have you done? Here you have had Abner with you. How could you let

him go? He has got clean away! You know Abner son 25
of Ner: he came meaning to deceive you, to learn all
about your movements and to find out what you are
doing.' When he left David's presence, Joab sent mes- 26
sengers after Abner and they brought him back from the
Pool of Sirah; but David knew nothing of all this. On 27
Abner's return to Hebron, Joab drew him aside in the
gateway, as though to speak privately with him, and
there, in revenge for his brother Asahel, he stabbed him
in the belly, and he died. When David heard the news 28
he said, 'I and my realm are for ever innocent in the
sight of the LORD of the blood of Abner son of Ner. May 29
it recoil upon the head of Joab and upon all his family!
May the house of Joab never be free from running sore
or foul disease, nor lack a son fit only to ply the distaff
or doomed to die by the sword or beg his bread!' So 30
Joab and Abishai his brother slew Abner because he had
killed their brother Asahel in battle at Gibeon. Then 31
David ordered Joab and all the people with him to rend
their clothes, put on sackcloth and beat their breasts for
Abner, and the king himself walked behind the bier. They 32
buried Abner in Hebron and the king wept aloud at the
tomb, while all the people wept with him. The king 33
made this lament for Abner:

> Must Abner die so base a death?
> Your hands were not bound, 34
> your feet not thrust into fetters;
> you fell as one who falls at a ruffian's hands.

And the people wept for him again.
They came to persuade David to eat something; but 35

45

it was still day and he swore, 'So help me God! I will not
36 touch food of any kind before sunset.' The people took
note of this and approved; indeed, everything the king
37 did pleased them. Everyone throughout Israel knew on
that day that the king had had no hand in the murder of
38 Abner son of Ner. The king said to his servants, 'Do
you not know that a warrior, a great man, has fallen this
39 day in Israel? King though I am, I feel weak and powerless
in face of these ruthless sons of Zeruiah; they are too
much for me; the LORD will requite the wrongdoer as he
deserves.'

✻ The sequel to Abner's negotiation with David is murder.
Ostensibly it is an act of revenge, but the fear of a powerful
rival at court might well also move Joab to act. The murder is
an embarrassment to David, as it might have lost him the
support of the other tribes; but it may be that for him too the
removal of such a man could in the end be advantageous.

22. *returned from a raid:* it would seem that the activities of
David the outlaw continued even after he came to be established at Hebron, as if he had merely moved his base of opera-
tions away from the Philistine-controlled Ziklag (cp. 1 Sam.
27). *after his dismissal:* we should add 'with a safe conduct' as
in verse 21. The phrase is repeated in verse 23 and possibly
should appear in verse 24. To a modern reader, such repetition
is unacceptable; but its refrain-like quality serves to underline
David's total lack of responsibility for Abner's death. He had
guaranteed his security.

24. *He has got clean away!:* a possible rendering of the text,
but it is more probable that a word has dropped out: 'he has
gone off under safe conduct' (cp. the Septuagint). Verse 25
may then begin: 'Do you not know...'

26. *Pool of Sirah:* presumably not far from Hebron. We may
note the stress in the phrase: *but David knew nothing of all this.*

27. *in the gateway:* this would be a large structure, having recesses on either side within it, presumably for the use of guards (cp. also 18: 24). *in the belly:* as in 2: 23 in the killing of Asahel. *in revenge for his brother Asahel:* the full phrase, now concealed in the N.E.B.'s rearrangement, stands at the end of the verse, by way of comment: 'Thus he died for the blood of Asahel' (cp. on verse 30).

28f. David's total repudiation of the death of Abner (cp. also verse 26 which prepares for this) is taken further in verses 31–9; his cursing of the whole family of Joab reappears at verse 39. *recoil:* or 'whirl like a storm' (cp. Jer. 23: 19 in a description of divine judgement). *fit only to ply the distaff:* i.e. effeminate; alternatively this has been interpreted as meaning 'crippled'. Such a curse, like a blessing (cp. that of Jacob in Gen. 27: 27–40), being a word of power, is believed to have irrevocable effect. The curse here is a terrible one, similar to that on the house of Eli in 1 Sam. 2: 31–4: the family is always to have weak members, diseased or effeminate, lacking warrior aptitude, or those doomed to violent death or poverty.

30. Another comment on the death of Abner as revenge, unexpectedly mentioning Abishai: possibly this verse and the last clause of verse 27 are two independent additions to the text. They may have been found by a copyist in two forms of the text and so he included them both. The Old Testament text quite often reveals such a tendency to keep two alternative readings side by side, no doubt out of reverence for what has been handed down.

31f. Here a very full description is given of funeral rites: we may note, as in 1: 11f., the demonstrative character of grief (cp. notes on those verses).

33f. As in 1: 17–27, David speaks a lament, which is set out in its poetic form. Its verse language and brief form suggest that we may have here only a fragment of a longer utterance. Literally its first phrase, almost proverbial in style, runs: 'Should Abner die the death of a fool?' The word for 'fool' (*nābāl*) is the same word as is used in the word-play on Nabal in 1 Sam. 25:25: 'Fool (N.E.B. "Churl") is his name; folly is his character.' The next pair of lines stress Abner's invincibility: he could never have become a captive. His death is an act of deceit. *ruffian:* better as a plural: 'men of deceit'. This last line is rich in assonance, a common device of Hebrew poetic diction.

35f. David's faithful adherence to what appears to be the full mourning custom wins the approval of *The people*: this must here mean the whole community.

37. *Everyone throughout Israel:* literally, and more correctly: 'the people (i.e. Judah) and all Israel (i.e. the other tribes)', though it could be rendered: 'all the people, namely all Israel'. But the distinguishing of Judah and Israel is fitting here, for it underlines the significance of David's pious behaviour both to his supporters and to those who, according to 3: 17, are already looking in his direction. A pointer forward is given to 5: 1–3.

38. This verse, in prose, looks like a paraphrase of a further line of the poetic lament, or of an alternative form of it.

39. The curse on Joab of verse 29 is here echoed. It is true to the succeeding narratives that David, though he is king, is unable to act firmly against Joab. But *the LORD will requite the wrongdoer as he deserves* is to find its sequel in the last words of David to Solomon (1 Kings 2: 5f.), and in the latter's action against Joab (1 Kings 2: 28–35). There is expressed in David's words a conviction that it is God alone who is the true judge of men's conduct. (Cp. Paul's use of this conviction in Rom. 12: 19, which alludes to Lev. 19: 18: 'You shall not seek revenge...I am the LORD.') ✶

THE DEATH OF ISHBOSHETH

4 When Saul's son Ishbosheth[a] heard that Abner had been killed in Hebron, his courage failed him and all
2 Israel was dismayed. Now Ishbosheth had[b] two officers,

[a] *So some MSS.; others om.*   [b] had: *prob. rdg.; Heb. om.*

who were captains of raiding parties, and whose names were Baanah and Rechab; they were Benjamites, sons of Rimmon of Beeroth, Beeroth being reckoned part of Benjamin; but the Beerothites had fled to Gittaim, where 3 they have lived ever since.

(Saul's son Jonathan had a son lame in both feet. He 4 was five years old when word of the death of Saul and Jonathan came from Jezreel. His nurse had picked him up and fled, but in her hurry to get away he fell and was crippled. His name was Mephibosheth.)

Rechab and Baanah, the sons of Rimmon of Beeroth, 5 came to the house of Ishbosheth in the heat of the day and went in, while he was taking his midday rest. Now 6 the door-keeper had been sifting wheat, but she had grown drowsy and fallen asleep, so Rechab and his brother Baanah crept in,*a* found their way to the room 7 where he was asleep on the bed, and struck him dead. They cut off his head and took it with them, and, making their way along the Arabah all night, came to Hebron. They brought Ishbosheth's head to David at Hebron and 8 said to the king, 'Here is the head of Ishbosheth son of Saul, your enemy, who sought your life. The LORD has avenged your majesty today on Saul and on his family.' David answered Rechab and his brother Baanah, the 9 sons of Rimmon of Beeroth, with an oath: 'As the LORD lives, who has rescued me from all my troubles! I seized 10 the man who brought me word that Saul was dead and thought it good news; I killed him in Ziklag, and that

[a] Now the door-keeper . . . crept in: *prob. rdg., cp. Sept.; Heb.* They came right into the house carrying wheat, and they struck him in the belly; Rechab and his brother Baanah were acting stealthily. They . . .

11 was how I rewarded him for his news. How much more when ruffians have killed an innocent man on his bed in his own house? Am I not to take vengeance on you now for the blood you have shed, and rid the earth of you?'

12 David gave the word, and the young men killed them; they cut off their hands and feet and hung them up beside the pool in Hebron, but the head of Ishbosheth they took and buried in Abner's tomb at Hebron.

---

* A narrative of treachery tells of the murder of Ishbosheth and of the execution of the assassins. The piety of David is underlined: he will show loyalty to the house of Saul and Jonathan, and will rest his confidence of victory in God alone.

1. *his courage failed him*: this fits the picture of Ishbosheth, dependent on Abner's superior power. The words literally denote loosely hanging hands (similarly used to express discouragement in Jer. 38: 4); its opposite is firmness and strength. *all Israel*: not altogether consonant with the statements in 3: 17–19, but the main negotiator was clearly a significant personage.

2*b*–3. *Beeroth being reckoned part of Benjamin . . .*: an explanatory note. At the time of this incident, this family lived in Benjamite territory – the assassins were of Saul's own tribe; subsequently (the N.E.B. has *had fled*, but 'fled' is more probable), they evidently moved elsewhere, possibly because of this treachery which would leave a stain on the whole family. The exact localities are uncertain. The note may be connected with 21: 1–14, since Beeroth is associated with Gibeon (cp. Josh. 9: 17).

4. This note about Jonathan's son is clearly out of place; the narrative proper continues at verse 5. But it does two things. It points forward to the subsequent story of this lame son in chapter 9 and in 16: 1–4; 19: 24–30. It also serves to underline the contrast between the treachery of these two Benjamites to

Saul's family and David's kindness and loyalty. *Mephibosheth:* the original name appears as Meribbaal (cp. 1 Chron. 8: 34: 'the Lord contends', i.e. so as to protect). For the change, cp. the note on Ishbosheth at 2: 8. The 'Mephi' form is obscure, possibly 'from the mouth of (Baal)'.

5. *his midday rest:* the siesta so advisable in a hot climate.

6f. It is evident that the text is confused; the Septuagint helps to provide a good sequence, but it is probable that there is a greater degree of disorder than the N.E.B. footnote shows, perhaps resulting from a conflation of alternative accounts. The story as presented suggests a very simple court life with only a woman on duty, and she asleep like the rest of the household.

9. David's response to this treachery is *an oath*: it underlines the point that it is God alone who saves and takes vengeance (cp. on 3: 39). *rescued me from all my troubles:* cp. the similar expression in 1 Sam. 26: 24.

10. *and that was how I rewarded him for his news:* cp. 1: 15f. The text is possibly defective, but the general sense is clear.

12. *they cut off their hands and feet:* such barbarity belongs to warfare and civil strife (cp. the treatment of Adoni-bezek and his treatment of his prisoners in Judg. 1: 6f.). *hung them:* the translation is ambiguous, and so is the text, but it is clear that it was the corpses that were hung up. The exposure of a criminal's body was common practice (cp. the law in Deut. 21: 22f., governing the length of time of such exposure, at least in somewhat later practice). *Abner's tomb:* cp. 3: 32.

The way is now open, with the removal of Ishbosheth, for the acceptance of David by the remaining tribes. His treatment of the assassins and his pious burial of Ishbosheth's head provide an appropriate prelude to this. *

David king in Jerusalem

DAVID KING OF ALL ISRAEL AND JUDAH

5 1*a* NOW ALL THE TRIBES of Israel came to David at
Hebron and said to him, 'We are your own flesh
2 and blood. In the past, while Saul was still king over us,
you led the forces of Israel to war and you brought them
home again. And the LORD said to you, "You shall be
shepherd of my people Israel; you shall be their prince."'
3 All the elders of Israel came to the king at Hebron; there
David made a covenant with them before the LORD,
4 and they anointed David king over Israel. David came
to the throne at the age of thirty and reigned for forty
5 years. In Hebron he had ruled over Judah for seven years
and a half, and for thirty-three years he reigned in Jerusalem over Israel and Judah together.

✶ The acceptance of David by all Israel is followed by a
chronological summary of his reign (cp. also 1 Kings 2: 10f.).
  1. *all the tribes*: naturally their representatives would come,
as in verse 3. But we may suspect that verses 1f. represent a
later interpretation of the total unity of Israel, and that the
original narrative was simpler. *We are your own flesh and blood*:
the claims of kinship are strong, and this underlines the unity
of all the people with the divinely chosen ruler.
  2. David's prowess as a military leader under Saul is indicated in such a passage as 1 Sam. 18: 5–7. The statement here
acknowledges that David was in a sense the true king, the
bringer of victory, even under Saul. "*You shall be shepherd . . .
you shall be their prince*": there is no precise previous statement

[a] Verses 1–3, 6–10: cp. 1 Chron. 11: 1–9.

to this effect, though the inference is strong in many of the narratives of 1 Sam. 16–31. The words are clearly linked to the important interpretative chapter 7, and perhaps should be seen to be dependent upon that chapter (cp. 7: 7f.). The designation of a ruler as *shepherd* is known elsewhere in the ancient Near East: Hammurabi of Babylon was, for example, so described (cp. also note on 1 Sam. 12: 2).

3. *All the elders of Israel:* the expected beginning of the narrative, linked to 3: 17f. It is on the basis of this that the previous verses have been introduced. These are the leaders of the northern tribes. *covenant:* the stipulation of the nature of the kingship and of its obligations on both parties. Such a negotiation, an unsuccessful one, is described in 1 Kings 12. *they anointed:* see note on 2: 4a.

4f. The chronology is idealized: a forty-year period is frequently used in the narratives of the judges (cp. also Eli in 1 Sam. 4: 18). Seventy years, as here allocated to David, is an ideal life-span (cp. Ps. 90: 10). *seven years and a half:* this appears to be a non-idealized figure. We may note that in 1 Kings 2: 11 it appears as only seven years. The mention of rule *in Jerusalem* anticipates the next narrative. *Israel and Judah:* correctly the two areas are separately designated. David is king of two realms which later separate (1 Kings 12). ✻

DAVID AND JERUSALEM

The king and his men went to Jerusalem to attack the 6 Jebusites, whose land it was. The Jebusites said to David, 'Never shall you come in here; not till you have disposed of the blind and the lame', meaning that David should never come in. None the less David did capture the 7 stronghold of Zion, and it is now known as the City of David. David said on that day, 'Everyone who would kill 8 a Jebusite, let him use his grappling-iron to reach the lame and the blind, David's bitter enemies.' That is why they say, 'No blind or lame man shall come into the LORD's house.'[a]

9 David took up his residence in the stronghold and called it the City of David. He built the city[b] round it,
10 starting at the Millo and working inwards. So David steadily grew stronger, for the LORD the God of Hosts was with him.

11[c] Hiram king of Tyre sent an embassy to David; he sent cedar logs, and with them carpenters and stonemasons,
12 who built David a house. David knew by now that the LORD had confirmed him as king over Israel and had made his royal power stand higher for the sake of his people Israel.

13 After he had moved from Hebron he took more concubines and wives from Jerusalem; and more sons
14[d] and daughters were born to him. These are the names of the children born to him in Jerusalem: Shammua,
15 Shobab, Nathan, Solomon, Ibhar, Elishua, Nepheg,
16 Japhia, Elishama, Eliada and Eliphelet.

✵ The order of the material is here significant, though probably not chronologically correct. The natural sequel to the anointing of David in 5: 3 is in 5: 17–25, the defeat of the Philistines: the capture of Jerusalem may belong somewhat later. But, as often in Old Testament presentations, where interpretation is an important factor, material is arranged in a meaningful way. David, king of all Israel, is followed by

[a] the LORD's house: *lit.* the house.
[b] the city: *prob. rdg., cp. 1 Chron. 11: 8; Heb. om.*
[c] *Verses 11–25: cp. 1 Chron. 14: 1–16.*
[d] *Verses 14–16: cp. 1 Chron. 3: 5–8; 14: 4–7.*

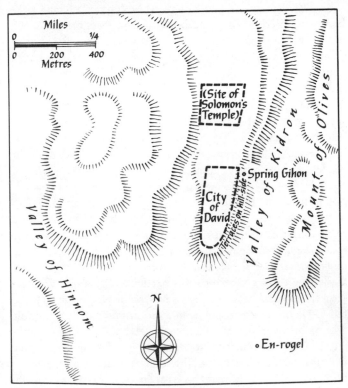

3. Plan of Jerusalem

David, king in Jerusalem. And the section underlines divine blessing (verses 10, 12) and also hints at the impregnability of the city which was in time to become so significant not simply for Israel's history but even more for Israel's faith.

The choice of Jerusalem, known from ancient documents as far back as before 2000 B.C. but so far not an Israelite city, and lying more or less between the northern and southern tribal areas, is a strategic one for David as he unites the two kingdoms in himself.

6. *The king and his men:* the royal bodyguard. That Jerusalem is captured by this elite body of troops suggests that it is to be regarded as David's own possession, royal property ('City of David', verse 7). *the Jebusites:* one of the native peoples of Canaan (cp. the lists, e.g. in Deut. 7: 1), here indicated as controlling Jerusalem and surrounding territory. According to Judg. 1: 21, 'the Jebusites have lived on in Jerusalem with the Benjamites till the present day', from which we may infer that the population of the city was mixed. The text does not in fact state that it was the Jebusites who made the apparently taunting statement: '*Never shall you come in here*...'; this attribution of the saying appears in 1 Chron. 11: 5. The text here could best be rendered: 'Now it was said that...' The saying appears to be a proverbial one, suggesting that the inhabitants will fight to the last man; even *the blind and the lame* will resist to the end. Then the final clause *meaning that David should never come in* may be seen as the applying of this proverb to this particular situation. We may see a fuller significance in this use of the proverb: the city will fall to David, but its reputation as an impregnable stronghold was to be an important feature of later thought. If it is the city of God, its security rests in him. This does not mean that it can never fall, but it may be held that this cannot happen without his leave. It may be handed over to the enemy as an act of divine judgement. These are themes to be fully developed in the prophecies of Isaiah, Jeremiah and Ezekiel, and in the whole presentation, the Deuteronomic History, of which 2 Samuel forms a part (cp. pp. 3f.).

7. This verse describes the capture of the city briefly. *the stronghold of Zion:* the location of this is uncertain, and the meaning of the name Zion is unknown. It is here identified with *the City of David* (see plan, p. 55). If it is to be distinguished from the city of Jerusalem, we can most naturally suppose it to be the central fortress.

8. The meaning of this verse is very uncertain. We may clearly see in the last clause an aetiological saying (cp. note on

2: 16), offering an explanation of the prohibition on blind and lame entering the temple. A later example may be seen in the story of the healing of the lame man who sits at the temple gate in Acts 3: 1–10. The explanation given here, by attachment to a specific event, is most improbable; the prohibition is likely to derive from a concern for purity in the temple, and the physically defective may be held to be the object of divine displeasure. Lev. 21: 17–21 has laws prohibiting such men from being priests, and it may be that this is the basic intention of the saying.

The first part of the verse is uncertain as to its text. There is a quite different text in 1 Chron. 11: 6 in which David promises the position of army commander to the first attacker, and explains that it was thus that Joab gained the position. The word translated *grappling-iron* or perhaps 'hook' (the Septuagint has 'dagger') has often been thought to denote a water-conduit, suggesting that a secret entry was made to the city via the water tunnel. Nor is it at all certain that the phrase *to reach the lame and the blind, David's bitter enemies*, really has this meaning. An alternative is: 'let him reach with the grappling-iron (?). The lame and the blind are abhorrent to David', or 'David hates the lame and the blind.' Perhaps something is missing. 1 Chronicles has no mention of the lame and the blind: but we must be cautious in making use of this fact. We shall observe a number of differences between this later text and that of 2 Samuel; the N.E.B. footnotes provide the references so that the reader may look at the texts in full. The Chronicler may have left out the references to the lame and blind because he did not understand the text, though it is more probable that he thought the words suggested weakness on David's part. For him the accession of David and his conquest of Jerusalem go through quite smoothly. To understand what the Chronicler does at any one point, we need to consider carefully the whole purpose of the later work. (See the commentaries on *1 and 2 Chronicles* and *Ezra–Nehemiah* in this series.)

9. This verse links up with verse 7 and adds information regarding David's building (or better 'rebuilding') of what is now to be his capital. Rulers, both in the Old Testament (cp. 1 Kings 12: 25) and elsewhere in the ancient Near East, are often described as great builders. The supreme Old Testament example is Solomon (1 Kings 5–7). *the Millo*: it is not known for certain what is meant. The word is connected with the verb 'to fill'; plausible suggestions are that it denotes either the terracing of the steep hillsides by which, as recent excavations have shown, the city was extended down almost to the valley level (see plan, p. 55); or to the filling of an enclosure with earth or rubble to make a platform for the construction of a building. In either case, retaining walls would hold a filling of earth and a level area be formed on which buildings could be constructed. In 1 Kings 9: 15, 24; 11: 27 Solomon is referred to as (re)building, i.e. repairing, the Millo. *inwards:* 'towards the house', i.e. temple or palace.

10. A summarizing statement of divine blessing on David (cp. 3: 1).

11. Trade relations with Phoenicia were to become even more significant in the reign of Solomon (cp. 1 Kings 5); this verse gives a very abbreviated statement of what may be assumed to be a treaty of friendship with Hiram of Tyre (see p. 11 and map, p. 85), who is to provide building materials and craftsmen for the construction of a royal palace. We are not told what David did in return. It is in fact probable that such a treaty belongs to the later period of David's reign, since it is unlikely that Hiram was yet on the throne. *cedar logs:* cedars enjoyed great repute as building materials in antiquity. An inscription of Gudea of Lagash (about 2000 B.C.) reads: 'In the Amanus, the Cedar Mountain, he formed into rafts cedar logs' for the temple of Ningursu (*A.N.E.T.* (see p. 240), p. 268).

12. Another summarizing comment which relates the establishing of Davidic royal power to the choice of Israel as the people of God. The theme of monarchy is thus integrated into that of God's election of Israel.

13–16. Some further family details (cp. 3: 2–5) indicating the building up of the royal establishment. *wives from Jerusalem:* perhaps better 'in Jerusalem', since there is no reason to suppose that they all came from one place. It is more likely that David was here too in some measure seeking diplomatic advantages. Of the eleven sons listed, only Solomon appears again, to be David's successor (cp. 12: 24f.; 1 Kings 1–2). The name *Eliada* appears in 1 Chron. 14: 7 as Beeliada, with the title *ba'al* used to replace the divine name El (cp. note on 2: 8). ✳

THE DEFEAT OF THE PHILISTINES

When the Philistines learnt that David had been anointed 17 king over Israel, they came up in force to seek him out. David, hearing of this, took refuge in the stronghold. The Philistines had come and overrun the Vale of 18 Rephaim. So David inquired of the LORD, 'If I attack the 19 Philistines, wilt thou deliver them into my hands?' And the LORD answered, 'Go, I will deliver the Philistines into your hands.' So he went up and attacked them at 20 Baal-perazim and defeated them there. 'The LORD has broken through my enemies' lines,' David said, 'as a river breaks its banks.' That is why the place was named Baal-perazim.[a] The Philistines left their idols behind 21 them there, and David and his men carried them off.

The Philistines made another attack and overran the 22 Vale of Rephaim. David inquired of the LORD, who said, 23 'Do not attack now but wheel round and take them in the rear opposite the aspens. As soon as you hear a rustling 24 sound in the tree-tops, then act at once; for the LORD will have gone out before you to defeat the Philistine

[a] *That is* Baal of Break-through.

25 army.' David did as the LORD had commanded, and drove the Philistines in flight all the way from Geba*a* to Gezer.

* David's supremacy is at once demonstrated in the permanent defeat of the Philistines. Two battles are briefly described, both set in the Vale of Rephaim. It is possible that two traditions of one battle are here combined; both have significant themes. The conclusion of this passage is perhaps to be seen in 6: 1 (see note on that verse).

17. *David had been anointed king:* this suggests that we have here the natural sequel to 5: 3. *took refuge in the stronghold:* since this is mentioned in verse 9, it is natural to think of the newly fortified city. But actually the text says: 'went down to the stronghold', not a natural expression for Zion, and more probably indicating Adullam (map, p. 29), so described in 23: 14 and 1 Sam. 22: 1-5. An alternative possibility is to suppose another fortified centre, with 'stronghold' perhaps really here a proper name.

18. *the Vale of Rephaim:* see map, p. 29, for its traditional site. It is by no means clear that it can be identified (cp. also note on 21: 16).

19. It is possible that here, as in 2: 1f., we should see two separate questions: 'Shall I attack?' 'Wilt thou deliver them into my power?' The answer represents a conflated reply.

20. *Baal-perazim:* an unknown place. Its name is here explained as deriving from this battle. The N.E.B. footnote gives the meaning and thus brings out the punning sense of David's saying. We may note that the divine title Baal is here quite properly applied to Israel's God: he himself is 'lord of breaking through'. We may also see a link in this name to the next narrative where a place-name Perez-uzzah is explained (6: 8). The point is made in the two uses that God's anger can break out both for Israel in victory and against Israel in judgement.

[a] Or, with 1 Chron. 14: 16 and Sept., Gibeon.

21. The carrying away of the Philistine idols, presumably to be displayed in triumph in the Israelite holy place, may be seen as the narrative's final answer to the defeat of Israel by the Philistines and the loss of the Ark in 1 Sam. 4–5.

22. The second battle begins in exactly the same way as the first, and this in itself suggests that we have alternative versions of one story.

23. Again we may see behind the divine answer a series of questions (cp. verse 19). *aspens:* balsam trees.

24. *a rustling sound in the tree-tops:* this rendering misses the real point of the narrative. What David is to hear is the sound of 'marching' in the tree- tops. The rational explanation of this may well be that the aspen leaves rustle in the wind. But it is interpreted as *the LORD* who *will have gone out before you*: God himself marches out first, and we may also better translate 'to smite the Philistine camp'. God will, it is here explained, bring victory for David by first producing panic in the camp on which David is advancing from the rear. The picture is much like that in the Gideon narrative of Judg. 7: 7–22 (cp. also the panic caused by God's thunder in 1 Sam. 7: 10f.). In effect, in all these instances the point is being made that it is God who defeats his enemies (cp. Ps. 2), not Israel who is only God's agent (cp. Ps. 44). Eventually the Old Testament will describe battles exclusively in symbolic terms as divine action against those who oppose him, and thus provide the basis for a rich use of military terms for the metaphor of spiritual warfare (cp. Eph. 6: 11–17).

25. *from Geba* (or 'Gibeon'; see the N.E.B. footnote) *to Gezer:* see map, p. 85. It is important to note that the defeat of the Philistines is not followed by the occupation of their territory. Cp. also the summary of the Philistine war in 8: 1, and contrast David's treatment of Moab, Ammon and the Aramaean territories (cp. chapters 8 and 11–12). The Philistines were contained within their own limits and no further indication appears of their attacking Israel. Other Philistine war themes appear in 21: 15–22; 23: 9–17. *

THE ARK – SYMBOL OF THE HOLY GOD

6 After that David again summoned the picked men of
2[a] Israel, thirty thousand in all, and went with the whole
army to Baalath-judah[b] to fetch the Ark of God which
bears the name of the LORD of Hosts, who is enthroned
3 upon the cherubim. They mounted the Ark of God
on a new cart and conveyed it from the house of Abinadab on the hill, with Uzzah and Ahio, sons of Abinadab,
4 guiding the cart. They took it with the Ark of God upon
it from Abinadab's house on the hill, with Ahio walking
5 in front. David and all Israel danced for joy before the
LORD without restraint to the sound of singing,[c] of harps
and lutes, of tambourines and castanets and cymbals.
6 But when they came to a certain threshing-floor, the
oxen stumbled, and Uzzah reached out to the Ark of
7 God and took hold of it. The LORD was angry with
Uzzah and struck him down there for his rash act.
8 So he died there beside the Ark of God. David was
vexed because the LORD's anger had broken out upon
Uzzah, and he called the place Perez-uzzah,[d] the name it
9 still bears. David was afraid of the LORD that day and
said, 'How can I harbour the Ark of the LORD after this?'
10 He felt he could not take the Ark of the LORD with him
to the City of David, but turned aside and carried it to
11 the house of Obed-edom the Gittite. Thus the Ark of

[a] *Verses 2–11: cp. 1 Chron. 13: 6–14.*
[b] to Baalath-judah: *prob. rdg., cp. 1 Chron. 13: 6; Heb.* from the lords
of Judah.
[c] without . . . singing: *prob. rdg., cp. 1 Chron. 13: 8; Heb.* to the
beating of batons.
[d] *That is* Outbreak on Uzzah.

the LORD remained at Obed-edom's house for three months, and the LORD blessed Obed-edom and all his family.

✷ The theme of this chapter is the bringing of the Ark to Jerusalem. It is told in two stages, the first of which shows the Ark as expressive of God's holy power, to bring disaster and blessing.

1. *the picked men of Israel, thirty thousand in all:* excessive for the fetching of the Ark. Possibly this verse was originally part of another battle narrative, continuing the previous verses. It is now being used to introduce the bringing up of the Ark and the *again* is perhaps designed to make a link with the capture of Jerusalem (cp. 5: 6). As we have seen (p. 54), the order of the narratives is not necessarily chronological; the real sequel to the capture of Jerusalem is the bringing into the new capital of the Ark as symbol of the presence of Israel's God.

2. *whole army:* but the text means 'all the people who were with him' and does not really refer back to verse 1. This suggests only a small company. In 1 Chron. 13: 2 it is 'the whole (religious) assembly', which extends the significance of the occasion. *Baalath-judah:* in 1 Sam. 6: 21 – 7: 1 the Ark is taken to Kiriath-jearim, a former Gibeonite city originally called Baalah (cp. map, p. 29 and Josh. 9: 17; 15: 9); the Chronicler has both names (1 Chron. 13: 5f.). It is strange to find the old name still being used, especially since the name so evidently refers to a female consort of the deity, given the title *ba'alāh*, 'lady'. The Hebrew text (cp. the N.E.B. footnote) has 'from the lords of Judah', which might be due to deliberate alteration to avoid the improper name. Certainly a place-name is needed.

the Ark of God: symbol of God's presence and particularly associated with him as leader of Israel's armies (cp. on 1 Sam. 4: 2f.), here suggested by the title *LORD of Hosts. Hosts* can mean both 'the heavenly host' and 'the army of Israel' (cp.

on 1 Sam. 1: 3). God is here given in addition the title *enthroned upon the cherubim* as in 1 Sam. 4: 4 – and cp. also 2 Sam. 22: 11; these are winged lions with human heads, thought also to bear the invisible deity in the inmost shrine (1 Kings 6: 19–28). An important additional point is made in the phrase *which bears the name*; literally 'over which the name of the LORD is called'. Jerusalem, or its temple, is so described, particularly in Deuteronomy (though without mention of the city by name; e.g. Deut. 12: 5), and in passages expressing the theological outlook of the Deuteronomic writers (e.g. Solomon's prayer, 1 Kings 8: 29, and such a sermonic passage, in Deuteronomic style, as Jer. 7: 10 which uses exactly the same expression as we have here). The presence of God in his temple or his city is an important theme, for men need to be able to establish contact with the deity who, by his very nature, must be remote and inaccessible. But if he is said to dwell in a temple, misunderstanding may easily arise; it may be supposed that the temple is impregnable (cp. Jeremiah's castigation of such a superstitious notion in the same sermonic passage, Jer. 7: 4), or it may be supposed that God is localized (a theme of Stephen's attack on his contemporaries in Acts 7). God cannot be so restricted: 'can God indeed dwell on earth? Heaven itself, the highest heaven, cannot contain thee; how much less this house that I have built!' (1 Kings 8: 27). Yet – and so the Deuteronomic theologians sought to meet the problem – the reality of his presence with men may be known and experienced, and this is expressed as his setting his name in his temple, or claiming ownership of temple and city by his name being 'called over it'. The name is understood as an extension of the person himself. God reveals his name (so Exod. 3: 14) so that men may invoke him. He is there, but he is there without any limitation being imposed on him.

3. *a new cart:* similar precautions were taken by the Philistines because of the holiness, and therefore the danger, of this sacred object (1 Sam. 6: 7). We may see here a deliberate echo

of that narrative. *the house of Abinadab on the hill:* possibly a holy place (cp. on 1 Sam. 6: 21 – 7: 1). *Uzzah and Ahio:* in 1 Sam. 7: 1, a son named Eleazar is mentioned as 'custodian' of the Ark. No explanation is given of his non-mention here. *Ahio* is a possible name (meaning 'Yahweh is brother', i.e. kin; cp. Abijah, 'Yahweh is father'), but the word could be translated 'his brother'. It is possible that there was originally no second name, and that Eleazar has been added in 1 Sam. 7: 1 in explanation of the text. Unnamed characters in stories tend to acquire names and particularly names that are suitable: Eleazar was a name closely associated with the priestly line (the son of Aaron and ancestor of the main priestly family; cp. 1 Chron. 6: 3–15).

4. The N.E.B. has ignored the last word of verse 3 'new' (cart) and thus overlooks the probability that a whole phrase has been accidentally repeated in the Hebrew text. We should read 'the cart with the Ark of God', omitting the remainder of this verse, except for the last phrase which should probably run: 'with Uzzah and his brother walking in front', making it clear that the two men were leading the procession.

5. A great celebration proceeds at the advance of the Ark (cp. the hymnic acclamation of the Ark in Ps. 24: 7–10, where it is not actually named, and Ps. 132: 8f.). *danced:* cp. verse 14 where a different word is used. The word here could be rendered 'made sport' as in Judg. 16: 25 where it is used of Samson in the Philistine shrine (cp. also 'join in single combat' in 2 Sam. 2: 14). It points to a type of religious activity less common in sober western practice than where religious joy is expressed without inhibitions. An accidental miswriting of letters has produced the nonsensical Hebrew text translated in the N.E.B. footnote; 1 Chron. 13: 8 has preserved the correct wording. The instruments which accompany the celebration are almost all mentioned in Ps. 150, a hymn of praise; a comparable celebration marks the return of a victorious army (e.g. 1 Sam. 18: 6; cp. note there).

6. *a certain threshing-floor:* could be 'threshing-floor of

Nachon' (1 Chron. 13: 9 has 'Kidon'). The word may however be an adjective suggesting 'firmness, preparedness', though there is also a possible word-play (*nākōn* = striking) on 'struck him down' (verse 7, *nākāh*). No comment is made on the place, but we may note the narrative of chapter 24 which leads up to the establishing of a holy place at such a threshing-floor. We could perhaps translate 'a prepared threshing-floor', and since the same word is used for setting an altar in position, see an allusion to a specially designated religious place. Is there perhaps a hint that *the oxen stumbled* because they knew (cp. the cows in 1 Sam. 6: 7–12 which are divinely controlled) that they were at a holy place, whereas David and his men had not recognized this? If so, Uzzah's 'rash act' in taking hold of the Ark occurs at a place where he, as one of the leaders of the procession, ought to have known better. (We may note in verse 13 that David subsequently takes due precautions.) *stumbled*: the meaning is uncertain, possibly 'let (it) fall', or 'tip'.

7. *for his rash act*: or 'irreverence'. Such a sense is possible and would fit the context well. But we may note that 1 Chron. 13: 10 has a longer phrase: 'because he had put out his hand to the Ark', of which the text here may be a mutilated fragment. The death of Uzzah is the result of the 'holiness of God', embodied in the Ark, being dangerous to anyone who approaches it with impiety. 'It is a terrible thing to fall into the hands of the living God' (Heb. 10: 31). Familiarity with the deity may suggest that he is harmless enough, but he is one whose love to men involves both judgement and saving power (cp. the story of Ananias and Sapphira in Acts 5: 1–12).

8. *David was vexed*: the N.E.B. rendering is too polite. David reacted in a display of anger, and, as the next verse indicates, of awe. The Old Testament is not embarrassed by the thought that the ways of God should seem so strange to men that they react thus. It depicts Jeremiah accusing God of duping him (Jer. 20: 7), and Job's speeches contain much

violent reaction against the activity of God. *he called:* better '(the place) was called'. *Perez-uzzah:* the theme of 'Outbreak' (N.E.B. footnote) or 'breaking through' echoes 5: 20.

9. David's awe at God's holiness raises doubts about his fitness to bring the Ark into the city. '*How can I harbour...*': literally 'how can the Ark come in to me?'

10. *He felt he could not take:* better 'he refused to take'. On *City of David,* cp. on 5: 7. *the house of Obed-edom the Gittite:* evidently at or near the threshing-floor. No explanation is given of who this man was. Later traditions portray him as an important religious official (1 Chron. 15: 18, 21, 24, where he is a Levite and a doorkeeper for the Ark). *Obed* means 'one who serves' or 'worships' (cp. Obadiah, 'worshipper of Yahweh'); perhaps *edom* conceals a divine title. His connection with Gath suggests an alien, unless Gittite simply refers to *gath* meaning 'wine-press' (but cp. 15: 18). Have we perhaps here an example, like that of the Gibeonites of Josh. 9, of a group of religious officials whose ancestry was non-Israelite, but who could claim a particular moment as authenticating their position in Israel's worship? If so we have a hint of ways in which Israel absorbed other groups and other religious traditions.

11. The beneficent effect of the Ark's presence in the house of Obed-edom makes a sharp and significant contrast to the death of Uzzah. A similar contrast was made in 1 Sam. 6: 13– 7: 1. ✻

THE ARK – TRIUMPHAL ENTRY AND MICHAL'S REJECTION

When they told David that the LORD had blessed 12[a] Obed-edom's family and all that was his because of the Ark of God, he went and brought up the Ark of God from the house of Obed-edom to the City of David with much rejoicing. When the bearers of the Ark of the 13

[a] *Verses 12–19: cp. 1 Chron. 15: 25–16: 3.*

LORD had gone six steps he sacrificed an ox and a buffalo.
14 David, wearing a linen ephod, danced without restraint
15 before the LORD. He and all the Israelites brought up the
Ark of the LORD with shouting and blowing of trumpets.
16 But as the Ark of the LORD was entering the City of
David, Saul's daughter Michal looked down through a
window and saw King David leaping and capering before
17 the LORD, and she despised him in her heart. When they
had brought in the Ark of the LORD, they put it in its
place inside the tent that David had pitched for it, and
David offered whole-offerings and shared-offerings before
18 the LORD. After David had completed these sacrifices,
he blessed the people in the name of the LORD of Hosts
19 and gave food to all the people, a flat loaf of bread, a
portion of meat,*a* and a cake of raisins, to every man and
woman in the whole gathering of the Israelites. Then all
20 the people went home. When David returned to greet
his household, Michal, Saul's daughter, came out to meet
him and said, 'What a glorious day for the king of Israel,
when he exposed his person in the sight of his servants'
21 slave-girls like any empty-headed fool!' David answered
Michal, 'But it was done in the presence of the LORD,
who chose me instead of your father and his family and
appointed me prince over Israel, the people of the LORD.
22 Before the LORD I will dance for joy, yes, and I will earn
yet more disgrace and lower myself still more in your*b*
eyes. But those girls of whom you speak, they will
23 honour me for it.' Michal, Saul's daughter, had no child
to her dying day.

[a] portion of meat: *mng. of Heb. word uncertain.*
[b] *So Sept.; Heb.* my.

* The day of David's successful bringing of the Ark to his city is also the day of Michal's rejection. The compiler has interwoven the two themes, and thereby again underlines the contrast between David and the family of Saul.

12. The blessing of Obed-edom and his family is a sign to David of the divine favour associated with the Ark. So now a successful move is made. The verse summarizes the story, and verses 13–19 set out the detail. Some Greek texts add before the words *he went*: 'and David said: I will turn the blessing to my house'.

13. *six steps:* the precise number suggests a particular ritual form, such as may be indicated by the allusive statements of Ps. 132, where verses 6–9 may allude to a rite. The story as told may reflect a ceremony carried out periodically. A crucial moment at the outset is marked by sacrifice, inviting divine favour on the procedure.

14. *David...danced:* not the same word as in verse 5. The word implies a circular motion, possibly 'whirling': in verse 16 it is rendered 'capering', and certainly we should not suppose the dancing to be an ordinary shuffle. For dancing in worship, cp. e.g. Ps. 87: 7. *a linen ephod:* not exclusively a priestly garment, but this is most naturally to be implied here (cp. on Samuel's ephod in 1 Sam. 2: 18). The relevance of this short garment is brought out in verse 20.

15. *shouting and blowing of trumpets:* the 'shout' of welcome is appropriate to the coming of the Ark as the symbol of God's presence (cp. 1 Sam. 4: 5). The trumpets are actually rams' horns, appropriate both to war and to religious ceremonial (cp. the blowing of rams' horns at Jericho in Josh. 6).

16. The verse is a parenthetic comment, pointing forward to the sequel in verses 20–3. It is an example of the compiler's skill in interweaving his themes. *looked down through a window:* perhaps we should simply take this literally, but it is worth noting that a frequent theme of ancient pictorial art is the portrayal of a woman at a window, goddess or (sacred) prostitute, and that this suggests the part Michal should be

playing in the ritual. Underlying the narrative here are indications of a ritual eventually held to be too alien for Israel, that of the 'sacred marriage': the ceremonial leading up to a marriage between king and queen as representative of god and goddess, and designed to bring fertility and well-being to the whole community. Another such example appears in the story of Jezebel's death (2 Kings 9: 30) where it would seem that she hoped to retain her place as queen at the side of the new king Jehu. The theme is also used of 'Lady Wisdom' in Prov. 7: 6: a close bond with her will preserve a man from the seductions of folly. *she despised him:* it is a mark of those who do not see clearly the ways of God that they undervalue those whom God chooses to honour. Michal places herself on the side of such men as the 'scoundrels' who had failed to acknowledge God's choice of her father Saul (1 Sam. 10: 27).

17. *in its place:* perhaps equivalent to 'its holy place', i.e. its tent-shrine. The tent is no ordinary secular structure. *David offered:* he is both king and priest.

18f. The completion of the ritual is described, again suggesting a regular procedure. *portion of meat:* an otherwise unknown term which could possibly mean 'cake of dates'. *a cake of raisins:* a term associated elsewhere with Canaanite fertility rituals (cp. Hos. 3: 1), another clue to the significance of verse 16.

20. Michal's attitude seems almost puritanical, and we might suppose that underlying it is the refusal of a member of a more conservative group to accept new and alien religious practices. It is an ironic comment – *What a glorious day*, better 'how the king today got honour for himself!' – but like many such, it serves to make a true statement. The bringing in of the Ark does mark a moment of glory: and when Michal describes David as *empty-headed* (*fool* is an unnecessary addition), she in fact reveals herself as the one who has no proper insight. The word implies 'men of no status' (cp. Judg. 11: 3, N.E.B. 'idle men').

21. Possibly David's reply should be expanded (with some

Septuagint texts) to read: 'I danced before the LORD: as the
LORD lives *who chose me...*' David underlines the divine
rejection of Saul and the choice of himself (cp. 1 Sam. 16:
8–10) as *prince* (literally 'head') *over Israel* and his care only for
the honour of God, not for his own dignity. Those who have
true insight will honour him.

22. *your eyes:* Hebrew (cp. the N.E.B. footnote) 'my eyes'.
Possibly altered in both Hebrew and Septuagint for reasons of
reverence from 'his (God's) eyes'. *those girls...:* the implication is that David will choose others rather than Michal to
consummate the celebration.

23. *Michal, Saul's daughter, had no child...:* the sting of the
story is in the tail. Again we are reminded of her family, and
there is a link to 3: 13–16 where the restoration of Michal to
David is related. The hope adumbrated there that a line of
kings descended from David and Michal could reconcile rival
groups is dashed. Michal is barren, a sign of divine displeasure (cp. 1 Sam. 1: 4f.). In this context it could also be
understood as marking Michal's refusal to participate in the
ritual; or as David's refusal to give her the child which she
might wish to have. But the text leaves no doubt that it is to
be understood as a divine decision.

The main theme of the Ark is for the moment over-
shadowed; but in fact the two themes are kept together so as
to be more fully developed in chapter 7, where the Ark theme
leads on into the temple theme, and the barrenness of Michal
into the promise of a royal dynasty. By bringing the Ark into
Jerusalem, his new capital, David may be seen to appropriate
to that dynasty the ancient symbol of God as 'LORD of Hosts'.
This was to be important for the legitimizing of religious ideas
associated with Jerusalem which developed beyond those of
earlier times and came to be central in much Old Testament
thought. By attempting the reconciliation with the house of
Saul, David appeared to be making a wise move; but his
intention was to be overruled by God who had chosen another
line of succession. That succession theme becomes increasingly

prominent in the subsequent chapters. A comparison may be made with the theme of succession to Abraham, where more than one false start is made before the establishment of Isaac as heir and as ancestor of Israel (cp. the narrative sequence in Gen. 15: 1–5; 16; 17: 15–22; 21–2).

We have also noted in this chapter the presence of details which suggest a formal ritual for the entry of the Ark. A fuller and much more elaborate account appears in 1 Chron. 15–16, incorporating much psalm material, and we may detect hints of the procedures both in Ps. 132 and in Ps. 24 which celebrates the triumphal entry of the Ark as symbol of the victorious deity. ✳

THE PROMISE OF THE DAVIDIC DYNASTY

7 1*ᵃ* As soon as the king was established in his house and the LORD had given him security from his enemies on all 2 sides, he said to Nathan the prophet, 'Here I live in a house of cedar, while the Ark of God is housed in cur- 3 tains.' Nathan answered the king, 'Very well, do what- 4 ever you have in mind, for the LORD is with you.' But 5 that night the word of the LORD came to Nathan: 'Go and say to David my servant, "This is the word of the LORD: Are you the man to build me a house to dwell in? 6 Down to this day I have never dwelt in a house since I brought Israel up from Egypt; I made my journey in a 7 tent and a tabernacle. Wherever I journeyed with Israel, did I ever ask any of the judges*ᵇ* whom I appointed shepherds of my people Israel why they had not built me 8 a house of cedar?" Then say this to my servant David: "This is the word of the LORD of Hosts: I took you from

[a] *Verses 1–29: cp. 1 Chron. 17: 1–27.*
[b] *Prob. rdg., cp. 1 Chron. 17: 6; Heb. tribes.*

the pastures, and from following the sheep, to be prince
over my people Israel. I have been with you wherever 9
you have gone, and have destroyed all the enemies in
your path. I will make you a great name among the great
ones of the earth. I will assign a place for my people 10
Israel; there I will plant them, and they shall dwell in
their own land. They shall be disturbed no more, never
again shall wicked men oppress them as they did in the
past, ever since the time when I appointed judges over 11
Israel my people; and I will give you peace from all your
enemies. The LORD has told you that he would build up
your royal house. When your life ends and you rest with 12
your forefathers, I will set up one of your family, one
of your own children, to succeed you and I will establish
his kingdom. It is he shall build a house in honour of my 13
name, and I will establish his royal throne for ever. I 14
-will be his father, and he shall be my son. When he does
wrong, I will punish him as any father might, and not
spare the rod. My love will never be withdrawn from 15
him as I withdrew it from Saul, whom I removed from
your path. Your family shall be established and your 16
kingdom shall stand for all time in my*a* sight, and your
throne shall be established for ever.'''

Nathan recounted to David all that had been said to 17
him and all that had been revealed.

* This chapter marks a climax: David's conquest of Jerusalem, his defeat of the Philistines, the entry of the Ark – all
lead up to the promise of God that his royal house will be
permanently established. Logically the details of David's wars
(chapters 8 and 10–12) ought to precede; but the compiler is

[a] *So some MSS.; others* your.

more concerned with significant order than with mere chronology. As the chapter finally stands – and it shows signs of elaboration of earlier material – it is set around a theme: David shall not build a house (temple) for me, but I will build a house (dynasty) for him (so especially verse 13). Close links may be seen between this chapter and Ps. 89, especially verses 19–37.

1. There is a deliberate echo here of Deut. 12: 10f.: 'he will grant you peace from all your enemies on every side' (the Hebrew words are the same as here); as Deuteronomy lays down, it will be at that time that the shrine which God has decreed will come into use. The moment of conquest is over; the full establishment of the Davidic house and of Jerusalem as the chosen holy place has come. The themes adumbrated in 1 Samuel are being drawn together (cp. the commentary on 1 Samuel in this series, especially pp. 7f., 231). Kings are often, in the ancient Near East, seen as temple builders or rebuilders (repairers); cp. note on Gudea on 5: 11. *was established:* the word could be translated 'sat enthroned'; it expresses his authority as ruler.

2. *Nathan the prophet:* as often in Old Testament narratives, new and significant personages appear unexplained. We know nothing of Nathan apart from the three incidents in which he appears: here, in chapter 12, the incident of David and Bathsheba, and in 1 Kings 1 in connection with the accession of Solomon. The three are in fact linked in that they are all concerned in one way or another with the eventual succession of Solomon (cp. comments on chapter 12). Nathan was not the only prophet of the period; Gad appears in chapter 24 (cp. also 1 Sam. 22: 5).

3. Nathan's approval of David's design to build a temple – implicit in the king's words in verse 2 – is strange, since it is immediately contradicted by the divine word of verses 5–7, and then modified yet again in verse 13. The present complex structure probably reflects different levels of thought. The ultimate significance of the Jerusalem temple was to be such

that its divine authorization could not be doubted by a pious writer. Yet there was evidently a strong tradition that a permanent temple was unsuited to a G⸰d whose initial relationship with Israel was traced to a pastoral wandering period. So 'tent' (verse 6; cp. 'housed in curtains' verse 2) and 'temple' are here seen as contrasting terms. But Solomon did build the temple, and in fact, as may be seen in 1 Sam. 1–3, a permanent building had certainly existed earlier at Shiloh. A distinction between 'tent' and 'temple' is in reality artificial, since in 6: 17 it is evident that a shrine is indicated. A particular theory of the development of Israel's religion, with a tent as more ancient than a temple, is here being propounded. It finds a counterpart, though there are theological differences, in the Priestly Writers' presentation of early Israel gathered around the Tabernacle (cp. especially *Exodus* (pp. 161f.) and *Numbers* (p. 22) in this series).

Why was David not permitted to build? It was to be explained as due to David's involvement in warfare (so 1 Kings 5: 3, and cp. 1 Chron. 22: 8); the later Chronicler made him carry out all the preparations (1 Chron. 22: 2–19; 28–9). We need also to recognize that in this chapter the primary concern with the divine promise of a dynasty to David has been combined with the temple theme, and that the two are not fully integrated.

4. *that night:* a divine revelation is commonly described as occurring at night, in vision or dream or by some other mechanism (cp. 1 Sam. 3). Many Hebrew manuscripts have a space in the text after *that night*: it has been suggested that this was to invite a cross-reference to Ps. 132, which could be understood as a comment on this passage (cp. also on 12: 13 and 16: 13).

5. *David my servant:* a frequent royal title, the king being in a special sense the servant or slave of the deity. *This is the word of the LORD:* the N.E.B. commonly renders thus the prophetic formula which runs literally: 'Thus the LORD has spoken', and thus does not distinguish this expression from

another which literally corresponds to the English: 'This is the word of the LORD.' There is a solemnity in the formulae which it is useful to preserve precisely. *Are you the man...?* the tone of the question implies 'not you, but Solomon', yet what follows suggests that any building is unwanted.

6. *I have never dwelt in a house:* but, as noted above, Shiloh was such a temple (cp. on 1 Sam. 1: 9f.). *tent...tabernacle:* as often in poetic language in Hebrew, the idea is expressed and emphasized by the use of two different words for one object. The notion of impermanence is made very clear. The word for Tabernacle belongs especially to the late Priestly Writers in Exodus to Numbers, and may be held to stress the willingness of God to 'tabernacle', that is to 'dwell in a tent' with his people. The Tabernacle for the later writers was particularly the place where God would meet with his people.

7. *judges:* the Hebrew for 'tribes' (see the N.E.B. footnote) differs in only one letter, an obvious scribal slip. *shepherds:* a common ancient Near Eastern metaphor for ruler (cp. on 5: 2). The two verses, 6f., like verses 22–4, serve also to stress the relationship between the past, when no temple was required, and the new situation in which a temple is to be seen as divinely commanded.

8f. A new theme is introduced here which is really the fundamental point in the divine promise to David. The choice of David, already stressed in 1 Samuel (cp. 16: 1–13 and the frequent emphasis on David as the true king-to-be), has already been stated in this manner in 6: 21. *from the pastures... from following the sheep:* cp. the similar claim for such divine choice in Amos 7: 15. The choice is followed by the continued support and guidance which God gives, and by the promise of *a great name*, the reputation of a great king, which was indeed to be that of David; later ages were to look back to him as an ideal and also look forward in hope to a new David, an anointed one, a Messiah.

10f. The establishing of the king is now associated with the greatness of *my people Israel*; the theme of the promised land, underlined especially in Deuteronomy and confirmed in the accounts of conquest and settlement in Joshua and Judges, is again set out as a promise. We may note too that the word rendered *place* suggests 'holy place', the temple itself. Such a thought is strongly brought out at the end of the long historical survey in Ps. 78. The choice of the temple site and the temple as focus for the people's life is a major theme in the books of Samuel and Kings.

Some of the phrases in these verses sound strange for the period of David, when the king's rule was established and Israel was occupying the land. But we need to recall here, as so often in the books of Samuel, that the eventual readership of the whole Deuteronomic History (cp. p. 4) was in the period of the exile, when the land was lost. *I will plant them:* cp. the vine symbol of Ps. 80: 8–16 and Ezek. 19: 10–14; this is a promise of a new and permanent settlement. *They shall be disturbed no more* is a reassurance to the exiles. The same theme, with slightly different wording, is found in Jer. 32: 37. There will be no more oppression such as there was *in the past*, which could be paraphrased 'in former times'. The writer is commenting on the whole history of his people; disobedience began with the settlement (cp. Judg. 2: 6–23 for a summarizing comment on that period), and was characteristic of the years that followed until final judgement came at the exile (cp. the comments in 2 Kings 17: 18–23; 23: 26f.). We may observe that a later generation still, after the exile, found itself confronted by the same situation when disobedience meant that they no longer possessed the land (so the long prayer-sermon of Neh. 9: 5–37, and especially verses 34–7). David's experience of 'security from his enemies' (verse 1 – the same word here rendered *give you peace*) is echoed in a promise for the people's future.

At the end of verse 11 we return to the theme of the dynasty, the *royal house* of David.

12. *I will set up one of your family:* this, in the light of verse 13, is certainly a possible interpretation of the text. But a

better alternative is to read verse 12 with verses 14–16 as a comment not on the individual heir, Solomon, but on the royal line. The word is 'seed' in the sense of 'descendants'; it is *his kingdom*, i.e. that of David's line of descendants, which is to be established perpetually.

13. The temple theme is brought in again here, the designation of Solomon as temple-builder being made explicit. The first part of the verse looks very much like a comment added to give this specific reference. The second part of the verse may simply be a variant on the last phrase of verse 12. (Cp. the use of this in 1 Kings in reference to Solomon, e.g. 5: 5.) An interesting comment may be seen in the fact that Ps. 127, concerned with the building of a house and the birth of sons, is traditionally associated with Solomon.

14–16. The point of verse 12 is continued. But an important qualification is introduced with the theme of God's relation to the king as of *father* to *son* (cp. Ps. 2: 7). The dynasty is established perpetually by God, but it is a dynasty under discipline. In contrast to the withdrawal of favour from Saul, the Davidic kingdom *shall stand for all time*. In verse 15 we should possibly read: 'I will not remove *My love* (or 'loyalty': *ḥesed*)'. But did not history contradict this promise? In 587 B.C. the Davidic kingdom came to an end; its last king, Zedekiah, was dead (2 Kings 25: 7 implies death in Babylon), the previous king, Jehoiachin, was in captivity (2 Kings 24: 15). What could the promise to David mean then? It seems evident that the hope of a new Davidic ruler remained, for 2 Kings closes with the release to favour of Jehoiachin (2 Kings 25: 27–30). In the event, this did not lead to a new kingship, though we find Zerubbabel, a Davidic descendant, as governor for a time (cp. Ezra 3–6; Hag. 2: 20–3). The longer-term outcome was to be a hope for an ideal Davidic anointed ruler, and royal oracles are to be found in the prophetic books (e.g. Jer. 32: 14–26), and were to be a source of hope for deliverance in a final age, as may be seen in the New Testament (e.g. Luke 1: 68f.) and in other later writings. A *midrash* (commentary)

on this chapter found in fragmentary form in Cave 4 at
Qumran has this to say about verse 14: '"I will be his father
and he will be my son": he is the shoot of David who will
stand with the interpreter of the Torah who will rise in Sion
in the end of days.'

The words of Nathan's oracle to David comment on the
nature and meaning of Davidic kingship. A number of elements – for example, his appointment (verses 9–11), the
demand for obedience (verse 14) – may be found in comparable expressions in ancient treaties between supreme rulers and
their subject princes. The writer has used patterns familiar to
his world to express his confidence in the enduring nature of
God's promises (verses 15–16). At the same time, the divine
words as here set out lay stress on another point to be echoed
in 1 Kings 8 (see especially verse 27). The temple may be seen
as a proper symbol of the presence of the deity and of his
willingness to hear his people's prayers. It must not be seen as
a confining of God to a single place; the loss of the temple,
whether in 587 B.C. or in A.D. 70 (the Roman destruction),
does not separate men from God.

The two themes, dynasty and temple, their relationship and
their enduring meaning, are being more fully stated.　✳

DAVID'S PRAYER

Then King David went into the presence of the LORD 18
and took his place there and said, 'What am I, Lord GOD,
and what is my family, that thou hast brought me thus
far? It was a small thing in thy sight to have planned for 19
thy servant's house in days long past. But such, O Lord
GOD, is the lot of a man embarked on a high career.[a]
And now what more can I say? for well thou knowest thy 20
servant David, O Lord GOD. Thou hast made good thy 21

[a] embarked on a high career: *prob. rdg.*, *cp. 1 Chron. 17: 17; Heb. om.*

word; it was thy purpose to spread thy servant's fame,
22 and so thou hast raised me to this greatness. Great indeed
art thou, O Lord GOD; we have never heard of one like
23 thee; there is no god but thee. And thy people Israel,
to whom can they be compared? Is there any other[a]
nation on earth whom thou, O God, hast set out to re-
deem from slavery to be thy people? Any other for whom
thou hast done great and terrible things to win fame for
thyself? Any other whom thou hast redeemed for thyself
from Egypt by driving out other nations and their gods
24 to make way for them[b]? Thou hast established thy people
Israel as thy own for ever, and thou, O LORD, hast be-
25 come their God. But now, LORD God, perform what thou
hast promised for thy servant and his house, and for all
26 time; make good what thou hast said. May thy fame be
great for evermore and let men say, "The LORD of Hosts
is God over Israel." So shall the house of thy servant
27 David be established before thee. O LORD of Hosts, God
of Israel, thou hast shown me thy purpose, in saying to
thy servant, "I will build up your house"; and therefore
28 I have made bold to offer this prayer to thee. Thou, O
Lord GOD, art God; thou hast made these noble promises
29 to thy servant, and thy promises come true; be pleased
now to bless thy servant's house that it may continue
always before thee; thou, O Lord GOD, hast promised,
and thy blessing shall rest upon thy servant's house for
evermore.'

[a] any other: *so Sept.; Heb.* one.
[b] by driving ... for them: *so Sept., cp. 1 Chron. 17: 21; Heb. unintelligible.*

✻ The prayer introduced at this point serves two purposes: it provides a fitting response to the promise of God set out in the divine word to Nathan in verses 8–16, and it provides a punctuating comment to the whole narrative sequence. In this latter respect, it is not unlike the speech of Samuel in 1 Sam. 12, which marks the end of the period of the judges and ushers in the monarchy. Here the monarchy of David, established as related in the intervening chapters – failure of Saul, rise of David – is shown in its final form. The Davidic dynasty, witness to God's enduring promise, is firmly established. What follows will be an exemplification of this, in failure and in success, to the establishment of Solomon. The narrator skilfully interweaves his themes of divine blessing, promise and judgement, with those of human response and rebellion.

18. *into the presence of the LORD*: clearly means 'into the shrine' (cp. also on 12: 16). The prayer opens in the use of a motif familiar from call narratives: *What am I...what is my family?*: cp. Gideon in Judg. 6: 15; Saul in 1 Sam. 9: 21. The self-deprecating note serves to exalt the wonder of divine choice (cp. Paul's disclaimer in 1 Cor. 15: 8).

19. The sense of this verse is not entirely clear, mainly because of obvious textual corruption in its latter part. The N.E.B. has followed the text in 1 Chron. 17: 17, but even that text is obscure. A possible emendation to the latter part of the verse could give: 'thou hast shown me generations to come for ever'. It is also possible to interpret the first part of the verse as follows: 'But this (i.e. the choice of David) was yet too small a thing...and thou hast even spoken concerning thy servant's family into the distant future and shown me generations to come...' This fits the context better, as there has been no suggestion of a predetermined plan by God to establish David's house.

21. The general sense is clear, but the text appears to be somewhat in confusion. An alternative rendering is: 'It is because of thy promise and thy nature that thou hast done this so as to show thy servant this greatness (i.e. this prospect of

greatness to come)'. Another possible sense, with a slightly emended text, is to begin the verse: 'For thy servant's sake, this dog (cp. on 3: 8) of yours...' (so the Jerusalem Bible).

22–4. A strongly hymnic passage speaks of the incomparable nature of God and the wonder of his action towards his people in the deliverance from Egypt and the establishing of them in their promised land. The verses strongly resemble other such descriptions, for example in Deut. 4: 32–40. The Hebrew text is again in some disorder, partly as a result of the somewhat repetitive nature of the passage and a desire on the part of a later scribe to avoid any suggestion that other gods might exist. An important feature of these verses, as also of verses 6f., is the relating of the new – the Davidic dynasty – to the old – the exodus and conquest themes. These are all part of the one purpose of God.

25. *But now:* used again in verses 28 and 29, but here serving to introduce the prayer proper. The same style is used in ancient letters, where the greeting and exposition, often elaborate, are followed by this 'but now' to lead into the main point (cp. Ezra 4: 11–16, where 'Now' should appear at the beginning of verse 13 as well as at verse 14). The style is common in documents outside the Old Testament such as the Elephantine letters (fifth century B.C.) written by a Jewish military colony in Egypt to various authorities (see *The Making of the Old Testament*, in this series, pp. 38–40). There is a close relationship between the forms of religious speech and those of everyday life.

25–9. David's prayer represents a repetition and hence an underlining of the words of the divine promise. This serves a double purpose: it stresses the acceptance by David – and hence by the people of which he may be seen to be the spokesman – of what God intends; it also underscores that promise. A reminder of what God has said is a source of hope and reassurance to those for whom the promises of God seemed to have been lost in disaster. ✳

DAVID'S CAMPAIGNS AND OFFICIALS

After this David defeated the Philistines and conquered **8** 1[a]
them, and took from them Metheg-ha-ammah. He de- 2
feated the Moabites, and he made them lie along the
ground and measured them off with a length of cord;
for every two lengths that were to be put to death one full
length was spared. The Moabites became subject to him
and paid him tribute. David also defeated Hadadezer 3
the Rehobite, king of Zobah, who was on his way to re-
erect his monument of victory by[b] the river Euphrates.
From him David captured seventeen hundred horse and 4
twenty thousand foot; he hamstrung all the chariot-
horses, except a hundred which he retained. When the 5
Aramaeans of Damascus came to the help of Hadadezer
king of Zobah, David destroyed twenty-two thousand
of them, and established garrisons among these Ara- 6
maeans; they became subject to him and paid him tribute.
Thus the LORD gave David victory wherever he went.
David took the gold quivers borne by Hadadezer's 7
servants and brought them to Jerusalem; and he also took 8
a great quantity of bronze[c] from Hadadezer's cities,
Betah and Berothai.

When Toi king of Hamath heard that David had 9
defeated the entire army of Hadadezer, he sent his son 10
Joram to King David to greet him and to congratulate
him on defeating Hadadezer in battle (for Hadadezer
had been at war with Toi); and he brought with him

[a] *Verses 1–14: cp. 1 Chron. 18: 1–13.*
[b] re-erect . . . victory by: *or* recover control of the crossings of . . .
[c] *Or* copper.

vessels of silver, gold, and copper, which King David
11 dedicated to the LORD. He dedicated also the silver and
12 gold taken from all the nations he had subdued, from
Edom[a] and Moab, from the Ammonites, the Philistines,
and Amalek, as well as part of the spoil taken from
Hadadezer the Rehobite, king of Zobah.

13　　David made a great name for himself by the slaughter
of eighteen thousand Edomites[b] in the Valley of Salt,
14 and on returning he stationed garrisons throughout
Edom, and all the Edomites were subject to him. Thus
the LORD gave victory to David wherever he went.

15[c]　　David ruled over the whole of Israel and maintained
16 law and justice among all his people. Joab son of Zeruiah
was in command of the army; Jehoshaphat son of Ahilud
17 was secretary of state; Zadok and Abiathar son of
Ahimelech, son of Ahitub,[d] were priests; Seraiah was
18 adjutant-general; Benaiah son of Jehoiada commanded[e]
the Kerethite and Pelethite guards. David's sons were
priests.

✻ The chapter contains two summarizing statements. Verses
1–14, picking up the theme of 7: 1, 'security from his enemies
on all sides', gather a number of notes on David's wars,
stressing (verses 6 and 14) the divine giving of victory. The
main places mentioned, so far as they can be identified, appear
on the map, p. 85. Verses 15–18, found in a variant form in
20: 23–6, name David's chief officials.

[a] *So some MSS.; others* Aram.
[b] *So some MSS.; others* Aramaeans.
[c] *Verses 15–18: cp. 20: 23–6; 1 Kings 4: 2–6; 1 Chron. 18: 14–17.*
[d] and Abiathar . . . Ahitub: *prob. rdg., cp. 1 Sam. 22: 11, 20; 2 Sam.
20: 25; Heb.* son of Ahitub and Ahimelech son of Abiathar.
[e] commanded: *so Vulg., cp. 2 Sam. 20: 23; 1 Chron. 18: 17; Heb.* and.

4. David's empire (mainly 2 Sam. 8 and 10–12)

1. *After this:* the loose chronological note enables the compiler to portray the victories of David as the direct sequel to the divine promises of chapter 7 (cp. especially the themes of victory and peace in verses 9 and 11), a point underlined at verses 6 and 14. The defeat of the Philistines, already related in 5: 17–25, is summarized, with a note of the extension of David's control. But it is not clear whether *Metheg-ha-ammah* is a place, unidentifiable (1 Chron. 18: 1 has 'Gath with its villages'), or whether the words have some other meaning: 'control' or 'supremacy' has been suggested, or 'the highroad of the mainland', or, by an emendation of the text, 'the Ark from Gath from Philistine control' which would offer a variant of the other Ark tradition. None of these meanings is verifiable. It is important to note that there is no mention, here or elsewhere, of either garrisons or tribute. David evidently held the Philistines to the coastal area which they controlled; that area did not become part of his extended kingdom. In the years that followed, Philistine areas were under their own control and played a part in the history of the kingdoms of Israel and Judah (cp. 1 Kings 15: 27; 2 Kings 18: 8).

2. The Moabites, however, became subject to him, paying tribute. The relation between Moab and Israel, the northern kingdom after the division, appears as an important political issue both in 2 Kings 3 and in the record on the Moabite Stone, a commemorative stele of the mid-ninth century B.C. (cp. *The Making of the Old Testament*, in this series, pp. 29–32). The record of the massacre of two-thirds of the prisoners makes the brutality of ancient warfare fully plain: there is no indication here of David's friendly relations with Moab in 1 Sam. 22: 3f.

3f. The defeat of Hadadezer of Zobah, an Aramaean kingdom, shows David's extension of control along the important trade-routes to the north-east (cp. also verses 5–8). Trade rivalry in this area was to result in a long struggle between the united kingdom of Aram and the northern kingdom of Israel, especially under the dynasties of Omri and Jehu (cp. 1 Kings

20; 22; 2 Kings 5–8; 10: 32f.; 13). Verse 4 as here rendered implies that David had little use for chariotry which was later to become a much more important factor in warfare. Verse 3 is, in fact, ambiguous; it could mean that David was on his way to set up *his monument of victory*. Only some manuscripts include the name *Euphrates*, though *the river* alone does often denote this particular one. But it is possible that the interpretation of the river as the Euphrates here derives from the kind of hyperbole found in Pss. 72: 8 and 89: 25 which speak of the extension of the Davidic kingdom 'from the River to the ends of the earth' (so 72: 8); such a poetic phrase may here have been given a literal sense. There is no adequate basis for supposing that David exercised so wide a political control. The N.E.B. footnote suggests an alternative interpretation, the text being literally 'to restore his hand (= power, or = victory-stele) at (on) the river'. Control of river-crossings would fit well with the trade aspects of the campaign, and it could be that at this time the Aramaeans were seeking to keep control of Jordan crossings, as later they were to claim trading-rights in Samaria (cp. 1 Kings 20: 34). There are, however, some indications of Aramaean conquests in the Euphrates region at this time, mentioned in later Assyrian documents (cp. on 10: 16).

5–8. These verses record further campaigns against the *Aramaeans of Damascus*, eventually to be the dominant group (cp. 1 Kings 11: 23f.). Here it is noted that *garrisons* were established (the word may also mean 'officers', but such officers would have to have supporting soldiery). The payment of tribute as a sign of subjection is to be distinguished from the booty of war, though it is possible that some of the tribute was paid in metal taken from palaces and cities (cp. the comparable payments made to Assyria by Hezekiah; 2 Kings 18: 14–16). Verse 6b underlines the divine giving of victory (cp. 14b). *gold quivers:* or 'shields' or some other military symbol, for ceremonial or religious purposes (cp. on 22: 35 and also 1 Kings 14: 26 which uses another Hebrew word for shields. A Qumran manuscript supports here an alternative Greek text which adds a cross-reference to that 1 Kings passage).

9f. A sidelight is cast on the internal warfare between Aramaean groups when Toi king of Hamath (see map, p. 85), an important kingdom in the later period, sent a peace embassy; it is evident that more than a friendly greeting is implied, since the king sent his son and a rich present. *Joram:* remarkable if an Aramaean prince has a Yahwistic name; 1 Chron. 18: 10 has Hadoram. *which King David dedicated to the LORD:* not in the Hebrew; the N.E.B. has added it to fit the sense.

11f. The present from Toi and all the spoils of war were 'dedicated to the LORD'. The mention of Edom anticipates verses 13f.; the alternative 'Aram' (the two words Aram and Edom look almost identical in Hebrew) is less likely since the last part of verse 12 gives the main reference to the Aramaean campaign. The mention of the Ammonites neatly anticipates the full story in chapters 10–12, where the long narrative also includes the Aramaeans and may therefore overlap verses 3–8 here (see especially 10: 15–19*a*). A defeat of Amalek (see map, p. 29) by David is to be found in 1 Sam. 30. That other campaigns took place is strongly supported by the brief catalogue of heroic deeds given in 21: 15–22; 23: 8–39.

13f. These verses allude briefly to a campaign against the Edomites (the reading 'Aramaeans' is clearly out of place). In 1 Chron. 18: 12 this victory is attributed to Abishai as military commander; the title to Ps. 60 (not printed by the N.E.B.) has: '...Joab returned and defeated Edom in the Valley of Salt, 12,000 (men).' *Valley of Salt:* see map, p. 85, for a probable location. Edom became subject at this stage; subsequently there was to be not-infrequent warfare between Edom and Judah (cp. e.g. 2 Kings 8: 20f.). The text makes the statement about *garrisons* twice, an example of two alternative readings being incorporated in the one text. Verse 14*b* again underlines the divine action (cp. 6*b*).

15–18. It is probable that this list of officials and the one in 20: 23–6 are simply variants, rather than reflections of different periods of David's reign. A similar but briefer statement appears for Saul in 1 Sam. 14: 49–51, suggesting a simpler form of organization; a comparable but fuller one for Solomon (1 Kings 4: 1–6 to which verses 7–19 add even more information) shows a further development.

15. This verse stresses the rule of David over a united kingdom, a concept which was to be influential in later pictures of David as ideal ruler. It also stresses his maintenance of *law and justice*, a feature of the ideal king (cp. on 23: 3f.; Isa. 11: 1–9, especially verses 2–4; Ps. 101, probably a royal psalm). Cp. further the notes on 15: 2–6.

16–18. The N.E.B. at 1 Kings 4: 2–6 sets out the officials as a list; this could equally well have been done here:

'Commander of the army: Joab son of Zeruiah' (cp. on 2: 18), already known from the narratives of chapters 2–3 and to appear again subsequently. He eventually lost his position to Benaiah when he supported Solomon's rival for the throne (1 Kings 1–2).

'Secretary of state: Jehoshaphat son of Ahilud'; the exact function is not clear. The title of the office, *mazkīr*, means something like 'remembrancer', and the term has important religious connections. Was it perhaps his responsibility to keep the king reminded of his duties, both secular and religious?

'Priests: Zadok and Abiathar' (oddly enough the same names appear for Solomon in spite of the fact that Abiathar had been dismissed; 1 Kings 2: 26f.). The text here is very muddled. Zadok, who appears without any explanation, is in fact described as 'son of Ahitub'; this may simply be due to a mistaken transposition of names, but it could represent one attempt at explaining Zadok's status by associating him with the older priestly line. Later he would be described as a direct descendant of Aaron's son Eleazar (1 Chron. 6: 3–8) and in that genealogy his father is named Ahitub. Who Zadok really

David king in Jerusalem

was remains unknown; it has often been thought that he was in reality the priest at the Jerusalem shrine from before David's conquest of the city, and this may be so. The names of earlier kings of Jerusalem suggest a connection, since they include the name element *zdq*, probably a divine title (meaning 'just, right'): Melchizedek, king of Salem (Jerusalem; Gen. 14: 18), and Adoni-bezek (probably deliberately altered from Adoni-zedek), apparently king of Jerusalem (Judg. 1: 5–7). David would then be taking over both shrine and priest, claiming both for the worship of his own God, but undoubtedly incorporating elements from the older Jerusalem cult. The text next has a phrase which is probably simply reversed: 'Ahimelech son of Abiathar'; Abiathar was quite clearly the priest who had succeeded his father Ahimelech at Nob (1 Sam. 21: 1) and was presumed to be of the Eli family (cp. 1 Kings 2: 27 and note on 1 Sam. 14: 3). Questions of priestly family are always complex, because family relationships are used to affirm status and authority. The same may be seen in the case of Obed-edom (cp. note on 6: 10).

'Adjutant-general: Seraiah' (Sheva or Sheja in 20: 25; Shavsha in 1 Chron. 18: 16; 1 Kings 4: 3 has 'Ahijah son of Shisha' which may indicate that the office remained in the same family or may suggest that the various names result from attempts at harmonizations). The functions of this official are not clear; the term is *sōphēr*, literally 'scribe', but the office often has military as well as civil aspects. Possibly he is to be regarded as the 'first executive officer', detailed to keep records and to carry out instructions.

'Superintendent (commander) of the royal bodyguard (named 'Kerethites and Pelethites'): Benaiah son of Jehoiada'. The names appear to point to (Philistine) mercenaries. The latter might be a dialect variant of Philistines; Kerethites may be linked with the place of origin, Crete. The text is corrupt here, but its proper sense may be supplied from 20: 23; literally the office is called 'Over the Kerethite and the Pelethite'. It is a form like that which appears in 20: 24 – an office not mentioned here – 'Over the forced-levy: Adoram'; and in 1 Kings 4: 6 – another office not mentioned here – 'Over the palace (house, household): Ahishar'.

The final clause is differently constructed and does not belong in the list. That *David's sons were priests* seems surprising. There is a different statement in 20: 26: 'Ira the Jairite was David's priest', and this may be a later interpretation designed to avoid the suggestion that the royal princes all held some kind of priestly office; it substitutes a sort of 'royal chaplain'. But what we know of the religious functions of the king (cp. the activities of David in chapter 6 and in 24: 25; or Solomon at the dedication of the temple in 1 Kings 8; and other later kings) makes it not at all improbable that such a priestly description should be used. We have no means of delineating their particular duties more fully. ✳

LOYALTY TO JONATHAN'S MEMORY

David asked, 'Is any member of Saul's family left, to **9** whom I can show true kindness for Jonathan's sake?' There was a servant of Saul's family named Ziba; and 2 he was summoned to David. The king asked, 'Are you Ziba?', and he answered, 'Your servant, sir.' So the 3 king said, 'Is no member of Saul's family still alive to whom I may show the kindness that God requires?' 'Yes,' said Ziba, 'there is a son of Jonathan still alive; he is a cripple, lame in both feet.' 'Where is he?' said 4 the king, and Ziba answered, 'He is staying with Machir son of Ammiel in Lo-debar.'

So the king sent and fetched him from Lo-debar, from 5 the house of Machir son of Ammiel, and when Mephibo- 6 sheth, son of Jonathan and Saul's grandson, entered David's presence, he prostrated himself and did obeisance. David said to him, 'Mephibosheth', and he answered,

7 'Your servant, sir.' Then David said, 'Do not be afraid;
I mean to show you kindness for your father Jonathan's
sake, and I will give you back the whole estate of your
grandfather*a* Saul; you shall have a place for yourself
8 at my table.' So Mephibosheth prostrated himself again
and said, 'Who am I that you should spare a thought for
9 a dead dog like me?' Then David summoned Saul's
servant Ziba to his presence and said to him, 'I assign
to your master's grandson*b* all the property that belonged
10 to Saul and his family. You and your sons and your slaves
must cultivate the land and bring in the harvest to provide
for your master's household,*c* but Mephibosheth your
master's grandson*b* shall have a place at my table.' This
11 man Ziba had fifteen sons and twenty slaves. Then Ziba
answered the king, 'I will do all that your majesty commands.' So Mephibosheth took his place in the royal*d*
12 household like one of the king's sons. He had a young
son, named Mica; and the members of Ziba's household
13 were all Mephibosheth's servants, while Mephibosheth
lived in Jerusalem and had his regular place at the king's
table, crippled as he was in both feet.

☆ The theme of loyalty here developed goes back to the bond
between David and Jonathan described in 1 Sam. 18: 1–4 and
further in 1 Sam. 20, especially there in verses 15f. which state
David's obligation to protect Jonathan's family 'When the
LORD rids the earth of all David's enemies'. It is thus with a
proper sense of order that this narrative has been placed here,
after the summary of David's campaigns. It is to have its
sequels in 16: 1–4; 19: 24–30. Another narrative concerning

[a] *Lit.* father.   [b] *Lit.* son.
[c] *So some Sept. MSS.; Heb.* son.   [d] *So Luc. Sept.; Heb.* my.

survivors of Saul's family appears in 21: 1–14; the relationship between the two narratives is by no means clear (cp. on 21: 7).

1. David's loyalty *for Jonathan's sake* extends to the whole family of Saul. A very different picture is given in 21: 1–14.

2. *Ziba:* evidently a man of substance himself, as we may judge from his family and retinue (cp. verse 10).

3. *the kindness that God requires:* literally 'kindness (loyalty, hesed) of God', which may mean what the N.E.B. translation indicates, or may mean 'great kindness', i.e. kindness such as goes beyond the normal (cp. 'mighty wind' for 'wind of God' in Gen. 1: 2). *cripple, lame:* 4: 4 has already related the cause.

4. *Lo-debar:* in Transjordan, towards the Aramaean border (cp. Amos 6: 13 and map, p. 85). The name *Machir* is associated with Manasseh, a part of which tribe was settled east of Jordan; evidently Machir was a man of some importance (cp. 17: 27).

6. *Mephibosheth:* the name Merib(b)aal changed to avoid the use of *ba'al* as a divine title (cp. on 2: 8 and 4: 4).

7. *Do not be afraid:* to be summoned from a remote place of refuge to the usurper's presence – for so Saul's family would view David – would hardly invite confidence. But Mephibosheth discovers the reality of David's loyalty to Jonathan. *the whole estate:* there is evidence of royal estates (cp. 1 Kings 21 for a story of the acquisition of such an estate, and 1 Chron. 27: 25–30 for a list indicating their wide geographical dispersion). There may well have been family property too. *my table:* for eating at the royal table, cp. the treatment of the captive king, Jehoiachin, in 2 Kings 25: 28f.

8. *a dead dog:* a common deprecatory title (cp. on 3: 8; 16: 9).

10f. *your master's household:* the Hebrew text has 'your master's son', which in fact makes good sense when it is recognized that the total proceeds are to be at Mephibosheth's disposal, for all who belong to him. The substitution of *household* would appear to be designed to make this clear.

Mephibosheth receives a fuller mark still of David's favour which is made clear by verse 11 specifying that he was treated like the royal princes. The phrase (*royal*) *household* is literally 'table' as in verses 7, 10 and 13.

12. *a young son*: there is no further mention of this boy, but we may observe that the narrator gives us just a hint that there might be a claimant to the throne, a theme which emerges later in regard to Mephibosheth. The further descendants of Saul's family are listed (in duplicate) in 1 Chron. 8: 34–40 and 9: 39–44. A hint at chronology is provided by this reference to Mica, since Mephibosheth is described (4: 4) as having been 'five years old' when Saul and Jonathan died.

13. *crippled as he was in both feet*: cp. 4: 4 and already mentioned here in verse 3. The repetition of the point (with different Hebrew words) paves the way for the sequel in 16: 1–4; 19: 24–30 where Mephibosheth's lameness is an operative factor. ✳

WAR WITH THE AMMONITES

10 1[a] Some time afterwards the king of the Ammonites 2 died and was succeeded by his son Hanun. David said, 'I must keep up the same loyal friendship with Hanun son of Nahash as his father showed me', and he sent a mission to condole with him on the death of his father. But when David's envoys entered the country of the 3 Ammonites, the Ammonite princes said to Hanun their lord, 'Do you suppose David means to do honour to your father when he sends you his condolences? These men of his are spies whom he has sent to find out how to 4 overthrow the city.' So Hanun took David's servants, and he shaved off half their beards, cut off half their gar- 5 ments up to the buttocks, and dismissed them. When

[a] *Verses 1–19: cp. 1 Chron. 19: 1–19.*

David heard how they had been treated, he sent to meet them, for they were deeply humiliated, and ordered them to wait in Jericho and not to return until their beards had grown again. The Ammonites knew that 6 they had fallen into bad odour with David, so they hired the Aramaeans of Beth-rehob and of Zobah to come to their help with twenty thousand infantry; they also hired the king of Maacah with a thousand men, and twelve thousand men from Tob. When David heard of it, he sent 7 out Joab and all the fighting men. The Ammonites came 8 and took up their position at the entrance to the city, while the Aramaeans of Zobah and of Rehob and the men of Tob and Maacah took up theirs in the open country. When Joab saw that he was threatened both 9 front and rear, he detailed some picked Israelite troops and drew them up facing the Aramaeans. The rest of his 10 forces he put under his brother Abishai, who took up a position facing the Ammonites. 'If the Aramaeans prove 11 too strong for me,' he said, 'you must come to my relief; and if the Ammonites prove too strong for you, I will come to yours. Courage! Let us fight bravely for our 12 people and for the cities*a* of our God. And the Lord's will be done.' But when Joab and his men came to close 13 quarters with the Aramaeans, they put them to flight; and when the Ammonites saw them in flight, they too 14 fled before Abishai and entered the city. Then Joab returned from the battle against the Ammonites and came to Jerusalem. The Aramaeans saw that they had 15 been worsted by Israel; but they rallied their forces, and 16 Hadadezer sent to summon other Aramaeans from the

[a] *Or* altars.

Great Bend of the Euphrates, and they advanced to
Helam under Shobach, commander of Hadadezer's
17 army. Their movement was reported to David, who
immediately mustered all the forces of Israel, crossed the
Jordan and advanced to meet them at Helam. There the
Aramaeans took up positions facing David and engaged
18 him, but were put to flight by Israel. David slew seven
hundred Aramaeans in chariots and forty thousand horsemen, mortally wounding Shobach, who died on the
19 field. When all the vassal kings of Hadadezer saw that
they had been worsted by Israel, they sued for peace and
submitted to the Israelites. The Aramaeans never dared
help the Ammonites again.

* The battle narrative consists of three separate elements,
after a preface (verses 1–6) which provides the setting: verses
7–14, Joab's battle against Ammon and Aram; verses 15–19,
David's battle against Aram (cp. 8: 3–8); 11: 1 and 12: 26–31,
Joab (and David) against Ammon. It is this battle narrative
which alone appears in the Chronicler's account in 1 Chron.
19: 1 – 20: 3. Into this group of stories, which refer to three
separate engagements, there has been inserted the story of
David and Bathsheba, 11: 2 – 12: 25, which makes use of an
incident in the Ammonite war to bring about the death of
Bathsheba's husband Uriah. It is a skilful interweaving of
themes (cp. further on chapter 12), leading to a climax in which
the birth of the successor, Solomon, neatly prefaces the successful conclusion of the war with Ammon.

1. *Some time afterwards:* not a true chronological note, but a
link phrase, of a kind commonly used in Samuel and Kings.

2. *loyal friendship:* the theme of loyalty provides a neat link
with chapter 9. It is evident that there was some kind of treaty
between David and Ammon. While nothing further is known
of this, it is understandable that David would be glad to

maintain a peaceful agreement with one of the neighbouring lands, as he also did with the Phoenicians (cp. 5: 11 and 1 Kings 5: 1; the latter passage similarly alludes to the treaty with Tyre during David's reign, without describing it in detail). *Hanun son of Nahash:* presumably Nahash is the same ruler as appears in the atrocity story of 1 Sam. 11. We may wonder whether his friendly relationship with David was in any way related to David's rivalry with Saul who delivered Jabesh-Gilead from Nahash.

3. *his condolences:* literally 'condolers'. The function of the ambassadors was to share in the mourning for the dead king and to give support to the new ruler. The same term is used of the friends, comforters, of Job (Job 2: 11-13). *These men of his are spies...:* a very free translation of the text which more literally runs: 'Has not David sent his servants to you to investigate the city (an alternative text has 'land') so as to spy it out and to overthrow it?' It is evident that the change of ruler has brought a change of policy; the folly of the young ruler is like that of Rehoboam after Solomon's death (1 Kings 12).

4. Hanun's action is designed to insult David by ridiculing and humiliating his envoys. Beards are symbols of status; the 'elder' is literally the 'bearded man'. Cp. 'shaving' as a symbol of judgement in Isa. 7: 20.

6. *they had fallen into bad odour:* possibly 'had acted shamefully' or 'had challenged'. It is clear that the action virtually constituted a declaration of war. The Ammonites gather various Aramaean mercenaries to assist them in their fight against Israel (cp. map, p. 85). *men from Tob:* or possibly 'the prince (literally 'man') of Tob'.

7. *all the fighting men:* literally 'the army, the warriors', and perhaps better 'both the army and the warrior corps', since a distinction is clear between the militia and the crack royal bodyguard.

8f. The implication of the narrative seems to be that by coming out of the city the Ammonites lured Joab into

advancing against them, while the Aramaean troops were still
out *in the open country*. Literally the text states that they were
'on their own', 'apart', implying that they were out of sight.
Joab, having advanced, discovered that the Aramaeans had
taken up a position to his rear. *the city:* we may assume this to
be the Ammonite capital, Rabbah (cp. 11: 1), elsewhere named
'Rabbath of the Ammonites' (so text at 12: 26; the N.E.B.
renders 'the Ammonite city of Rabbah').

12. *for our people and for the cities of our God:* the N.E.B.
footnote offers an alternative 'altars'. It is possible, however,
that the word for 'cities' is intrusive, resulting from a double
copying of two Hebrew letters, and that we should read
simply 'for our God'. We may compare the battle-cry in
Judg. 7: 18: 'For the LORD and for Gideon'. Another suggestion is that we should read 'for the Ark of our God' (cp.
11: 11). The final phrase indicates acknowledgement that it is
God alone who gives victory.

13f. Total victory is achieved. The enemy retreats to the
capital and the victorious army withdraws. The campaign is
over.

15–19. These verses appear to relate a quite independent
incident, with very exaggerated numbers; perhaps we have
here an alternative and parallel account to 8: 5–8. The Ammonites are not mentioned, except at the very end in verse 19*b*,
which probably belongs with verses 1–14. We may note that
this campaign is led by David himself, not by Joab. *from the
Great Bend of the Euphrates:* the text simply says 'from beyond
the river (Euphrates)' (cp. the Assyrian evidence noted on
8: 3f.). Helam is unknown, though it has been thought to be
the same as Alema in northern Transjordan (cp. 1 Macc. 5: 26;
map, p. 85. A slight change would give: 'and they brought
their army'. The Aramaeans are here under their commander
Shobach, not directly under the king, Hadadezer. Victory
leads to the submission of Hadadezer's *vassal kings*, and peace
is established, with the Aramaeans in a subject position. ✶

DAVID AND BATHSHEBA

At the turn of the year, when kings take the field,[a] **11**
David sent Joab out with his other officers and all the
Israelite forces, and they ravaged Ammon and laid siege to
Rabbah, while David remained in Jerusalem. One even- 2
ing David got up from his couch and, as he walked about
on the roof of the palace, he saw from there a woman
bathing, and she was very beautiful. He sent to inquire 3
who she was, and the answer came, 'It must be Bathsheba
daughter of Eliam and wife of Uriah the Hittite.' So he 4
sent messengers to fetch her, and when she came to him,
he had intercourse with her, though she was still being
purified after her period, and then she went home. She 5
conceived, and sent word to David that she was pregnant.
David ordered Joab to send Uriah the Hittite to him. 6
So Joab sent him to David, and when he arrived, David 7
asked him for news of Joab and the troops and how the
campaign was going; and then said to him, 'Go down to 8
your house and wash your feet after your journey.' As
he left the palace, a present from the king followed him.
But Uriah did not return to his house; he lay down by the 9
palace gate with the king's slaves. David heard that 10
Uriah had not gone home, and said to him, 'You have
had a long journey, why did you not go home?' Uriah 11
answered David, 'Israel and Judah are under canvas,[b]
and so is the Ark, and my lord Joab and your majesty's
officers are camping in the open; how can I go home to
eat and drink and to sleep with my wife? By your life, I

[a] when . . . field: *so some MSS.*, *cp. 1 Chron. 20: 1; others* when messengers set out.　　　[b] under canvas: *or* at Succoth.

12 cannot do this!' David then said to Uriah, 'Stay here another day, and tomorrow I will let you go.' So Uriah
13 stayed in Jerusalem that day. The next day David invited him to eat and drink with him and made him drunk. But in the evening Uriah went out to lie down in his blanket^a among the king's slaves and did not go home.

☆ The narrative which begins here – strictly after verse 1 which is part of the battle story – needs to be read as a single unit. It is vividly told, and the development is relentless. It may be conveniently divided into four stages, of which 11: 1–13 is the first, consisting of two scenes: verses 2–5 and verses 6–13.

1. *At the turn of the year:* the beginning of the campaign season, after the end of the rain, but before the heat is too great. Hebrew distinguishes the 'going out of the year' (Exod. 23: 16, N.E.B. footnote), i.e. New Year in the autumn, and 'the turning back of the year' as here, i.e. the spring (also a New Year in a calendar system which Israel knew; this system was used in Babylonia, and cp. Exod. 12: 2 where passover is described as falling in the first month). *kings:* the N.E.B. footnote indicates the alternative 'messengers' which results from a departure from the normal spelling. There appears to be no link made between this campaign against Ammon and the one described in 10: 1–14. *David remained in Jerusalem:* a normal procedure, as in 10: 1–14, though David on other occasions took the field himself (so 10: 17; cp. notes on 18: 3; 21: 17).

2. *from his couch:* after the afternoon rest, during the hottest part of the day. The evening was the time for a cool breeze (cp. Gen. 3: 8), especially on the roof-top. *a woman bathing:* verse 4 indicates that the washing was a purification rite after menstruation.

3. *Eliam* (reversed as Ammiel in 1 Chron. 3: 5): an Eliam

[a] in his blanket: *or* on his pallet.

son of Ahithophel is mentioned in 23: 34 among the heroes, but we do not know if they are one and the same. There is no adequate reason for linking Bathsheba with the Ahithophel who appears in 15: 12 and plays an important part in Absalom's rebellion. *Uriah the Hittite:* one of the 'thirty' heroes, according to 23: 38. Since a number of those listed are non-Israelite, we may suppose him to be one such. But his name Uriah, in which the 'iah' is the name of Yahweh, Israel's God, suggests a full member of the community. It is possible that 'Hittite' was a nickname, or that his father had already become part of the Israelite community. The Hittites at an earlier date were a great imperial power in Asia Minor; by this date there were small states in northern Syria which could be regarded as 'Hittite'. The term is, however, also used in the Old Testament to suggest simply alien people (cp. the scathing description of Jerusalem, Samaria and Sodom as sisters, with a Hittite mother and an Amorite father (Ezek. 16: 45f.). This is not genealogy; it is a denunciation of evil ways). The effect of this name here is, however, to suggest that Uriah the alien is to be contrasted for his piety with David the true king.

4. *though she was still being purified...*: if the N.E.B. rendering is correct, then David is being accused of infringement of a ritual law (cp. Lev. 20: 18) as well as of adultery. It may be so, but more probably the phrase simply means that the rites of purification were now complete.

5. The first scene ends with the emergency created by Bathsheba's pregnancy. The punishment for an adulterous wife was death (cp. Num. 5: II–3I for one account of legal procedure).

6–13. The second scene shows David's attempt to get Uriah to father the child. We are naturally to see Uriah as entirely unsuspecting and to presume that David, as in the next part of the story, had sent the appropriate secret instructions to Joab.

7f. The excuse for Uriah's recall appears to be the conveying of news of the campaign. A kindly encouragement to him to go home is accompanied by a royal present, probably a special dish of food (cp. Gen. 43: 34), ostensibly in return for the good news he has brought.

11. Uriah's refusal to go home at all is explained in terms of his rigorous piety. The order of words in the Hebrew is more emphatic than in the N.E.B. It begins: 'The Ark (the symbol of God's presence in battle) and Israel and Judah are under canvas' (the N.E.B. footnote indicates that the word for 'tents' might be a proper name, and that would simply indicate the campaign headquarters; though Succoth – see map, p. 29, for a possible site – is rather far from the capital of Ammon). *sleep with my wife:* a neatly ironical comment in view of what David is endeavouring to contrive. *By your life:* possibly this should be preceded by 'As Yahweh lives'. Uriah pronounces a firm and solemn oath; he cannot be guilty of infringing battle procedure – abstinence from sexual intercourse (cp. note on 1 Sam. 21: 5), or possibly, more simply, from enjoying relaxation. The former is more likely, since the writer clearly wishes to contrast the piety of Uriah with David's sin.

12f. The point is underlined by repetition. Uriah drunk is more pious than David sober. *

THE MURDER OF URIAH CONTRIVED

14 The following morning David wrote a letter to Joab
15 and sent Uriah with it. He wrote in the letter, 'Put Uriah opposite the enemy where the fighting is fiercest and then fall back, and leave him to meet his death.'
16 Joab had been watching the city, and he stationed Uriah at a point where he knew they would put up a stout fight.
17 The men of the city sallied out and engaged Joab, and some of David's guards fell; Uriah the Hittite was also
18 killed. Joab sent David a dispatch with all the news of the
19 battle and gave the messenger these instructions: 'When

you have finished your report to the king, if he is angry 20
and asks, "Why did you go so near the city during the
fight? You must have known there would be shooting
from the wall. Remember who killed Abimelech son of 21
Jerubbesheth.[a] It was a woman who threw down an
upper millstone on to him from the wall of Thebez and
killed him! Why did you go so near the wall?" – if he
asks this, then tell him, "Your servant Uriah the Hittite
also is dead." '

So the messenger set out and, when he came to David, 22
he made his report as Joab had instructed. David was
angry with Joab and said to the messenger, 'Why did
you go so near the city during the fight? You must have
known you would be struck down from the wall.
Remember who killed Abimelech son of Jerubbesheth.
Was it not a woman who threw down an upper millstone on to him from the wall of Thebez and killed him?
Why did you go near the wall?'[b] He answered, 'The 23
enemy massed against us and sallied out into the open;
we pressed them back as far as the gateway. There the 24
archers shot down at us from the wall and some of your
majesty's men fell; and your servant Uriah the Hittite
is dead.' David said to the man, 'Give Joab this message: 25
"Do not let this distress you – there is no knowing where
the sword will strike; press home your attack on the city,
and you will take it and raze it to the ground"; and tell
him to take heart.'

When Uriah's wife heard that her husband was dead, 26
she mourned for him; and when the period of mourning 27

[a] Jerubbaal *in Judg. 9: 1.*
[b] David was angry . . . near the wall?': *so Sept.; Heb. om.*

was over, David sent for her and brought her into his house. She became his wife and bore him a son. But what David had done was wrong in the eyes of the LORD.

* The stratagem of David as here related is not altogether unlike that of Jezebel in her bringing Naboth to his death (1 Kings 21): it is murder, concealed in what is designed to look like a normal sequence of events. The writer makes no comment on Joab's part in this; he is simply the loyal commander who does what he is ordered. It is part of the irony of the whole story that David at the end of his life (1 Kings 2: 5f.) recalls Joab's murder of Abner and Amasa (20: 4–13), and that both at the murder of Abner (3: 23–39) and when Joab's brother Abishai demands Shimei's death (19: 21–3), we see David unable to control 'these ruthless sons of Zeruiah' (3: 39). A modern writer might well have tied these loose ends together; the biblical writer leaves the elements of tragedy side by side.

14. *David wrote a letter to Joab:* the normal procedure would be for the scribe to undertake this and for Joab's scribe to read it to him. The inference is that Uriah cannot read, unless we should suppose a sealed document.

16. *Joab had been watching:* this rendering implies 'examining its defences', whereas the more probable sense is 'guarding'. *where...they would put up a stout fight:* better, more literally, 'where there were warriors stationed', crack troops presumably at a vulnerable point in the fortifications.

19–21. The text is remarkable at this point. Joab, not unreasonably, anticipates David's anger at the loss of members of his bodyguard, and is ready to have that met with an adroit mention of Uriah's death; but in addition, he foresees the rather curious analogy of the death of Abimelech (cp. Judg. 9: 50–7 for the actual incident). Then in verse 22 (see the N.E.B. footnote), the Hebrew text omits the whole of this from David's speech, and it is added from the Septuagint. To

our way of thinking, it would be more natural for the analogy
to appear only in David's speech; but to the ancient writer the
repetition was an effective stylistic device. It underlines the
point.

21. *Abimelech son of Jerubbesheth:* cp. the N.E.B. footnote
for the name. This is another example of the removal of the
divine title *ba'al* (cp. note on 2: 8). Actually, the more familiar
name of Abimelech's father is Gideon, and his name Jerubbaal
is explained in a story in Judg. 6: 25–32. It is possible that
two quite separate groups of traditions have been combined in
Judg. 6–8. The analogy is odd in that Abimelech was hardly a
hero; his story as told in Judg. 9 is an indictment of an upstart
king who came to a bad end; and the point made in the incident of his death is that he lost his life ignominiously because
of a woman's action. The story as related is grimly humorous,
suggesting that in spite of Abimelech's attempt to cover up
what had happened, it had become almost proverbial to refer
to him with the sneering remark: 'A woman killed him' (cp.
Judg. 9: 54). It is also possible that the reference to Abimelech
here is designed to point to a disastrous example of kingship
and to imply how far David went astray from the ideal. This
is another skilful cross-linkage in the whole narrative sequence.

22. On the long addition from the Septuagint, cp. the note
on verses 19–21.

25. David's reversal of attitude is simply stated; the reader
is left to imagine it and to draw his own conclusions. The
writer makes no effort to spare David's reputation. *take it:* not
actually in the text.

26f. The narrator gives us no insight into the attitude of
Bathsheba. When she heard of her husband's death, *she
mourned for him*: she carried out the proper rites, probably for
seven days (cp. 1 Sam. 31: 13). Then, just as apparently she
had accepted David's advances, she became his wife. Later, in
1 Kings 1–2, we find her as a forceful character, fighting for
her son Solomon and also, apparently misguidedly, trying to
influence him in favour of his rival Adonijah. But here she is a

passive figure; it is David who is at the centre. And the
narrator adds his own laconic comment at the end: *what
David had done was wrong in the eyes of the LORD*. This provides a cue for the entrance of the next character. ✻

THE JUDGEMENT OF DAVID

12 The LORD sent Nathan the prophet[a] to David, and
when he entered his presence, he said to him, 'There
were once two men in the same city, one rich and the
2 other poor. The rich man had large flocks and herds,
3 but the poor man had nothing of his own except one
little ewe lamb. He reared it himself, and it grew up in
his home with his own sons. It ate from his dish, drank
from his cup and nestled in his arms; it was like a daughter
4 to him. One day a traveller came to the rich man's
house, and he, too mean to take something from his
own flocks and herds to serve to his guest, took the poor
5 man's lamb and served up that.' David was very angry,
and burst out, 'As the LORD lives, the man who did this
6 deserves to die! He shall pay for the lamb four times over,
7 because he has done this and shown no pity.' Then Nathan
said to David, 'You are the man. This is the word of the
LORD the God of Israel to you: "I anointed you king
8 over Israel, I rescued you from the power of Saul, I
gave you your master's daughter[b] and his wives to be
your own, I gave you the daughters[c] of Israel and Judah;
and, had this not been enough, I would have added other
9 favours as great. Why then have you flouted the word of
the LORD by doing what is wrong in my eyes? You

[a] the prophet: *so some MSS.; others om.*
[b] *Prob. rdg.; Heb.* house.   [c] *So Pesh.; Heb.* house.

106

have struck down Uriah the Hittite with the sword; the
man himself you murdered by the sword of the Ammonites, and you have stolen his wife. Now, therefore, 10
since you have despised me and taken the wife of Uriah
the Hittite to be your own wife, your family shall never
again have rest from the sword." This is the word of the 11
LORD: "I will bring trouble upon you from within your
own family; I will take your wives and give them to
another man before your eyes, and he will lie with them
in broad daylight. What you did was done in secret; 12
but I will do this in the light of day for all Israel to see." '
David said to Nathan, 'I have sinned against the LORD.' 13
Nathan answered him, 'The LORD has laid on another the
consequences of your sin: you shall not die, but, because 14
in this you have shown your contempt for the LORD,*a*
the boy that will be born to you shall die.'

✻ The appearance of Nathan serves a twofold purpose. Like
so many of the other great prophets of Israel, he is here the
mediator of the divine word of judgement. The closest
parallel is again in the story of Ahab and Naboth (1 Kings 21;
cp. above on 11: 14–27), in which Elijah appears to pass a
similar judgement on the royal house. Subsequently, in verses
24f., Nathan is instrumental in conveying a word of promise.
The two themes, judgement on David, promise of his successor Solomon, are tied together in that the same prophet is
responsible for both. Such a pattern of judgement and promise
is to be found repeatedly in the presentation of the words of
the great prophets (cp. the promise at the end of the book of
Amos in 9: 11–15). To the prophetic movement as a whole,
the word of God is two-edged, and its effect depends on the
response that men make. A commentator added a note to

[*a*] the LORD: *prob. rdg.; Heb.* the enemies of the LORD.

the book of Hosea as a reminder of this: 'Let the wise consider these things and let him who considers take note; for the LORD's ways are straight and the righteous walk in them, while sinners stumble' (Hos. 14: 9). A similar point is repeatedly made in the teaching of Deuteronomy (cp. e.g. the sermon in Deut. 30, and especially verses 15–20).

It has often been observed that the Nathan section of the material in this chapter (verses 1–14 together with the opening of verse 15; cp. note below) could have been inserted into an existing narrative in which the judgement is not explained, but comes simply as a divine response to David's wrongdoing. The same may be true of Nathan's appearance in 1 Kings 1, and there are other examples of narratives in which prophets appear and disappear in such a way as to suggest that the final compiler has sought to underline and to interpret the themes of the stories. The point cannot be fully proved, but we may note that the story can be read at more than one level, and that there is a skilful interweaving of themes. We may observe too that the themes which are here brought out are handled in another manner in Prov. 6: 20–35 in which there is reflection on the folly and the evil of such conduct.

1–4. The story related by Nathan is a parable and possibly one which should be set out in poetic form. Another such parable may be seen in Judg. 9: 8–15 on the theme of false kingship. Clearly, like other parables and particularly those of Jesus found in the Gospels, the story which Nathan tells is exaggerated to bring the point out more forcibly. The extreme of contrast between the *rich man* and the *poor* one invites an immediate response where a more balanced story would not necessarily do so (cp. the similar contrast of rich and poor in Luke 16: 19–31). The purpose of a parable, as we see it here, is to involve the hearer and call for a response which commits him to a certain line of thought and action. In particular here, as often, the involvement is an act of self-judgement.

The style of the story must not be overlooked. Nathan is not represented as putting forward a particular legal case which the king is to resolve. David, and with him the reader, hears a fictional case and it is not to be supposed that he for one moment thinks that he is dealing with actuality. His response is an inevitable and natural reaction, but it commits him to the acceptance of judgement upon himself. *too mean:* literally 'he spared to take', a phrase echoed in verse 6 in the words 'shown no pity', literally 'did not spare'.

5f. David's response is what we might expect; it is made in anger at such injustice and in unawareness of the degree to which he is thereby committing himself. *deserves to die:* literally 'a son of death'; we might paraphrase by some such word as 'archvillain', but we should also observe that the Hebrew suggests that the man already in a sense belongs within the realm of death. This is not a death sentence, for such would be inappropriate for the particular offence of theft committed; it is the spontaneous response of righteous indignation to an intolerable action. It is also immediately clear that there is irony in the response, for it is completely apposite to David who is to be declared a murderer (verse 9). *four times over:* the Septuagint has 'seven times' (cp. Prov. 6: 31, in the passage already mentioned above). The hyperbole of this ideal figure is perhaps to be seen as preferable to the exact legal penalty of fourfold restitution which is in accordance with the law (clearly stated in Exod. 22: 1). David is not making a legal pronouncement; he is involving himself in the story. *and shown no pity:* cp. note on 'too mean' (verse 4). A very simple emendation would give: 'but spared what belonged to himself', which makes a better contrast with the preceding phrase.

7. But the real point is that by his comment David has committed himself. So Nathan's pronouncement of judgement, *You are the man*, turns David's words back upon himself. The grounding of the judgement is then stated more fully to be the divine favour to which David ought to have responded in gratitude, not in greed.

8. Twice in this verse (see the N.E.B. footnote) the Hebrew text has 'house' – 'house of your master', 'house of Israel'; the N.E.B., probably correctly, has substituted *daughter* (i.e. Michal) and *daughters* (i.e. David's other wives). The Hebrew text broadens the reference to David's receiving the kingdom of Saul and indeed of all Israel. *his wives to be your own:* this is a point not mentioned elsewhere, but it corresponds to known ancient practice. The dead king's harem belongs to his successor (cp. on 16: 21); possession of the king's wife or wives could be seen as a claim to the throne. (Cp. the stories of Abner and Rizpah in 3: 7 and of Adonijah and Abishag in 1 Kings 2: 13–25: in the latter case, the request for David's last wife by Adonijah is seen as such a claim to the throne, as we may see from Solomon's words (verse 22): 'Why do you ask for Abishag the Shunammite as wife for Adonijah? you might as well ask for the throne.')

9. David's crime is wife-stealing and murder. *flouted the word of the LORD:* cp. 'you have despised me', in verse 10. The same verb is used for both, and possibly 'the word of' is an insertion. The text in these two verses appears to incorporate duplicate readings. It actually states the murder of Uriah twice; the phrase *the man himself...Ammonites* should stand, as it does in the Hebrew, at the end of the verse. This alternative underlines the means by which the murder was carried out.

10. Such a crime is not viewed merely as a social evil; it is an act against God and its penalty should be death. The penalty is here described in terms of continual warfare, a reflection on the whole troubled history of the Davidic dynasty. If this is an exaggerated statement, it nevertheless corresponds closely enough to what actually happened, for periods of real peace were relatively few. The writer is here showing his belief that the whole of his people's experience has a pattern, related to David's behaviour.

11f. The judgement has been pronounced. But a more specific penalty is here added to make a direct link between

David's crime and an event interpreted as its sequel. *trouble . . . within your own family:* chapters 13–19 are devoted to this in the story of Absalom's rebellion. *I will take your wives and give them to another man:* better 'to your close companion', i.e. Absalom. The precise fulfilment of this is given in 16: 21–3. This is making the punishment fit the crime; but more significantly it is an example of a prophecy-fulfilment pattern frequently set out in detail in the Deuteronomic History (cp. e.g. 1 Kings 13: 2 and 2 Kings 23: 17).

13. David's acknowledgement of his sin leads to a partial withdrawal of doom: the same kind of sequel is to be found in the Ahab/Naboth story (cp. 1 Kings 21: 27–9). It is a reminder of the continuing graciousness of God and of his willingness to forgive, even though doom is only transferred or (as in the Naboth case) postponed. As at 7: 4 (see note), a space in the text of some manuscripts suggests a cross-reference, here to Ps. 51, a psalm of penitence, where the title, not printed by the N.E.B., has: '. . . when Nathan the prophet came in to him because he had had intercourse with (literally 'come into') Bathsheba'. This is indicative of a correlating of psalm and narrative which provides an early type of commentary on both. *The LORD has laid on another:* this rendering implies that the unborn child is to bear the judgement which ought to fall on David. Such an interpretation is quite possible, but the text may simply mean: 'The LORD has removed', i.e. caused to pass over. It is better then to end the sentence with the words *you shall not die.*

14. This verse modifies the forgiveness; the child of adultery must not live. *you have shown your contempt for the LORD* (cp. verse 10): a later scribe evidently inserted 'the enemies of' to avoid the terrible statement of the text (cp. the N.E.B. footnote). If that phrase is inserted, we should have to paraphrase: 'you have caused the enemies of the LORD to blaspheme', i.e. you have made a mockery of God's commands so that his enemies will fail to understand his true nature. One of the psalmists, tempted to deny the equity of God's ways,

felt himself constrained by the thought that he would then have 'betrayed the family of God', the loyal members of the community (Ps. 73: 15).

We should add here the opening words of verse 15, rendered simply: 'Then Nathan went home.' ✳

THE BIRTH OF SOLOMON

15 When Nathan had gone home, the LORD struck the boy whom Uriah's wife had borne to David, and he was 16 very ill. David prayed to God for the child; he fasted and went in and spent the night fasting, lying on the ground. 17 The older men of his household tried to get him to rise from the ground, but he refused and would eat no food 18 with them. On the seventh day the boy died, and David's servants were afraid to tell him. 'While the boy was alive,' they said, 'we spoke to him, and he did not listen to us; how can we now tell him that the boy is dead? He may 19 do something desperate.' But David saw his servants whispering among themselves and guessed that the boy was dead. He asked, 'Is the boy dead?', and they answered, 20 'He is dead.' Then David rose from the ground, washed and anointed himself, and put on fresh clothes; he entered the house of the LORD and prostrated himself there. Then he went home, asked for food to be brought, 21 and when it was ready, he ate it. His servants asked him, 'What is this? While the boy lived you fasted and wept for him, but now that he is dead you rise up and eat.' 22 He answered, 'While the boy was still alive I fasted and wept, thinking, "It may be that the LORD will be gracious 23 to me, and the boy may live." But now that he is dead, why should I fast? Can I bring him back again? I shall

go to him; he will not come back to me.' David consoled 24
Bathsheba his wife; he went to her and had intercourse
with her, and she gave birth to a son and called*a* him
Solomon. And because the LORD loved him, he sent 25
word through Nathan the prophet that for the LORD's
sake he should be given the name Jedidiah.*b*

✻ As this section of the story now stands, it is to be read as the
carrying through of God's word of judgement spoken by
Nathan. But it follows in fact somewhat better as a sequel to
11: 27, since the endeavour of David to save the child's life is
less appropriate after the absoluteness of judgement stated in
verse 14. There has been skilful interweaving, but the style of
the story here is less overtly theological than the Nathan
section. Although the main part of the passage is concerned
with the death of Bathsheba's first child, the real point comes
at the end in the birth of Solomon, its significance underlined
by the comment in the new appearance of Nathan in verse 25.
David's sin is turned by God into the promise for the future,
the successor, the temple-builder. A comparison may be made
with the fuller exposition of such a theme in the Joseph story,
where the climax is in the words of Joseph to his brothers:
'You meant to do me harm; but God meant to bring good
out of it by preserving the lives of many people' (Gen. 50:
20).

15. *the LORD struck the boy...*: possibly the original sequel
to 11: 27, i.e. 'But what David had done was wrong in the
eyes of the LORD and so...'

16. *he fasted and went in:* David entered the shrine to spend
the night fasting and prostrate before God; he undergirds his
prayer with appropriate action. A Qumran text adds a reference to 'in sackcloth' after *lying.*

17. It is evident that David's actions were felt to be carrying

[*a*] and called: *or, as otherwise read,* and he called.
[*b*] *That is* Beloved of the LORD.

privation to a dangerous extreme; we are to assume that he performed the same actions each night for seven nights.

18f. The picture conveyed of courtiers and an irascible king is very vivid. *something desperate:* the word means 'a calamity', which could well befall the servant who brought the bad news.

20f. David's actions – washing, anointing with oil, *fresh clothes* – are appropriate signs of return to normal after fasting (cp. Matt. 6: 17f. for a comment on the external customs). The strangeness of David's behaviour is linked with the normal practice of mourning customs (cp. 1: 12f.; 3: 31f.). His eating has been interpreted as a funeral meal, but in this context appears rather as a sign of his acceptance of God's will. This is explained in verse 22.

23. *Can I bring him back again?:* the absoluteness of death is thus accepted. David will join his son in Sheol, the realm of the dead; but none can return from there. It is known, in fact, in the ancient Near East as the 'Land of no return'. For very vivid language describing notions of the realm of the dead cp. Job 3: 13–19 and Isa. 14: 9–18.

24. *and called him Solomon:* naming might be by the mother (cp. Gen. 35: 16–18 and 1 Sam. 4: 21 where the text has 'she named the boy', as in fact some manuscripts have here) or by the father (cp. footnote and Abraham's naming of Isaac in Gen. 21: 3). In fact the text may be simply rendered 'he was called', i.e. 'one called', an impersonal construction. The name Solomon is connected with the Hebrew word *shālōm*, peace, well-being, prosperity: in this context it emphasizes the restoration of divine favour, and might also carry the sense of 'restitution', i.e. the second son as a replacement for the lost first one. It may also be observed that both this name and that of Absalom, incorporating the same element *shālōm*, may be seen to have a link with the name Jerusalem (Salem in Gen. 14: 18) in which the same element may possibly denote the name or title of a deity. *the LORD loved him:* the phrase may, as in the Hebrew text, be joined to what

precedes. The purpose of God is declared in this apparently
arbitrary choice of the child of David and Bathsheba. The
sequel comes only in 1 Kings 1 where there is, however, no
reference back to this passage; but we are invited to read the
story of the court intrigue there in the light of what we already
know. It is possible too that a contrast is intended between
Bathsheba through whom the successor comes and Michal the
barren (6: 23); the divine choice is as mysterious here as in the
choice of Jacob rather than Esau (cp. Mal. 1: 2f. and Rom. 9:
13 for comments).

25. *he sent word through Nathan the prophet*: this is better
seen as an addition underlining the choice of Solomon with
prophetic, and hence with divine, authority. The second
naming is not explained, though a number of Old (and New)
Testament personages have two names, one of which may
designate purpose or character (cp. Jacob–Israel, Gen. 32: 28;
Simon–Peter, Matt. 16: 18). Here *Jedidiah*, 'Beloved of the
LORD' (cp. the N.E.B. footnote), further emphasizes what
Solomon is to be, though curiously this name does not
appear again. There is some evidence for throne-names in
Israel (cp. on 21: 19 and the naming of the last kings of Judah
in 2 Kings: Eliakim–Jehoiakim, 23: 34; Mattaniah–Zedekiah,
24: 17). If so, we may suppose Jedidiah to have been the original name and Solomon the throne-name; but this is merely
supposition. ✲

VICTORY OVER THE AMMONITES

Joab attacked the Ammonite city of Rabbah and took 26[a]
the King's Pool. He sent messengers to David with this 27
report: 'I have attacked Rabbah and have taken the pool.
You had better muster the rest of the army yourself, 28
besiege the city and take it; otherwise I shall take the
city and the name to be proclaimed over it will be mine.'

[a] *Verses 26–31: cp. 1 Chron. 20: 1–3.*

29 David accordingly mustered his whole forces, marched
30 to Rabbah, attacked it and took it. He took the crown
from the head of Milcom, which weighed a talent of
gold and was set with*[a]* a precious stone, and this he placed
on his own head. He also removed a great quantity of
31 booty from the city; he took its inhabitants and set them
to work with saws and other iron tools, sharp and tooth-
ed, and made them work in the brick-kilns. David did
this to all the cities of the Ammonites; then he and all his
people returned to Jerusalem.

✻ The story of the Ammonite war is resumed and concluded.
   26. *the King's Pool:* the text has 'the royal city', but since
verse 27 has 'the water city' (N.E.B. 'the pool'), we may
suppose that what is meant is a specially fortified area controlling access to the water-supply, a vital matter to a besieged city. A number of great constructions have been found,
e.g. at Megiddo, designed to enable access to the spring which
lies outside the city through a staircase and tunnel. Special
fortification would presumably also be needed outside the
city, especially where in peacetime access to the water would
be by the normal route out through the city gate (sometimes
known as the 'Water-Gate', cp. Neh. 3: 26).
   27. With the control of the water-supply in Israelite hands,
the fall of the city is imminent.
   28. *the name to be proclaimed over it will be mine:* just as
Jerusalem was called the 'City of David' (5: 7). The anxiety
of Joab to have David present is a strong expression of loyalty
since he could claim the honour for himself. The statement
appears to indicate a custom of warfare.
   30. *the crown from the head of Milcom:* Milcom is known to
us as the name, or better, as the title, of the Ammonite deity
(cp. 1 Kings 11: 33 for a list of the deities of various peoples).

[a] was set with: *so Pesh.; Heb. om.*

Milcom, derived from *melek*, king, would be descriptive of the deity as supreme ruler. But the text actually has *malkām* which means 'their king', and since David places the crown, or perhaps the *precious stone, on his own head*, this seems a better sense. This may then be understood to mean that David was deposing the Ammonite king and was considering himself as taking over the kingship there. The weight of the crown – *a talent of gold* might be about 30 kg (66 lb) – though more suited to an idol, is not really an objection to this view. We may in any case allow for some measure of exaggeration.

31. The sequel to victory is plunder and servitude: *all the cities of the Ammonites* are reduced to total subjection. The precise nature of the tools mentioned is not clear. The text would seem to indicate (as the N.E.B. does) subjection to forced labour, though earlier it was believed that it denoted torture.

The end of the Ammonite war marks David's supremacy. Having brought his readers to this climax, the compiler moves at once into the major threat to the kingdom's well-being, the rebellion of Absalom. ✵

Absalom's rebellion

✵ The N.E.B. heading's reference to 'other conflicts' here is inappropriate. The section from 13: 1 – 19: 8 is entirely concerned with Absalom's rebellion, and it is only in what follows that 'other conflicts' are handled. ✵

THE RAPE OF TAMAR

Now David's son Absalom had a beautiful sister 13 named Tamar, and Amnon, another of David's sons, fell in love with her. Amnon was so distressed that 2 he fell sick with love for his half-sister; for he thought

it an impossible thing to approach her since she was a
3 virgin. But he had a friend named Jonadab, son of David's
4 brother Shimeah, who was a very shrewd man. He said
to Amnon, 'Why are you so low-spirited morning after
morning, my lord? Will you not tell me?' So Amnon
told him that he was in love with Tamar, his brother
5 Absalom's sister. Jonadab said to him, 'Take to your
bed and pretend to be ill. When your father comes to
visit you, say to him, "Please let my sister Tamar come
and give me my food. Let her prepare it in front of me,
so that I may watch her and then take it from her own
6 hands."' So Amnon lay down and pretended to be ill.
When the king came to visit him, he said, 'Sir, let my
sister Tamar come and make a few cakes in front of me,
7 and serve them to me with her own hands.' So David
sent a message to Tamar in the palace: 'Go to your
brother Amnon's quarters and prepare a meal for him.'
8 Tamar came to her brother and found him lying down;
she took some dough and kneaded it, made the cakes in
9 front of him and baked them. Then she took the pan and
turned them out before him. But Amnon refused to eat
and ordered everyone out of the room. When they had
10 all left, he said to Tamar, 'Bring the food over to the
recess so that I may eat from your own hands.' Tamar
took the cakes she had made and brought them to
11 Amnon in the recess. But when she offered them to him,
he caught hold of her and said, 'Come to bed with me,
12 sister.' But she answered, 'No, brother, do not dishonour
me, we do not do such things in Israel; do not behave
13 like a beast. Where could I go and hide my disgrace? –
and you would sink as low as any beast in Israel. Why

not speak to the king for me? He will not refuse you leave 14
to marry me.' He would not listen, but overpowered
her, dishonoured her and raped her.

Then Amnon was filled with utter hatred for her; his 15
hatred was stronger than the love he had felt, and he said
to her, 'Get up and go.' She answered, 'No. It is wicked 16
to send me away. This is harder to bear than all you have
done to me.' He would not listen to her, but summoned 17
the boy who attended him and said, 'Get rid of this
woman, put her out and bolt the door after her.' She 18
had on a long, sleeved robe, the usual dress of unmarried princesses; and the boy turned her out and bolted
the door. Tamar threw ashes over her head, rent the long, 19
sleeved robe that she was wearing, put her hands on her
head and went away, sobbing as she went. Her brother 20
Absalom asked her, 'Has your brother Amnon been
with you? Keep this to yourself, he is your brother; do
not take it to heart.' So Tamar remained in her brother
Absalom's house, desolate. When King David heard the 21
whole story he was very angry; but he would not hurt
Amnon because he was his eldest son and he loved him.[a]
Absalom did not speak a single word to Amnon, friendly 22
or unfriendly; he hated him for having dishonoured his
sister Tamar.

* The space given to Absalom's rebellion (13: 1 – 19: 8)
emphasizes its significance: David nearly lost his throne
entirely, and had this happened, subsequent history would
have been very different. The narrator combines various
motifs in this narrative. There are indications of David's weakness and partiality; there is Absalom's ambition; there is

[a] but he . . . loved him: *so Sept.; Heb. om.*

evident some measure of discontent and rivalry within the various tribes and areas which make up the kingdom. It is a vivid story, so vivid that many scholars have believed it to be nearly contemporary with the events it describes; and this has indeed been supposed for the larger section 2 Sam. 9–20; 1 Kings 1–2 (cp. p. 10). But the interlinkages between all these chapters and what precedes and follows suggest that, whatever the compiler inherited, he used it with some freedom. And the story of Absalom contains various elements which are not entirely dovetailed; we may note the degree of theological interpretation either explicit or implicit, the presence of non-historical elements in the presentation (see especially the comments on chapter 15), and see that this section fits into the overall pattern of 2 Samuel. The promise of succession is being worked out; immediately after the designation of Solomon as God's loved one, the story of the greatest threat to the succession is introduced. The narrator, as a good writer, knows how to hold his readers in suspense, waiting to see the outcome. This serves also to underline the mystery and at the same time the absoluteness of divine action; human affairs are to be seen as overruled by God.

1. *Now:* the text actually begins: 'Now after this' which the N.E.B. renders 'some time afterwards' in 10: 1. The link is not in any way a precise chronological one, and indeed it is impossible on the evidence available to us to put all the David narratives in a completely satisfactory sequence. *Absalom... Tamar...Amnon:* cp. the family list in 3: 2–5 and notes there. Amnon and Absalom were half-brothers, sons of David but by different mothers. *beautiful:* cp. for David (1 Sam. 16: 12), for Absalom (2 Sam. 14: 25) and for Adonijah (1 Kings 1: 6).

2. The description of love-sickness is very vivid, as indeed the whole of this narrative shows what today would be called 'psychological insight'. The narrator did not need any modern jargon to enable him to appreciate the nature of human behaviour. *he fell sick* with: great subtlety, the Hebrew uses

exactly the same word in verse 5 to mean 'pretend to be ill'.
since she was a virgin: this suggests both a concern here about
possible penalties, though this is not eventually a deterrent,
and a hint that, as was proper, unmarried girls, and particularly those of the royal house, would be carefully guarded. A
woman's value, particularly that of a princess, useful in
political alliance, was lowered by loss of virginity (cp. Deut.
22: 28f., which makes clear that in an ordinary case financial
compensation would be required).

3. *Jonadab:* Amnon's cousin. *a friend:* since Amnon was the
eldest son and perhaps therefore heir-presumptive to the
throne, this friend could possibly be the special officer and
associate who would in due course become the 'King's
Friend' (cp. on 15: 37 for a fuller note on his position). *a very
shrewd man:* the word used is *ḥākām,* wise, and this indicates an
important aspect of the Hebrew idea of wisdom: 'skill' or
'craft', 'ability to attain an end'.

5–7. We cannot fully understand the stratagem, though it
is evident that it involved an intelligible request which David
accepted at its face value. Some special merit is thought to
belong to food prepared in the sick man's presence and
administered to him by a young woman, perhaps especially if
she were a virgin. The nearest parallel is in the attempt to
revive David in old age by the use of the virgin Abishag
(1 Kings 1: 1–4), for though there the problem is warmth, the
idea of the transference of vitality is also present. *a few cakes:*
or 'two cakes'. The word is used only here; it might mean
'heart-shaped', possibly having religious significance (cp.
'crescent-cakes', i.e. moon-shaped, for the queen of heaven
in Jer. 7: 18), or it may express the idea of 'desirable food'.
a meal (verse 7): better simply 'food' as in verse 5.

8. *baked:* the word means 'boil' and is distinguished from
another Hebrew word meaning 'bake'. We should not
assume that what is meant corresponds closely to our modern
ideas.

10. *to the recess:* or 'the inner room'. *from your own hands:*

there is perhaps thought to be some special merit in direct physical contact.

12. *do not dishonour me:* or 'humiliate', a word particularly used for violent sexual action. *we do not do such things in Israel:* an appeal to normal and accepted standards of right conduct. *do not behave like a beast:* a very free translation, designed to bring out the force of a word which means 'folly' or 'impiety', i.e. something which is contrary to proper ways. It is the same word as appears as a proper name Nabal in 1 Sam. 25 (cp. the note there on verse 25). The fool is the man who has no proper regard for either the divine will or the proprieties of human conduct; he may be described as 'brutish' or as a 'mere beast' (cp. Ps. 73: 22).

13. *as any beast:* cp. previous note; literally 'as one of the fools', the churls, the impious. Tamar appeals to Amnon's better nature; marriage between half-brother and half-sister was evidently possible, though later laws (e.g. Lev. 18: 9) forbid it. We are not told whether Tamar had any feelings about such a marriage, any more than we are told what Bathsheba thought about David's approaches. As a dutiful daughter, she would accept the obligations of her position (cp. the attitude of Rebecca in Gen. 24: 58).

15. *his hatred was stronger than the love he had felt:* a modern novelist might spend pages analysing such a reaction. The biblical writer simply speaks from knowledge and experience of human nature and particularly of the irrationality of sexual attraction and revulsion.

16. The text is not completely clear. A possible emendation is: 'No, my brother, to send me away (now) is a greater evil than the other which you have done me.' But it is possible that an originally longer text has been accidentally curtailed. At this point, Tamar's one hope might seem to rest in persuading Amnon to put the matter right by asking David's consent to marriage.

17. *this woman:* a derogatory term expressive of his hatred.
18. The clauses in this verse are clearly out of order. The

comment on the *long, sleeved robe* really belongs as a note to
verse 19; this is explained as being the customary wear for
the *unmarried princesses*. Change of dress-style at marriage is
common in the Near East.

19. Tamar's actions are typical of mourning; it is as if she
sees herself as already dead as a result of the evil which has
been done to her.

20. Absalom's protection of his sister is to be the first basis
for his rupture with his father, but as yet no hint is given of
this. *desolate*: the same word is used of a 'deserted wife' in Isa.
54: 1. What happened to Tamar is not specified; as her
brother, Absalom was offering protection, against any imposing of penalty on her which would be a matter of family
duty.

21. The second half of the verse is missing in the Hebrew,
but is an essential part of the text. Partiality towards his sons
was a failing to appear again in David's handling of Absalom.

22. *friendly or unfriendly*: i.e. total silence. It is a silence not
of unwillingness to act, but of waiting for an unguarded
moment.

The use of this incident as the first cause of Absalom's
subsequent rebellion shows the narrator's skill. He has shown
David's sin with Bathsheba as evoking a divine judgement
upon the royal house; now he shows another such sin as
initiating that judgement. *

ABSALOM'S REVENGE AND EXILE

Two years later Absalom invited all the king's sons to 23
his sheep-shearing at Baal-hazor, near Ephron.[a] He 24
approached the king and said, 'Sir, I am shearing; will
your majesty and your servants come?' The king answer- 25
ed, 'No, my son, we must not all come and be a burden

[a] *Prob. rdg.; Heb.* Ephraim.

to you.' Absalom pressed[a] him, but David was still un-
26 willing to go and dismissed him with his blessing. But
Absalom said, 'If you cannot, may my brother Amnon
come with us?' 'Why should he go with you?' the king
27 asked; but Absalom pressed[a] him again, so he let Amnon
and all the other princes go with him.

28   Then Absalom prepared a feast fit for a king.[b] He gave
his servants these orders: 'Bide your time, and when
Amnon is merry with wine I shall say to you, "Strike."
Then kill Amnon. You have nothing to fear, these are
29 my orders; be bold and resolute.' Absalom's servants did
as he had told them, whereupon all the king's sons
mounted their mules in haste and set off for home.

30   While they were on their way, a rumour reached
David that Absalom had murdered all the royal princes
31 and that not one was left alive. The king stood up and
rent his clothes and then threw himself on the ground;
all his servants were standing round him with their
32 clothes rent. Then Jonadab, son of David's brother Shimeah, said, 'Your majesty must not think that they have
killed all the young princes; only Amnon is dead;
Absalom has looked black ever since Amnon ravished
33 his sister Tamar. Your majesty must not pay attention
to a mere rumour that all the princes are dead; only
Amnon is dead.'

34   Absalom made good his escape. Meanwhile the sentry
looked up and saw a crowd of people coming down the
hill from the direction of Horonaim.[c] He came and

[a] *So Sept.; Heb.* broke out on . . .
[b] Then Absalom . . . king: *so Sept.; Heb. om.*
[c] *Prob. rdg.; Heb.* from a road behind him.

reported to the king, 'I see men coming down the hill from
Horonaim.'^a Then Jonadab said to the king, 'Here 35
come the royal princes, just as I said they would.' As he 36
finished speaking, the princes came in and broke into
loud lamentations; the king and all his servants also
wept bitterly.

But Absalom went to take refuge with Talmai son of 37
Ammihur king of Geshur; and for a long while the king
mourned for Amnon.

✻ Absalom, by waiting two years, creates a sense of false
security for Amnon. He takes his revenge, but it begins to
emerge that he is concerned with more than this.

23. *sheep-shearing:* not surprisingly, this important event in
the farmer's year is an occasion for a great feast (cp. 1 Sam.
25: 4). *Baal-hazor, near Ephron:* possibly north-east of Jerusalem, but its identity is uncertain.

24. The invitation to the king is a skilful device; had David
accepted, Absalom could afford to await another opportunity.

25. *pressed him:* cp. the N.E.B. footnote; the same
confusion of words occurs in verse 27 and in 1 Sam. 28:
23.

26. *my brother Amnon:* it would seem natural, since David
refused, to invite the eldest son who would be regarded as the
king's representative. David's question neither demands nor
excludes the possibility of a suspicion in his mind about
Absalom's intentions.

28. *a feast fit for a king:* more literally 'a feast like a royal
feast'. There is a subtle implication here that Absalom is
behaving already as if he were king (cp. on 15: 1–6).

29f. In the panic which followed Amnon's murder, the
other royal princes took to flight, and we are to assume that a
fugitive who had only partly observed what was going on

[a] He came ... from Horonaim': *so Sept.; Heb. om.*

came quickly ahead with grim news. *mules:* royal mounts (cp. 18: 9).

31. The king and his courtiers perform the customary mourning rites.

32. Jonadab shows himself to be shrewd and observant. Where David, apparently too indulgent to his sons (cp. on verse 21), does not see clearly, Jonadab has observed Absalom's patient waiting on his opportunity. *has looked black:* a strange word is used which may denote a 'scowl' or 'frown' (an inauspicious look) on the face of Absalom. Or we might render: 'By the mouth of Absalom it has been settled.'

34. *Absalom made good his escape:* this could be better regarded as the last part of Jonadab's words. The section of narrative from here to verse 39 interweaves the scenes at court with the escape of Absalom. It may be that some of the clauses are out of order – thus the second half of verse 37 would seem to belong really with verse 36. But we may also see in the arrangement the skill of a writer who holds our interest in the two aspects of the story, David's behaviour and Absalom's fortunes. The same technique is more fully developed in chapters 15–18. *Horonaim:* the dual form (ending in *aim*) appears to refer to the two places Upper and Lower Beth-horon (see map, p. 85). The copyist's eye seems to have jumped from the first to the second occurrence of the name, and at a later stage still the name itself was miscopied to give: 'from the direction (road) behind him' (i.e. to the west; cp. the N.E.B. footnote).

37. *Talmai...king of Geshur:* the father of Absalom's mother Maacah (cp. 3: 3).

Verses 38f., attached to this section in the N.E.B., are in part repetitive, and may perhaps best be viewed as the beginning of the next section. ✻

JOAB CONTRIVES ABSALOM'S RETURN

Absalom, having escaped to Geshur, stayed there for 38
three years; and David's heart*ᵃ* went out to him with 39
longing, for he became reconciled to the death of Amnon.

Joab son of Zeruiah saw that the king's heart was set **14**
on Absalom, so he sent to Tekoa and fetched a wise 2
woman. He said to her, 'Pretend to be a mourner; put
on mourning, go without anointing yourself, and behave
like a bereaved woman who has been long in mourning.
Then go to the king and repeat what I tell you.' He then 3
told her exactly what she was to say.

When the woman from Tekoa came into the king's 4
presence,*ᵇ* she threw herself, face downwards, on the
ground and did obeisance, and cried, 'Help, your
majesty!' The king asked, 'What is it?' She answered, 5
'O sir, I am a widow; my husband is dead. I had two 6
sons; they came to blows out in the country where there
was no one to part them, and one of them struck the
other and killed him. Now, sir, the kinsmen have risen 7
against me and they all cry, "Hand over the man who
has killed his brother, so that we can put him to death for
taking his brother's life, and so cut off the succession."
If they do this, they will stamp out my last live ember
and leave my husband no name and no descendant upon
earth.'*ᶜ* 'Go home,' said the king to the woman, 'and I 8
will settle your case.' But the woman continued, 'The 9
guilt be on me, your majesty, and on my father's house;

[a] David's heart: *so Targ.; Heb.* David.
[b] came . . . presence: *so some MSS.; others* said to the king.
[c] *See note on verse 15.*

10 let the king and his throne be blameless.' The king said,
'If anyone says anything more to you, bring him to me
11 and he shall never molest you again.' Then the woman
went on, 'Let your majesty call upon the LORD your
God, to prevent his kinsmen bound to vengeance from
doing their worst and destroying my son.' The king
swore, 'As the LORD lives, not a hair of your son's head
shall fall to the ground.'

12   The woman then said, 'May I add one word more,
13 your majesty?' 'Say on', said the king. So she continued, 'How then could it enter your head to do this
same wrong to God's people? Out of your own mouth,
your majesty, you condemn yourself: you have refused
14 to bring back the man you have banished. We shall all
die; we shall be like water that is spilt on the ground and
lost; but God will spare the man who does not set him-
15*a* self to keep the outlaw in banishment. I came to say this to
your majesty because the people have threatened me.
I thought, "If I can only speak to the king, perhaps he
16 will attend to my case; for he will listen, and he will save
me from the man who is seeking*b* to cut off me and my
17 son together from Israel, God's own possession." I
thought too that the words of my lord the king would
be a comfort to me; for your majesty is like the angel of
God and can decide between right and wrong. The
18 LORD your God be with you!' Then the king said to the
woman, 'Tell me no lies: I shall now ask you a ques-
19 tion.' 'Speak on, your majesty', she said. So he asked,
'Is the hand of Joab behind you in all this?' 'Your life

[a] *Probably verses 15–17 are misplaced and should follow verse 7.*
[b] who is seeking: *so Sept.; Heb. om.*

upon it, sir!' she answered; 'when your majesty asks a
question, there is no way round it, right or left. Yes,
your servant Joab did prompt me; it was he who put the
whole story into my mouth. He did it to give a new turn 20
to this affair. Your majesty is as wise as the angel of
God and knows all that goes on in the land.'

The king said to Joab, 'You have my consent; go 21
and fetch back the young man Absalom.' Then Joab 22
humbly prostrated himself, took leave of the king with a
blessing and said, 'Now I know that I have found favour
with your majesty, because you have granted my humble
petition.' Joab went at once to Geshur and brought Ab- 23
salom to Jerusalem, but the king said, 'Let him go to his 24
own quarters; he shall not come into my presence.' So
Absalom went to his own quarters and did not enter the
king's presence.

✶ Joab adopts a stratagem to persuade David to recall
Absalom. In one way, what he does is like Nathan's telling of
his parable (12: 1–4); the story told by the wise woman
evokes a response from David, and he discovers that he has
committed himself to restoring Absalom, his heir. In another
way, the woman's action is like an acted symbol, of a kind
well known among the prophets: the carrying out of the
action is itself part of the divine message (cp. 1 Sam. 15: 27f.
and note; cp. e.g. Jeremiah's breaking of the jar as symbol of
judgement in Jer. 19). In this, the woman's mourning garments are symbolic of the state of Israel, lacking an heir to the
throne (cp. on verse 14). A similar intervention by a wise
woman is related in chapter 20, and the parallel strongly suggests that the motive is essentially the same in each case: to
preserve the life of the people and kingdom. But this is implied
rather than stated.

38f. Verse 38 is resumptive. *David's heart:* the Hebrew text actually has 'David the king'; the reading 'the king's heart' ('spirit') is also to be found in a Qumran manuscript. The meaning of the opening part of the verse is not at all clear. We should not see in David's change of attitude any callousness about Amnon's death, but more evidently his affection for his sons combined with a concern for the future of the kingdom. So Absalom appears as the eldest remaining son, the natural heir to the throne, even though there does not seem to have been any regular rule (cp. the narrative of 1 Kings 1). At this point in the narrative, the outcome is unclear. Amnon the eldest son is dead. Chileab, mentioned in 3: 3, is not named again. Absalom is in exile. Where does the succession lie? The danger to the kingdom is the theme of the wise woman's story.

14: 1. *the king's heart was set on Absalom:* this phrase picks up the motif of the previous verse. At this point the emphasis of the story is on David's affection for his son, unchanged by the murder of Amnon. *Tekoa:* see map, p. 29; the home of the prophet Amos (Amos 1: 1). *a wise woman:* as often in the Old Testament, wisdom consists of the ability to use words to give sound advice or to bring about a desired effect. The wise woman of 20: 16–22 was similarly gifted. The significance of her home being in Tekoa is not indicated. The supposition that it was a place which had a tradition of wisdom is not borne out by any other evidence, though some scholars have claimed to find such evidence in wisdom themes and language in Amos. Chapter 20 shows another place where such a woman was to be found.

2. Whereas Nathan spoke a parable, the wise woman is to act as if she were a mourner of long-standing.

3. The N.E.B. rendering *exactly what she was to say* suggests that her wisdom was hardly relevant; Joab is described as 'putting the words into her mouth'.

4. The woman's action is a clear indication that, in a difficult case, appeal could be made to the king. This is indicated

by 15: 1–6 too, and also by 1 Kings 3: 16–28. We do not know the precise customs involved, but may observe that Deut. 17: 8f., in a law which may well envisage the later, post-monarchical situation, speaks of 'any lawsuit...beyond your competence', i.e. that of the local community.

5. *O sir:* a strong particle meaning 'indeed', 'truly'. *I am a widow; my husband is dead:* the repetitive statement underlines the first aspect of the problem.

6. *I had:* literally, the polite form 'your handmaid had'. *two sons; they came to blows out in the country:* the story is here reminiscent of that of Cain and Abel (Gen. 4: 8). *to part them:* literally 'to rescue them'.

7. *the kinsmen:* literally 'the whole clan'. *Hand over the man who has killed his brother...:* murder is punishable by death (cp. e.g. Exod. 21: 12); but it is here that the other aspect of the problem appears. *and so cut off the succession:* this is expressed rather curiously as if it were part of the kinsmen's words; it would be more natural to read 'and so they will cut off...'. If the second son is killed, there will be none remaining to *leave my husband* a *name* and a *descendant* (literally 'remnant', 'one who survives'). The same theme is essential to the book of Ruth (cp. Ruth 1: 11f.), where the dilemma is resolved by the marriage of Ruth to her dead husband's kinsman Boaz. The custom of levirate marriage (marriage to a brother-in-law (Latin *levir*) or other close relative) was aimed at meeting such a problem. The surviving son could by marriage and children preserve the dead husband's name and lineage (cp. Deut. 25: 5–10 and the story in the Gospels, e.g. Matt. 22: 23–33). The problem here lies in the meeting of two legal principles: punishment by death for murder, and preservation of name and line. In such a situation, it may well appear that an appeal to a higher authority can alone resolve the dilemma.

After verse 7, as the N.E.B. footnote indicates, it may be proper to insert verses 15–17. It will be seen that these verses appear to be out of place where they stand and they would make good sense here. Their present position may be the result of accidental misplacing; or it may be that a copyist who wished to draw out more precisely the similarity between the woman's hypothetical case and that of David and Absalom transposed the words. Thus the phrases in verse 16 'me and my son' and 'Israel, God's own possession' point to David and Absalom and they hint also at the theme of danger to the community, which would be left less than perfect if one member family is lost (cp. comments on 20: 16–22).

9–11. The king's response in verse 8 appears to settle the matter, but since the real concern is to commit David to action in a different question, these verses serve to underline the point.

9. *The guilt be on me:* more than a polite formula, this is a recognition that responsibility for transgressing the law must be laid somewhere. *let the king and his throne be blameless:* points also to the real concern with David and his successor.

11. *to prevent his kinsmen bound to vengeance:* there is a reference here to the 'kinsman of blood', or perhaps better the 'avenger of blood', sometimes believed to be an official, or a person specially designated, to resolve the difficult case of whether a man in such a situation was guilty of murder or of manslaughter. The point is not raised in this narrative, but no clear evidence was necessarily available to prove whether or not the brother had intended murder (cp. the laws on cities of refuge in Deut. 19: 6 and the comment on this point in *Deuteronomy* in this series). David's oath that the son will not be harmed commits him firmly to doing the same for Absalom. *from doing their worst:* more literally 'from totally destroying'.

13. The point of the story is now made plain in its direct application to Absalom, *the man you have banished.*

14. This is a problematic verse. The second part makes it clear that the reference is still to the problem of Absalom, *the outlaw.* The first half appears to be a general comment on life and death (cp. 12: 23). But in that case the last part of the verse

is unattached. It is therefore better to consider the whole verse as having reference to the condition of the community. If Absalom remains an outlaw, then the king has no successor – for the purpose of the argument, it is the loss of the eldest son and successor which is at stake – then we, the community, perish. The metaphor of spilling water on the ground is a vivid way of expressing irretrievable loss.

15–17. On these verses, cp. the note after verse 7.

17. *be a comfort to me:* an appropriate word to the woman's story, but even more appropriate to the community. It is a word often translated 'rest' – cp. on 7: 1 – and suggestive of a divinely blessed people settled in the land where 'rest' is to be found (cp. Ps. 95: 11). *like the angel of God:* the king is especially close to God and may therefore be his 'messenger' (angel), able to decide a difficult case and also to mediate well-being (cp. verse 20 and 1 Sam. 29: 9).

18. This verse is to be linked to verse 14.

19. David immediately detects the hand of Joab. The woman's reply again emphasizes the nature of royal discernment. It will be observed that if verses 15–17 are read after verse 7, this statement neatly balances the statement of verse 17 standing within the woman's narrative. *no way round it, right or left:* truth lies exactly in what the king has said.

20. *to give a new turn to this affair:* an expression which suggests a comparison with 1 Kings 12: 15 where God is described as acting in and through Rehoboam's folly and 'had given this turn to the affair' (literally 'a turn about', a reversal). The action of Joab and the woman is now reinforced by David's resolve, but we may see in the concluding comment of this verse that it is the king's wisdom, linked to the divine world, which makes plain that what is happening is divinely overruled. Again we may observe the irony of the narrative; this 'turn about in the affair' will bring back Absalom, but not to succession and well-being for the kingdom. David's security will be radically threatened; Absalom will die.

24. The refusal of David to see Absalom represents the vacillation between favour and disfavour; it is as if the king cannot make up his mind to full reconciliation. ✳

ABSALOM RESTORED TO FAVOUR

25 No one in all Israel was so greatly admired for his beauty as Absalom; he was without flaw from the crown 26 of his head to the sole of his foot. His hair, when he cut his hair (as he had to do every year, for he found it heavy), weighed two hundred shekels by the royal 27 standard. Three sons were born to Absalom, and a daughter named Tamar, who was a very beautiful woman.

28 Absalom remained in Jerusalem for two whole years 29 without entering the king's presence. He summoned Joab to send a message by him to the king, but Joab refused to come; he sent for him a second time, but he 30 still refused. Then Absalom said to his servants, 'You know that Joab has a field next to mine with barley growing in it; go and set fire to it.' So Absalom's ser-31 vants set fire to the field. Joab promptly came to Absalom in his own quarters and said to him, 'Why have 32 your servants set fire to my field?' Absalom answered Joab, 'I had sent for you to come here, so that I could ask you to give the king this message from me: "Why did I leave Geshur? It would be better for me if I were still there. Let me now come into your majesty's presence 33 and, if I have done any wrong, put me to death."' When Joab went to the king and told him, he summoned Absalom, who came and prostrated himself humbly before the king; and he greeted Absalom with a kiss.

✻ 25-7. These verses interrupt the narrative to give some detail about Absalom. He was a strongly attractive personality, as may be seen from the measure of adherence to him in the rebellion (cp. chapters 15-16). We note here similar indications of personal appearance as in the David tradition (cp. 1 Sam. 16: 12, 18); and indeed Saul too was evidently of impressive stature (1 Sam. 9: 2; 10: 23f.). Loyalty to a leader may well be linked to personal attraction. The statement about Absalom's hair (verse 26) is clearly exaggerated: *two hundred shekels by the royal standard* might be about 2.3 kg (5 lb). A weight from Gezer marked 'for the king' demonstrates the existence of such a royal standard. But it is not simply a matter of personal beauty, since hair is a mark of virility and power (cp. the story of Samson, especially Judg. 16). We may wonder whether this fragment has been added here to comment on verse 11 'not a hair of your son's head shall fall', applied to Absalom. *Three sons:* but cp. 18: 18 which has another and contradictory note about Absalom. *a daughter named Tamar:* she could have been named after Absalom's sister (chapter 13), though it is possible that this isolated note contains a hint of an alternative tradition that it was his daughter rather than his sister whom Amnon raped.

28. The narrative of verse 24 is resumed.

29. Joab's refusal to respond to Absalom's summons may be expressive of a fear lest another approach to David would occasion anger against him. A king's displeasure may easily be incurred by injudicious action (cp. Esther 4: 11).

30. Absalom resorts to extreme measures to gain Joab's attention. The verse is of interest as providing a small note on the lands of royal princes, though we have little on which to build up a clear picture of custom. A Qumran text (cp. the Septuagint) adds: 'Joab's young men came to him with their garments rent and said: "The servants of Absalom have set fire to the field"', a natural link line which may have been omitted inadvertently.

32. *if I have done any wrong, put me to death:* the sense of this

is to invite a death sentence if guilt deserving death has been incurred. The judicial position is not simple. Amnon should have been punished for his wrong-doing; Absalom took justice into his own hands and that merited punishment. But a precise decision would not be easy.

33. David meets Absalom with complete reconciliation, a situation which is strong in irony since it is related as the introduction to the rebellion. ✳

ABSALOM THE REBEL

15 After this, Absalom provided himself with a chariot and
2 horses and an escort of fifty men. He made it a practice to rise early and stand beside the road which runs through the city gate. He would hail every man who had a case to bring before the king for judgement and would ask him what city he came from. When he answered, 'I
3 come, sir, from such and such a tribe of Israel', Absalom would say to him, 'I can see that you have a very good
4 case, but you will get no hearing from the king.' And he would add, 'If only I were appointed judge in the land, it would be my business to see that everyone who brought
5 a suit or a claim got justice from me.' Whenever a man approached to prostrate himself, Absalom would stretch
6 out his hand, take hold of him and kiss him. By behaving like this to every Israelite who sought the king's justice, Absalom stole the affections of the Israelites.

7 At the end of four[a] years, Absalom said to the king, 'May I have leave now to go to Hebron to fulfil a vow
8 there that I made to the LORD? For when I lived in Geshur, in Aram, I made this vow: "If the LORD brings me back

[a] *So Luc. Sept.; Heb.* forty.

to Jerusalem, I will become a worshipper of the LORD in
Hebron." *a* The king answered, 'Certainly you may go'; 9
so he set off for Hebron at once. Absalom sent runners 10
through all the tribes of Israel with this message: 'As
soon as you hear the sound of the trumpet, then say,
"Absalom is king in Hebron." ' Two hundred men 11
accompanied Absalom from Jerusalem; they were invited and went in all innocence, knowing nothing of the
affair. Absalom also sent to summon Ahithophel the 12
Gilonite, David's counsellor, from Giloh his city, where
he was offering the customary sacrifices. The conspiracy
gathered strength, and Absalom's supporters increased in
number.

✻ These verses provide the introduction to the rebellion.
Verses 1–6 depict a skilful man paving the way for drawing
adherents to his side (cp. verse 12). Verses 7–12 show the actual
start of rebellion, centred on Hebron.

   1. *After this:* again there is no note of chronology. *a chariot
and horses and an escort of fifty men:* it is clear that these belong
to one who is already claiming full royal status (cp. Adonijah's similar behaviour in 1 Kings 1: 5). Thus Absalom is
shown to be making a bid for royal power.

   2. Verses 2–4 and 6 describe a particular method of gaining
allegiance. The king appears again as court of appeal in cases of
difficulty; a neat link is made with David's position in
chapter 14 (cp. on verse 4) as the one to whom appeal is made.
The statement here is abbreviated; we may assume that
Absalom inquired into the details of the case. It is not clear
whether the use of *Israel* here means the whole people or refers
to the northern tribes; it has sometimes been thought that here
and in verse 10 we have the fostering of support from the
north, whereas the start of the rebellion in verses 7–12 con-

[a] in Hebron *so Luc. Sept.; Heb. om.*

137

centrates on gathering Judaean support. But it may be doubted if such a distinction is intended.

3. Absalom's assurances are no doubt a matter of diplomatic flattery. *but you will get no hearing:* literally 'there is no one to hear you', i.e. presumably, 'you will find no advocate of your case in the royal court'. An interesting parallel may be found in one of the Ras Shamra (Canaanite) texts (cp. *The Making of the Old Testament* in this series, pp. 25–9). The son of King Keret reproaches his father with failing to perform his royal duties, in particular for not caring for widows and fatherless, and for not helping the oppressed. 'Come down from your throne', he says, 'that I may rule.'

4. The arbitrary claim does not need to be justified; it is like the pre-election promises of many a political candidate.

5. A new motif is here introduced: Absalom at least pretends to be impatient of the forms of submission to royalty.

6. The question of justice is resumed, and the undermining of confidence in David goes hand-in-hand with Absalom's gaining popular acclaim.

7. *four years:* the Hebrew has 'forty' (see the N.E.B. footnote), which may be a simple slip or may be designed to suggest a pattern like that of the period of judges. We might be tempted to ask why Absalom waited even four years before fulfilling his vow. Chronology is not a primary interest of the writer. *to Hebron:* these words come in the text after *a vow . . . to the LORD.* While the N.E.B. rendering is perfectly natural, an alternative is to understand 'a vow . . . to Yahweh-in-Hebron', i.e. to Yahweh as he is known or as he has manifested himself in that holy place. Deut. 6: 4 stresses that 'the LORD . . . our God (is) one LORD', and this may be understood to mean: 'There is only one Yahweh; you are not to suppose that because he has revealed himself in more than one place, there is more than one Yahweh.' The pressure for a single sanctuary on which Deuteronomy lays such stress is in part an attempt to avoid such a pluralistic view. The confusion between local manifestations of a deity – popularly readily understood as

separate – and the one supreme deity may also be seen in Canaanite religion where there is not always a clear distinction possible between the great supreme god (Hadad, often entitled Baal, lord) and local manifestations called 'baals' (*baalīm*). To some simple worshipper 'Our Lady of Lourdes' may well be distinguishable from the Virgin who is acknowledged and invoked in some other great centre. The same point is made at the end of verse 8 in the addition of 'in Hebron' (cp. the N.E.B. footnote).

9. As in the case of Amnon's murder, David is unable to detect any other motive in Absalom's request, so far as we can tell (cp. on 13: 26).

10. *runners:* more literally 'spies', suggesting that their activity was not in public. *the sound of the trumpet:* this implies a prearranged moment at which a trumpet (strictly 'ram's horn') signal in many centres will simultaneously evoke the response: *"Absalom is king* (has become king) *in Hebron".* The formula (cp. e.g. 1 Kings 15: 1) is normal for accession to the throne.

11. Those who went with Absalom *in all innocence* were placed in a difficult position. If they tried to return to David, they would probably be killed; if they stayed with Absalom, David would assume their complicity.

12. The significant part to be played by Ahithophel is brought out in 16: 15–23, and cp. 15: 31, 34. His name appears to mean 'my brother (i.e. kin, used as a title for a deity) is folly', but this would appear to be a deliberate alteration of his name as a comment on his failure. The wise counsellor is being sarcastically described as foolish. The original form and meaning of the name remain unknown. *to summon:* the word is missing by accident in the Hebrew text. *from Giloh:* cp. map, p. 85. *The conspiracy gathered strength:* the link to verses 1–6 is implied rather than stated.

The proclamation of Absalom as king in Hebron is significant. Clearly he needed a centre which would enable him to organize the rebellion and provide a rallying point. The choice of Hebron, which had been David's centre until he captured Jerusalem (5: 1–5), may suggest that there were those who viewed the move to the new capital with disfavour. ✳

DAVID'S FLIGHT

13 When news reached David that the men of Israel had
14 transferred their allegiance to Absalom, he said to those who were with him in Jerusalem, 'We must get away at once; or there will be no escape from Absalom for any of us. Make haste, or else he will soon be upon us and bring disaster on us, showing no mercy to anyone in the
15 city.' The king's servants said to him, 'As your majesty thinks best; we are ready.'

16 When the king departed, all his household followed him except ten concubines, whom he left in charge of
17 the palace. At the Far House the king and all the people
18 who were with him halted. His own servants then stood*a* beside him, while the Kerethite and Pelethite guards and Ittai*b* with the six hundred Gittites under him marched
19 past the king. The king said to Ittai the Gittite, 'Are you here too? Why are you coming with us? Go back and stay with the new king, for you are a foreigner and,
20 what is more, an exile from your own country. You came only yesterday, and today must you be compelled to share my wanderings? I do not know where I am going. Go back home and take your countrymen with you; and
21 may the LORD ever be your steadfast friend.'*c* Ittai swore to the king, 'As the LORD lives, your life upon it, wherever you may be, in life or in death, I, your servant, will be

[a] *Prob. rdg.; Heb.* passed.   [b] and Ittai: *prob. rdg.; Heb. om.*
[c] and may . . . friend: *so Sept.; Heb.* constant love and truth.

there.' David said to Ittai, 'It is well, march on!' So 22
Ittai the Gittite marched on with his whole company and
all the dependants who were with him. The whole 23
country-side re-echoed with their weeping. And the king
remained standing*a* while all the people crossed the gorge
of the Kidron before him, by way of the olive-tree in the
wilderness.*b*

Zadok also was there with all the Levites; they were 24
carrying the Ark of the Covenant of God, which they set
down beside Abiathar*c* until all the people had passed
out of the city. But the king said to Zadok, 'Take the 25
Ark of God back to the city. If I find favour with the
LORD, he will bring me back and will let me see the Ark
and its dwelling-place again. But if he says he does not 26
want me, then here I am; let him do what he pleases
with me.' The king went on to say to Zadok the priest, 27
'Can you make good use of your eyes? You may safely
go back to the city, you and Abiathar,*d* and take with
you the two young men, Ahimaaz your son and Abiathar's son Jonathan. Do not forget: I will linger at the 28
Fords of the Wilderness until you can send word to
me.' Then Zadok and Abiathar took the Ark of God 29
back to Jerusalem and stayed there.

David wept as he went up the slope of the Mount of 30
Olives; he was bare-headed and went bare-foot. The
people with him all had their heads uncovered and wept
as they went. David had been told*e* that Ahithophel was 31

[a] *Prob. rdg.; Heb.* passing.
[b] by way . . . wilderness: *prob. rdg.; Heb. obscure.*
[c] beside Abiathar: *prob. rdg.; Heb.* and Abiathar went up.
[d] you and Abiathar: *prob. rdg., cp. verse 29; Heb. om.*
[e] *So Sept.; Heb.* David told.

among the conspirators with Absalom, and he prayed, 'Frustrate, O LORD, the counsel of Ahithophel.'

32 As David was approaching the top of the ridge where it was the custom to prostrate oneself to God, Hushai the Archite was there to meet him with his tunic rent and
33 earth on his head. David said to him, 'If you come with
34 me you will only be a hindrance; but you can help me to frustrate Ahithophel's plans if you go back to the city and say to Absalom, "I will be your majesty's servant; up to now I have been your father's servant, and now I
35 will be yours." You will have with you, as you know, the priests Zadok and Abiathar; tell them everything that
36 you hear in the king's household. They have with them Zadok's son Ahimaaz and Abiathar's son Jonathan, and through them you may pass on to me everything you
37 hear.' So Hushai, David's friend, came to the city as Absalom was entering Jerusalem.

* The narrative of David's flight covers a series of incidents up to 16: 14, and again we may see how the compiler dovetails different elements. We follow David through various incidents, some of which are needed for us to understand what Absalom does. Then at 16: 15 we return to trace the course of events in Jerusalem, and this continues to 17: 23. The remaining verses of chapter 17 revert to a David incident, and the stage is set for the battle and its aftermath in chapters 18 and 19, where we observe a kind of tidying-up operation in which a number of incidents during David's flight are recalled. Again in the battle narrative we are taken skilfully from one scene to another, kept aware of the different moments. The whole account, to the end of chapter 19, should also be read as a single unit to get the overall impact.

The first section 15: 13–37 falls into four short units.

In the first, verses 13–15, the panic and flight are swiftly depicted.

13. The text refers to a messenger who brought the news, though it seems evident that, as in the case of the murder of Amnon, there is exaggeration of the nature of what had happened. *the men of Israel had transferred their allegiance:* it is difficult to know to what extent the northern tribes had accepted Absalom, and indeed uncertain whether Israel here really means this (cp. on verse 2). Certainly some from Hebron and the south were on his side, so the division is not between a Judah loyal to David and a disloyal north.

14. It must remain a puzzle to understand why David fled from Jerusalem. The city was a strong one (cp. 5: 6–8) and was later to withstand much more powerful besiegers than Absalom. Did he fear treachery? It would not be impossible, since Absalom's action must undermine confidence. Or is there here a hint of something in addition to a tradition of the events of the rebellion? We shall need to consider the possible incorporation into this narrative of elements which belong not to a historical account but to a sort of 'procession' theme. David, expelled by enemies from his city, is to return in triumph to it. Is he being portrayed as the true king, assailed by hostile forces, afflicted and humiliated, who will return when God has overthrown his enemies? Is an apparently historical narrative in reality in part at least to be read for its theological motivation (cp. below p. 148)? Such a suggestion, made to offer an explanation for some elements in the story, would mean recognizing that the story of an actual rebellion is being told under the influence of forms which belong to worship, in which the humiliation and triumph of the king are celebrated not as historical events but as indications of the king's relationship to God.

15. There is almost a contrasting calm and confidence in the acceptance by David's servants of whatever decision he will choose to make. *thinks best:* literally 'chooses'. *we are ready:* literally 'behold your servants', i.e. 'at your service'.

The second unit covers verses 16–23; central to this is the figure of Ittai the Gittite.

16. *ten concubines, whom he left in charge of the palace:* this paves the way for the carrying through of Nathan's judgement of David in 12: 11 (cp. 16: 20–2).

17. *the Far House:* some of the early translations have in verse 18 a reference to 'the olive-tree of the wilderness' which the N.E.B. has incorporated in verse 23. Some commentators have thought that this phrase might belong here. If the text is correct, then presumably there is some topographical reference, or perhaps an allusion simply to the last house of the city. We note that the king halts here and again at the edge of Kidron (verse 23), while others advance. Is there here some hint of a prescribed processional route, with appropriate halting places?

18. *stood beside him:* as the N.E.B. footnote shows, both here and in verse 23, there is some confusion in the text, as if a later scribe were trying to puzzle out the reasons for the oddity of David's behaviour on his apparently speedy flight. *the Kerethite and Pelethite guards:* cp. note on 8: 16–18. Together with these royal bodyguards, mercenary troops, we find Ittai the Gittite and his *six hundred Gittites.* Obed-edom, noted in connection with the Ark in 6: 10f., is also described as a Gittite. Ittai's particular position, then and later, might point to a special bodyguard, perhaps connected with religious duties (cp. the reference to a temple guard in 2 Kings 11: 4–8, modified further in 2 Chron. 23: 4f.; and note also the almost military action of the officers in the temple in Jer. 26: 10. A temple guard is clear in New Testament times; cp. Luke 22: 52).

19. *the new king:* the text actually has 'the king', as if David is acknowledging that Absalom has taken over the kingdom. Could there be here an allusion to a rite in which for a limited period some person is appointed to take over the royal duties while the real king is humiliated or in flight? *exile:* might imply that he had lost favour in his homeland,

but more probably simply depicts him as living in a land to which he has no natural allegiance.

20. *I do not know where I am going:* a rather pedestrian translation of a sentence which runs literally: 'as for me, I am going where I am going', suggesting (cp. also verses 25f.) David's acceptance that his fate is in God's hands.

21. The response of Ittai, 'a foreigner' and 'an exile' from his own country (verse 19), shows a remarkable loyalty; it contrasts sharply with the betrayal and disloyalty of Absalom and his followers.

23. *The whole country-side re-echoed with their weeping:* the weeping is not that of Ittai and his men, but of all the population. Literally the text speaks of 'the land (i.e. all the people) weeping with a loud noise'. It is not inappropriate to the distress at David's ignominious flight, but since weeping is so commonly part of religious celebration (cp. Joel 2: 17), we may again have here a hint of a cultic procession. *the gorge of the Kidron:* the steep valley to the immediate east of Jerusalem, between the city and the Mount of Olives (cp. verse 30; see plan, p. 55). *the olive-tree in the wilderness:* cp. on verse 17. Again we note how there is a curious formality in the way the king takes up his stand as the people move across.

The third unit is in verses 24-30 and interweaves two themes: that of the Ark in verses 24-6 and 29, and that of the spies in verses 27f. (cp. 17: 15-22). The flight itself continues in verse 30.

24. *Zadok:* we note that he appears alone here, and that Abiathar is mentioned almost in an aside. In fact, as the N.E.B. footnote shows, the reference to Abiathar is probably an addition to the text, as if a scribe, observing that he had not been mentioned, put in a reminder: 'Abiathar (too) went up.' His name has been added again in verse 29 when the Ark goes back to the city. The reference to *the Levites* is also a later gloss (cp. 1 Chron. 15: 2). The whole verse is problematic. Since Zadok was eventually seen as the ancestor of the true priestly line in Jerusalem, it would appear that whoever was respon-

sible for this account took that view of him. Another possibility is to render: 'and Abiathar offered (sacrifices) and poured out (libations)' in place of *which they set down beside Abiathar.*

the Ark of the Covenant of God: the simpler title in verse 25 is more original; the fuller phrase here emphasizes God's covenant with David (cp. chapter 7).

25f. The attitude of David is remarkable (cp. on verse 20). To take *the Ark of God* with him could be interpreted as suggesting that he is sure of the presence of God which it symbolizes. But for David, the matter rests entirely with God. He will come back or he will not come back, entirely as God has decreed. This may be described as religious fatalism; it may be better seen as total submission to the divine will. *its dwelling-place:* i.e. the shrine or sacred precincts. So the Ark is taken back (verse 29).

27f. These two verses are interwoven with the Ark theme. As the material stands, David's conduct is reminiscent of the advice before battle: 'Trust in God and keep your powder dry.' Here we find David taking precautions and ensuring a source of information about Absalom's plans. *Can you make good use of your eyes?:* this rendering takes the expression literally, with Zadok (and Abiathar, who is not in fact mentioned in the text; cp. the N.E.B. footnote: *you and Abiathar* is added) to act as an observer of what goes on and ready to report to David who *will linger at the Fords of the Wilderness* (cp. 17: 16). These are presumably the Jordan crossings (cp. 16: 14; 17: 21f.), though the phrase could also denote 'narrow desert defiles' to the west of the Jordan.

The words addressed to Zadok could however be rendered: 'Are you a seer?', using one of the words that the Old Testament employs for a prophet (cp. note on 1 Sam. 9: 9). If this is the correct sense, then Zadok the priest is being asked as a religious leader if he has such prophetic powers as may enable him to gain insight into Absalom's activities and so inform David. We shall see that the theme of Zadok (and Abiathar) is somewhat loosely tied in with the alternative theme of Hushai the counsellor (cp. verses 35f.; 17: 15f.).

30. The narrative of the flight is apparently resumed here. We note again the degree of ceremonial acted out by David and the people – weeping, *bare-headed* (or possibly 'with heads covered'), *bare-foot*. This looks less like flight from urgent danger and more like a penitential ritual, and the rhythmic character of the language also suggests this.

The fourth unit is in verses 31–7 (the N.E.B. paragraphing separates the first of these verses from its clear sequel). The theme is the frustrating of Ahithophel's counsel.

31. This verse recalls the event noted in verse 12. David's prayer is skilfully placed so as to lead directly into the answer, the appearance of Hushai who will carry through what is needed. The sequel to this is to be found in 17: 7–14.

32. *where it was the custom to prostrate oneself to God*: this suggests the presence of a holy place on the Mount of Olives; it is also possible to see here another moment in a processional ritual. *Hushai the Archite*: his status as 'King's Friend' is more clearly defined in verse 37, but the title should probably be added here (cp. the Septuagint). The Archites, according to Josh. 16: 2, belonged near Bethel.

33f. An extra courtier adds to the burden, but David counts on the wisdom and skill of Hushai *to frustrate Ahithophel's plans*, no easy task in view of the authority which this counsellor evidently had (cp. 16: 23).

35f. A different function is here given to Hushai. He is not here thought of as providing advice to counter that of Ahithophel, which is his function in the main sequel, but simply as a spy. This overlaps a function already assigned to Zadok (and Abiathar). Faced with alternative stories about the one event, the compiler has harmonized them into a complex whole.

37. *David's friend*: the 'King's Friend' is listed in 1 Kings 4: 5 among the royal officers. So we should have a capital for 'Friend' here and recognize a precise designation. Unfortu-

nately we have little information from which to reconstruct just what this officer did; he was evidently close to the king, perhaps even in some things his deputy. Such a 'friend' is mentioned also in Gen. 26: 26: Ahuzzath, friend of the Philistine king, Abimelech, at Gerar. The office could be much older and of non-Israelite origin. The nearest analogy is the friend of the bridegroom; in Judg. 14: 20 we are told that 'Samson's wife was given in marriage to the friend who had been his groomsman', as if he had a status as deputy in certain circumstances (cp. also on 3: 8 and 13: 3).

It is already clear that this narrative uses more than one element of tradition. It would appear likely that various stories were in circulation concerning David and Absalom, their closeness and the separation produced by Absalom's rebellion. They told in various ways how David escaped and was eventually victorious. But, as we have noted, there has not only been a welding together of different story elements, but also an overlaying of the story with elements of another kind, belonging apparently to religious practice; it is as if a great penitential ritual is also being alluded to, presented in a dramatic narrative form. We have noted the possible relationship between Pss. 24 and 132 and a procession of the Ark which appears in some elements of chapter 6 (and cp. also 1 Sam. 4–6). Ps. 89 suggests a moment of rejection and humiliation for the Davidic king (see especially Ps. 89: 38–45) from which God will bring him back in triumph and glory. We have seen the possibility that the allusion to Absalom as king (cp. verse 19) invited comparison with the role played by a substitute king in some ancient ceremonials. It is one thing to see such possible allusions; it is quite another to try to reconstruct either ceremonials or beliefs for Israel with any precision. We must simply note the possibility of such influences on the narrative presentation. ✻

DAVID AND THE FAMILY OF SAUL

When David had moved on a little from the top of the **16**
ridge, he was met by Ziba the servant of Mephibosheth,
who had with him a pair of asses saddled and loaded with
two hundred loaves, a hundred clusters of raisins, a hundred bunches of summer fruit, and a flagon of wine.
The king said to him, 'What are you doing with these?' 2
Ziba answered, 'The asses are for the king's family to ride
on, the bread and the summer fruit are for the servants
to eat, and the wine for anyone who becomes exhausted
in the wilderness.' The king asked, 'Where is your master's 3
grandson?' 'He is staying in Jerusalem,' said Ziba, 'for he
thought that the Israelites might now restore to him his
grandfather's throne.' The king said to Ziba, 'You shall 4
have everything that belongs to Mephibosheth.' Ziba
said, 'I am your humble servant, sir; may I continue to
stand well with you.'

As King David approached Bahurim, a man of Saul's 5
family, whose name was Shimei son of Gera, came out,
cursing as he came. He showered stones right and left on 6
David and on all the king's servants and on everyone,
soldiers and people alike. This is what Shimei said as he 7
cursed him: 'Get out, get out, you scoundrel! you man
of blood! The LORD has taken vengeance on you for the 8
blood of the house of Saul whose throne you stole, and
he has given the kingdom to your son Absalom. You
murderer, see how your crimes have overtaken you!'

Then Abishai son of Zeruiah said to the king, 'Why 9
let this dead dog curse your majesty? I will go across and
knock off his head.' But the king said, 'What has this to 10

do with you, you sons of Zeruiah? If he curses and if the
LORD has told him to curse David, who can question it?'
11 David said to Abishai and to all his servants, 'If my son,
my own son, is out to kill me, who can wonder at this
Benjamite? Let him be, let him curse; for the LORD has
12 told him to do it. But perhaps the LORD will mark my sufferings[a] and bestow a blessing on me in place of the curse
13 laid on me this day.' David and his men continued on their
way, and Shimei moved along the ridge of the hill parallel
to David's path, cursing as he went and hurling stones
14 across the valley at him and kicking up the dust. When the
king and all the people with him reached the Jordan,[b]
they were worn out; and they refreshed themselves there.

✻ Two further incidents are here associated with David's
flight, but they refer to a different aspect of the larger subject
of the succession to the kingdom. While the issue is in doubt
between David and Absalom, there is a brief glance at hopes
still attaching to the family of Saul. David's kindness to
Mephibosheth (chapter 9) appears to have led to a somewhat
ill-judged attempt at recovering the kingdom for Saul's line
(verses 1–4). Animosity against David and loyalty to Saul are
vividly expressed by Shimei (verses 5–13).

1. Ziba provides *a pair of asses* for riding and a surely
immense supply of food and drink as a token of his loyalty.
Some of the supporters of Saul, it appears, adhere whole-
heartedly to David, though the truth of the matter is in this
instance not easy to discover (cp. 19: 24–30). *summer fruit:*
various kinds, belonging to the later summer, e.g. figs, and
perhaps pomegranates.

2. *servants:* or 'young men', i.e. soldiers.

[a] So Sept.; Heb. my wickedness.
[b] the Jordan: so Luc. Sept.; Heb. om.

3f. Mephibosheth is said to be *staying in Jerusalem,* believing that he might profit by the confusion of David's absence during Absalom's rebellion to regain the throne for the house of Saul. While we might think that the chances of a lame man gaining the kingship at this point were very remote, we need to recognize that there was a strong sense of allegiance to Saul and his family. If Ziba's report is accurate, then the story of Mephibosheth reflects a theme familiar already from that of Saul and David (cp. e.g. 1 Sam. 24: 9–15), namely that of David's loyalty and kindness contrasted with Saul's (here Mephibosheth's) opposite response. It is conceivable that the narrator has interwoven the Mephibosheth story with that of Absalom to draw out the point. The next narrative underlines it with a contrasting motif. *grandson...grandfather:* literally 'son', 'father'. *he thought:* the Hebrew more vividly presents the following clause in direct speech: 'The house of Israel will now restore to me...' *I am your humble servant:* literally, 'I prostrate myself.' *stand well:* or 'enjoy your favour'.

5. *Bahurim:* see map, p. 29. *Shimei:* not otherwise known. There is a Shimeah (or Shimeam) in 1 Chron. 8: 32 (9: 38), but with a different father's name. *Gera* is the name of a Benjamite clan in Gen. 46: 21.

6. The picture is clarified by verse 13. *soldiers and people:* the warrior band and the militia.

7. Shimei's curse picks up two ideas: *man of blood* (which appears first in the text: the N.E.B. reverses the order) means 'murderer' as it is rendered in the next verse; and *scoundrel:* literally 'man of *belī'al'*, of 'confusion', or of 'the swallower' (Sheol), one who belongs to the hostile realm of death (cp. note on 1 Sam. 1: 16; and also 2 Sam. 20: 1 and 22: 5f.). Both are used here as general terms to describe David's actions in the usurpation of royal authority. We may note another narrative in 21: 1–14 which points to more direct action against members of Saul's family, but no precise correlation is given.

8. *whose throne you stole:* rather a strong rendering of the

text which has the more neutral 'in whose place you are king'. The rebellion of Absalom is here interpreted as judgement upon David for his actions against Saul; this is a different interpretation from that of Nathan's statement in 12: 10–12 where judgement is linked to David's sin over Uriah and Bathsheba. *You murderer, see how your crimes have overtaken you:* literally 'Look at you (now) in disaster because you are a murderer.'

9. *this dead dog:* a derogatory expression (cp. 9: 8 and also 3: 8). *knock off:* literally 'remove', better 'cut off'.

10f. David's response is in line with what we have seen in 15: 20 and 25f. *if the LORD has told him to curse David:* this emphasizes David's acceptance of the possibility of judgement. Shimei's cursing is placed alongside Absalom's rebel activity: the two interpretations of God's judgement are thus drawn together. *for the LORD has told him...:* probably better again here: 'if...'

12. *my sufferings:* or possibly 'my lowly state', 'humiliation' (cp. Ps. 89: 38–45). The text (cp. the N.E.B. footnote) has 'my wickedness', a very similar word, in the sense of 'the wickedness, evil done to me (David)'. God is called on to act to change *the curse* into *a blessing* having regard to David's now low state. A curse is a terrible thing, because of the power believed to inhere in actual words: the effective counter to such dangerous words is a blessing which brings well-being and life. Again in this verse we see David's experiences given a deeper meaning: the relation between what happened and its celebration in worship is being brought out (cp. p. 148).

13. The precise situation (cp. verse 6) is here made clearer. If we may rightly picture David and his men proceeding along a narrow path in a valley, Shimei appears to be on *the ridge of the hill parallel to David's path.* The text might be rendered more precisely 'on the rock (escarpment) of the hillside', i.e. Shimei is part way up the hillside, able to move parallel to David but out of reach, and able to make the fugitives uncomfortable without being seriously in danger himself. *across*

the valley: not in the text, which repeats the word for 'parallel to him' from the preceding phrase. *kicking up the dust:* or better 'pelting with dust'.

Again in this verse (cp. on 7: 4 and 12: 13) a space in the Hebrew manuscripts may be seen as a point at which Ps. 3 could be read; its title (not printed by the N.E.B.) runs: 'when he fled from Absalom his son'. A *midrash* (Jewish commentary) on verse 3 of the psalm has: 'How can there be salvation for a man who had taken the lamb captive and slew the shepherd and who caused Israel to fall by the sword?', thus underlining the way the psalmist rests all his confidence in God alone.

14. The section of narrative concludes with the arrival at the agreed halting place, *the Jordan* (accidentally missing from the Hebrew text). Now we pause to see what has been happening in Jerusalem, and to wait for the news which determines the next stage for David.

The sequel to the Ziba–Mephibosheth incident is in 19: 24–30; that to the Shimei incident in 19: 16–23 (note the reverse order), and further in 1 Kings 2: 8f., 36–46. ✲

THE COUNSEL OF AHITHOPHEL

By now Absalom and all his Israelites had reached 15 Jerusalem, and Ahithophel with him. When Hushai the 16 Archite, David's friend, met Absalom he said to him, 'Long live the king! Long live the king!' But Absalom 17 retorted, 'Is this your loyalty to your friend? Why did you not go with him?' Hushai answered Absalom, 'Be- 18 cause I mean to attach myself to the man chosen by the LORD, by this people, and by all the men of Israel, and with him I will remain. After all, whom ought I to serve? 19 Should I not serve the son? I will serve you as I have served your father.' Then Absalom said to Ahithophel, 20

21 'Give us your advice: how shall we act?' Ahithophel
answered, 'Have intercourse with your father's concubines whom he left in charge of the palace. Then all
Israel will come to hear that you have given great cause
of offence to your father, and this will confirm the resolu-
22 tion of your followers.' So they set up a tent for Absalom
on the roof, and he lay with his father's concubines in
23 the sight of all Israel. In those days a man would seek
counsel of Ahithophel as readily as he might make an
inquiry of the word of God; that was how Ahithophel's
counsel was esteemed by David and Absalom.

* This passage serves to confront Ahithophel and Hushai, and
so paves the way for the real conflict between them described
in chapter 17.

15. *all his Israelites:* the Hebrew text has alternative readings:
'the people', i.e. his followers, or 'the men of Israel', i.e. the
whole people. Either is possible; the N.E.B. conflates the two.
and Ahithophel with him: it is by such a skilful touch that the
narrator introduces the most important personage and recalls
15: 12 and 31-7.

16. On *Hushai* and *David's friend* cp. 15: 32-7.

17. Hushai's repeated and thus emphasized assurance of
acceptance of Absalom's kingship not surprisingly evokes a
question about *your loyalty to your friend*. In the conversation
there is a subtle irony: Hushai is in fact loyal to David. But
Absalom's doubts of Hushai are readily overcome by flattery
and the assurance of divine choice (verse 18).

18. The choice of a king is here described in terms which
stress both divine action and human acceptance. We may
compare the progress of David to supreme kingship, e.g.
2: 1-4; 5: 1-5; and Rehoboam's seeking of the people's
ratification of his kingship in 1 Kings 12: 1-15.

19. Again the irony: Hushai will serve Absalom by betrayal.

20. The interlude (verses 16–19) introducing Hushai in preparation for chapter 17 is now followed by the first example of Ahithophel's advice.

21. To take the harem of the deposed ruler is to be understood as indicating the full claim to the rights of the throne (cp. on 12: 8); Absalom is thus declaring an absolute breach with David, and the die is cast for the overthrow of either David or Absalom. The significance of David's leaving the ten concubines in Jerusalem now becomes clear in making real the judgement on David (cp. on 12: 11f.; 15: 16). *you have given great cause of offence:* the same word is used as in 10: 6, in the incident of David's ambassadors to Ammon. It may mean 'made yourself stink' or better 'acted shamefully', i.e. so as to put David to shame. The fugitive king is put in a position of embarrassment or impotence by his usurper's taking over of all his rights. It is also possible that the word should be given the sense of 'challenged'.

22. *a tent for Absalom on the roof:* the procedure is used to emphasize the public nature of the act. Thus it corresponds precisely to Nathan's words in 12: 11. We may, however, wonder whether there is concealed in this some special practice of a religious kind, connected with the royal (sacred) marriage, utilized here for a different purpose (cp. on 6: 16). The bridal tent or canopy is a regular part of marriage ritual (cp. Ps. 19: 5 of the sun as bridegroom); it survives in current Jewish practice.

23. The concluding comment is a remarkable testimony to the status of Ahithophel. It equates the *counsel of Ahithophel* with the seeking of *the word of God,* an activity particularly associated with prophecy. It becomes clear that there are various means by which God's will is thought to be mediated to men. Among these the three most important may be seen to be the priestly directive (*tōrāh*), the prophetic word or vision, and the counsel of the wise or the elders. These three types appear together in Jer. 18: 18 and Ezek. 7: 26; the former refers to 'wise', the latter to 'elders', which may in this

context be seen as equivalents, for wisdom may often be seen to reside in those whose experience gives them a sound basis for advising. Counsel or advice in this context is not simply sound judgement, though it may well be that; it is a word spoken with power to influence events. It is in this way that we may understand much of the collected wisdom of such a book as Proverbs. Political sagacity and the wisdom which comes from God are not to be set in any sharp contrast; the true politician is concerned for man's well-being. The wise man who gives true counsel may, however, be contrasted with those who are 'wise in your own eyes' (cp. Isa. 5: 21).

That Ahithophel's counsel is so estimated provides the lead into the next passage; what may be seen to be wise advice is frustrated, the wisdom of Ahithophel rejected in an act of folly (cp. 1 Kings 12: 13f. for a similar case). But the narrator is showing how God acts to frustrate Absalom (cp. 17: 14). *

HUSHAI FRUSTRATES AHITHOPHEL'S COUNSEL

17 Ahithophel said to Absalom, 'Let me pick twelve
2 thousand men, and I will pursue David tonight. I shall overtake him when he is tired and dispirited; I will cut him off from his people and they will all scatter; and I
3 shall kill no one but the king. I will bring all the people over to you as a bride is brought to her husband. It is only one man's life that you are seeking;[a] the rest of the people
4 will be unharmed.' Absalom and all the elders of Israel
5 approved of Ahithophel's advice; but Absalom said, 'Summon Hushai the Archite and let us hear what he too
6 has to say.' Hushai came, and Absalom told him all that Ahithophel had said and asked him, 'Shall we do what he says? If not, say what you think.'

[a] as a bride . . . seeking: *so Sept.; Heb.* as the whole returns, so is the man you are seeking.

Hushai said to Absalom, 'For once the counsel that 7
Ahithophel has given is not good. You know', he went 8
on, 'that your father and the men with him are hardened .
warriors and savage as a bear in the wilds robbed of her
cubs. Your father is an old campaigner and will not spend
the night with the main body; even now he will be 9
lying hidden in a pit or in some such place. Then if any
of your men are killed at the outset, anyone who hears
the news will say, "Disaster has overtaken the followers
of Absalom." The courage of the most resolute and lion- 10
hearted will melt away, for all Israel knows that your
father is a man of war and has determined men with him.
My advice is this. Wait until the whole of Israel, from 11
Dan to Beersheba, is gathered about you, countless as
grains of sand on the sea-shore, and then you shall march
with them in person.[a] Then we shall come upon him 12
somewhere, wherever he may be, and descend on him like
dew falling on the ground, and not a man of his family or
of his followers will be left alive. If he retreats into a city, 13
all Israel will bring ropes to that city, and we will drag it
into a ravine until not a stone can be found on the site.'
Absalom and all the men of Israel said, 'Hushai the Arch- 14
ite gives us better advice than Ahithophel.' It was the
LORD's purpose to frustrate Ahithophel's good advice
and so bring disaster upon Absalom.

Hushai told Zadok and Abiathar the priests all the 15
advice that Ahithophel had given to Absalom and the
elders of Israel, and also his own. 'Now send quickly to 16
David,' he said, 'and warn him not to spend the night at
the Fords of the Wilderness but to cross the river at once,

[a] with them in person: *so Sept.; Heb.* in person in the battle.

before a blow can be struck at the king and his followers.'
17 Jonathan and Ahimaaz were waiting at En-rogel, and a
servant girl would go and tell them what happened and
they would pass it on to King David; for they could not
18 risk being seen entering the city. But this time a lad saw
them and told Absalom; so the two of them hurried to
the house of a man in Bahurim. He had a pit in his court-
19 yard, and they climbed down into it. The man's wife
took a covering, spread it over the mouth of the pit
and strewed grain over it, and no one was any the wiser.
20 Absalom's servants came to the house and asked the
woman, 'Where are Ahimaaz and Jonathan?' She
answered, 'They went beyond the pool.'[a] The men
searched but could not find them; so they went back to
21 Jerusalem. When they had gone the two climbed out of
the pit and went off to report to King David and said,
'Over the water at once, make haste!', and they told him
22 Ahithophel's plan against him. So David and all his
company began at once to cross the Jordan; by day-
break there was not one who had not reached the other
bank.

23   When Ahithophel saw that his advice had not been
taken he saddled his ass, went straight home to his own
city, gave his last instructions to his household, and
hanged himself. So he died and was buried in his father's
grave.

* This narrative combines two themes already indicated. In
verses 1–14, 23, the advice given by Ahithophel is skilfully
countered by Hushai (cp. 15: 31–4); in verses 15–22, the spy

[a] Heb. *word of uncertain mng.*

operation by Zadok and Abiathar and their sons is carried through, and combined with the activity of Hushai (cp. 15: 27f., 35f.). It is quite evident that these are in reality separate and alternative traditions telling how the rebellion of Absalom was defeated. They are placed together and loosely linked.

1–3. *Ahithophel's* advice (cp. 16: 20) is presented here; no precise relationship is established with 16: 21f., but since speed is of the essence of its success (note *tonight* in verse 1), it is difficult to dovetail it satisfactorily with what precedes. The advice has three aspects. First, a speedy action by a picked body of men. *twelve thousand* appears a very large number for what must surely more appropriately be a surprise attack. Second, an attack on David alone. *I will cut him off*: this depends on a different and dubious understanding of the Hebrew word, where the normal rendering would be 'I will put him in a panic', a common military stratagem (cp. the Gideon story in Judg. 7); this is an entirely suitable sense. Third, an attraction to Absalom of the loyalty of the whole people. A vivid metaphor – *as a bride is brought to her husband* – suggests the closeness of the bond to be established and the joyfulness with which Absalom will be fully recognized as king. The Hebrew text (cp. the N.E.B. footnote) has a slip in the order of the letters of the word for 'bride', and the accidental omission of two further words. The advice is skilful. It avoids civil war, and it envisages David taken by surprise at an unguarded moment.

4. The acceptance of the advice appears to be a foregone conclusion, but Absalom, led, as the narrator will comment (verse 14), by the divine will, hesitates sufficiently to ask Hushai to judge.

6. The last clauses may be rendered: 'Shall we do what he says or not? Say what you think.'

7. Hushai's task is to persuade Absalom and his followers to reject Ahithophel's sound advice. He does this by evoking fear and by suggesting great military glory and honour for Absalom. It is not stated that he suggests that Ahithophel's advice

involved giving to himself rather than to Absalom the major achievement of capturing David and bringing over the loyalty of all Israel. But we may see this implied, especially in verse 11.

8f. Here the theme of fear is used. Hushai uses a vivid comparison – *a bear in the wilds robbed of her cubs* – to suggest the risk. He points to David's probable anticipation of just such a stroke as Ahithophel advises. A failure in any speedy action will lead to exaggerated rumour of failure; the phrase *anyone who hears* strongly suggests the spread of rumour (cp. 13: 30; 15: 13).

11. Hushai here turns to the idea of great military glory. Again a vivid, if familiar, image is used for the immense army to be gathered, *countless as grains of sand on the sea-shore* (cp. Gen. 22: 17). *then you shall march with them in person:* Hushai appeals to Absalom's vanity by suggesting his leadership of the successful campaign. Literally the text runs: 'with your person (your face) going in the midst' (so the Septuagint – cp. the N.E.B. footnote – rather than 'in the battle'). *Dan to Beersheba:* cp. on 3: 9f.

12f. The glory element is pursued, first by yet another vivid picture of the totality of the disaster to be brought about: no opponent will be spared, any more than there can be a spot upon which *dew* does not fall. A similar use of this picture is to be found in Mic. 5: 7, where a hostile sense is equally implied (see *Amos, Hosea and Micah* in this series, p. 180). Second, we have a fanciful portrayal of the overthrow of any city in which David might think to find refuge. The ruthlessness of the idea contrasts markedly with the narrative in 20: 14–22. *stone:* or more vividly 'pebble'.

14. The acceptance of Hushai's advice has its sequel in verse 23. Here the narrator comments that *It was the LORD's purpose to frustrate Ahithophel's good advice.* The future of the kingdom does not lie with Absalom.

It is worth noting that the speeches of Ahithophel and Hushai provide us with excellent examples of the narrator's skill. The vividness of the pictures used, their almost proverbial quality, suggests a man trained in the art of speech and writing such as we find in the scribal schools known to us in Egypt and elsewhere. Though no reference is made to such schools in the Old Testament, Israel too must have had its training methods for public officers such as secretaries and government servants. It is from the time of David and Solomon onwards that we should expect to find such men, needed to organize the more complex administration of the kingdom.

15f. In the verses which follow, it appears as if the action advised by Ahithophel is about to be carried out (cp. verse 21). A warning must be sent to David to hasten across Jordan, away from such a surprise attack. It is evident that the two themes, frustration of Ahithophel's advice and the spies, are here combined. *Fords of the Wilderness:* cp. note on 15: 27f. *before a blow can be struck at the king:* more vividly and precisely, 'lest the king and those with him be swallowed up'.

17. *En-rogel:* just outside the city (cp. plan, p. 55). This verse envisages a situation in which the two young men have been employed on their intelligence errand more than once without being seen. A *servant girl* could go to and fro without any notice being taken.

18. *Bahurim:* cp. 16: 5.

19. *strewed grain over it:* a similar device for concealment is described in Josh. 2: 6. The meaning of the word translated 'grain' is uncertain; the Targum has 'dates'. Clearly it must be some product which needs drying in the sun.

20. *beyond the pool:* a word of very uncertain meaning, for which no satisfactory explanation has been found. Simple emendations would give 'from here to the waters' or 'a short while ago to the waters', but the meaning is still unclear.

21f. *they told him Ahithophel's plan against him:* cp. on verses 15f. The haste with which David and his men *cross the Jordan* makes it evident that a speedy surprise attack is expected.

23. The narrative of verses 1–14 is concluded. Ahithophel's position is doubly impossible. His involvement in the con-

spiracy from its outset (15: 12) and his clarity of outlook, enabling him to foresee disaster, make it not surprising that he should take the way out of suicide. Equally the countering of his advice, in the light of the view presented in 16: 23 of its divinely inspired authority, may be said to undermine his whole status as counsellor. He is shown as calm; *his household* is left in order. *he died and was buried in his father's grave:* no stigma attaches to suicide.

A question remains about Ahithophel. Why did he join the conspiracy at all? The supposition that he was grandfather to Bathsheba (cp. note on 11: 3) is without adequate basis. Nothing in the narratives suggests any connection between them; the idea that he resented what David had done is pure conjecture. His position as counsellor to David (16: 23) reveals him as a close supporter who transferred his allegiance, just as we find Joab and Abiathar supporting Adonijah in 1 Kings 1. No reasons are given. We are invited to see the hand of God at work, removing the threat to David, and Ahithophel as an instrument of God in this.

A link may be seen with this passage and with other elements in the story of David's flight and his betrayal by Ahithophel in the way in which the story of Jesus' betrayal by Judas is presented. Crossing the Kidron (15: 23) may provide the basis for John 18: 1; the route towards the Mount of Olives and the weeping and prayer (15: 30f.) are suggestive of Gethsemane; the suicide of Judas (Matt. 27: 5) is described in words which are exactly those of the Septuagint text of 17: 23. The narrative of Jesus' passion is deeply enriched with such Old Testament allusion and analogy. *

PREPARATIONS FOR BATTLE

24 By the time that Absalom had crossed the Jordan with
25 the Israelites, David was already at Mahanaim. Absalom had appointed Amasa as commander-in-chief instead of

Joab; he was the son of a man named Ithra, an Ishmaelite,[a] by Abigal daughter of Nahash and sister to Joab's
mother Zeruiah. The Israelites and Absalom camped in 26
the district of Gilead. When David came to Mahanaim, 27
he was met by Shobi son of Nahash from the Ammonite
town Rabbah, Machir son of Ammiel from Lo-debar,
and Barzillai the Gileadite from Rogelim, bringing 28
mattresses and blankets, bowls and jugs.[b] They brought
also wheat and barley, meal and parched grain, beans and
lentils,[c] honey and curds, sheep and fat cattle, and offered 29
them to David and his people to eat, knowing that the
people must be hungry and thirsty and weary in the
wilderness.

David mustered the people who were with him, and **18**
appointed officers over units of a thousand and a hundred.
Then he divided the army in three, one division under the 2
command of Joab, one under Joab's brother Abishai son
of Zeruiah, and the third under Ittai the Gittite. The king
announced to the army that he was coming out himself
with them to battle. But they said, 'No, you must not 3
come out; if we turn and run, no one will take any
notice, nor will they, even if half of us are killed; but you[d]
are worth ten thousand of us, and it would be better
now for you to remain in the city[e] in support.' 'I will 4
do what you think best', answered the king; and he then
stood beside the gate, and the army marched past in their

[a] *So one form of Sept., cp. 1 Chron. 2: 17; Heb.* an Israelite.
[b] bringing . . . jugs: *prob. rdg.; Heb.* a couch, bowls and a potter's
vessel.
[c] *So Sept.; Heb. adds* and parched grain.
[d] you: *so Sept.; Heb.* now.
[e] in the city: *so Sept.; Heb.* from a city.

5 units of a thousand and a hundred. The king gave orders to Joab, Abishai, and Ittai: 'Deal gently with the young man Absalom for my sake.' The whole army heard the king giving all his officers this order to spare Absalom.

* The section 17: 15–22 has bridged the gap between the scenes with Absalom and those with David. The confrontation is now brought about as the battle draws near.

24. The juxtaposition of David's arrival *at Mahanaim* (cp. map, p. 29) and Absalom's crossing of *the Jordan* brings the two into the same scene. It is not at all clear whether we are to suppose that Absalom is following Hushai's advice, though he is in fact himself leading the army.

25. *Amasa:* cousin of Joab, of part Ishmaelite stock if, as seems probable, we should follow the evidence of the Septuagint and Chronicles (cp. the N.E.B. footnote). The narrative of 20: 4–13 tells of his death at Joab's hand. *Nahash:* 1 Chron. 2: 16 makes both Abigal (Abigail) and Zeruiah, mother of Joab, daughters of Jesse and sisters of David. If this is correct, there would appear to be intense family disputes involved in the political conflicts.

27–9. These verses are an aside, commenting on David at Mahanaim, just as verses 25f. comment on Absalom's actions. Recognition of David's kingship and of his army's material needs comes from a group of important men of Transjordan. *Shobi son of Nahash:* since he comes from Rabbah (cp. 11: 1; also called Rabbath-Ammon), we may guess him to be of the royal house, perhaps brother to Hanun (10: 1), though this is not stated. He would in any case represent Ammonite loyalty to their overlord. On *Machir...from Lo-debar,* cp. note on 9: 4. Perhaps we are to relate his loyalty to David's kindly treatment of Mephibosheth. *Barzillai the Gileadite from Rogelim* (an unknown locality): he is the only one of these three to be mentioned again (cp. 19: 31–9 and 1 Kings 2: 7). The range of supplies is considerable, and must represent an important contribution to victory, since provisioning a rapidly moving army is inevitably a difficult matter.

18: 1f. *units of a thousand and a hundred:* such army units (and fifties and tens) probably imply simply larger and smaller groupings with commanding officers of particular status, rather than precise numbers. The threefold division of the army is one commonly adopted in ancient warfare (cp. Gideon's use of the procedure in Judg. 7: 16). *he divided:* so some Septuagint texts, where the Hebrew has 'he despatched'.

3. David's announcement that he will lead the army (verse 2) is countered in a remarkable statement. It is claimed that neither the flight of the Israelite army nor the death of half its numbers will count, *but you are worth ten thousand of us.* The king's life is so valued that its loss must not be risked. A similar claim for the king's status is made in 21: 17 where he is described as 'the lamp of Israel'. King and people are bound together; the life of the king is as the life of the whole people, and what a king is, good or evil, results in divine approval or judgement on the whole people (cp. the comments in 1 and 2 Kings on the rulers of Israel and Judah, e.g. 1 Kings 15: 1-8).

4. So David *stood beside the gate*, as if transmitting his beneficent strength to the soldiers as they marched out to the battle.

5. '*Deal gently with the young man Absalom for my sake*': the order, overheard by *The whole army*, was to be of importance in the moment of battle (cp. verses 9-17). The appeal reveals the continuing affection of David for the rebel who has nearly cost him life and kingdom. *

THE DEATH OF ABSALOM

The army took the field against the Israelites and the 6
battle was fought in the forest of Ephron.*a* There the 7
Israelites were routed before the onslaught of David's

[a] *Prob. rdg.; Heb.* Ephraim.

men; so great was the rout that twenty thousand men
8 fell that day. The fighting spread over the whole country-
side, and the forest took toll of more people that day
than the sword.

9   Now some of David's men caught sight of Absalom.
He was riding a mule and, as it passed beneath a great
oak,*a* his head was caught in its boughs; he found himself
10 in mid air and the mule went on from under him. One
of the men who saw it went and told Joab, 'I saw
11 Absalom hanging from an oak.' While the man was
telling him, Joab broke in, 'You saw him? Why did you
not strike him to the ground then and there? I would
12 have given you ten pieces of silver and a belt.' The man
answered, 'If you were to put in my hands a thousand
pieces of silver, I would not lift a finger against the king's
son; for we all heard the king giving orders to you and
Abishai and Ittai that whoever finds himself near the
13 young man Absalom must take great care of him. If
I had dealt him a treacherous blow, the king would soon
have known, and you would have kept well out of it.'
14 'That is a lie!' said Joab. 'I will make a start and show
you.'*b* So he picked up three stout sticks and drove them
against Absalom's chest while he was held fast in the
15 tree and still alive. Then ten young men who were
Joab's armour-bearers closed in on Absalom, struck at
16 him and killed him. Joab sounded the trumpet, and
the army came back from the pursuit of Israel because
17 he had called it off. They took Absalom's body and
flung it into a great pit in the forest, and raised over

[*a*] *Or* terebinth.
[*b*] I will . . . show you: *or* I can waste no more time on you like this.

it a huge pile of stones. The Israelites all fled to their homes.

The pillar in the King's Vale had been set up by Ab- 18
salom in his lifetime, for he said, 'I have no son to carry on my name.' He had named the pillar after himself; and to this day it is called Absalom's Monument.

* 6. *the forest of Ephron:* the N.E.B. (see the footnote) assumes that the text which has 'Ephraim' must be wrong, because the battlefield must be east of Jordan. It is, however, conceivable that another place than the main tribal area had this name. But it is not even clear that Ephron fits (cp. on 13: 23), and another suggestion is 'forest of Mahanaim' (cp. 17: 24). The nature of the forest described here and in verse 8 is not an orderly tree-planted area, but rough country with trees and scrub and uneven ground, dangerous terrain for both battle and flight.

7. It is made very plain here that the whole army of Israel was defeated by *David's men,* literally 'servants'. This appears to be a victory for the orderly troops, relatively few in number, under the control of skilled officers and with strict discipline, over the loosely organized though numerous supporters of Absalom. The battle indicates an important point in the development of warfare in ancient Israel.

8. *the forest took toll...:* literally 'devoured'. The picture is of an army routed, meeting death by accident more than from their opponents.

9. *caught sight of Absalom:* or 'Absalom was encountered by chance'. *beneath a great oak:* better 'beneath the branches (or network of branches)...' *oak:* the N.E.B. footnote has the alternative 'terebinth', the turpentine tree. The names of the two trees are very similar in Hebrew and may well have been confused. *his head was caught:* it has often been supposed (already by Josephus, the first-century historian), because of the reference to Absalom's mass of hair in 14: 26, that he was

caught by his hair; but this is not what the text says. We may picture the fugitive Absalom, riding rapidly; failing to stoop to clear the branches in the rough country, he is left suspended, himself a victim of the wild forest. *found himself:* better 'was left hanging' as in a Qumran manuscript. The general statement of verse 8 about the forest is thus seen to be an anticipation of the leader's death.

11. *ten pieces of silver and a belt:* both monetary reward and a mark of military honour (cp. 2: 21).

12f. The man's reply is shrewd. Not only does he remind Joab of David's explicit orders (verse 5) and thereby show his respect for the royal command; he is well aware that high officers have a way of disclaiming responsibility when it comes to the point. *whoever finds himself...:* the text is not clear and may be an error for 'protect (for me) the young man...'. *If I had dealt him a treacherous blow:* or, possibly, 'If I had myself acted treacherously.' *you would have kept well out of it:* more literally and precisely 'you would just have stood there'.

14. *'That is a lie!':* the N.E.B. footnote offers an alternative and well-supported rendering, effectively meaning 'I cannot delay here exchanging arguments with you.' *stout sticks:* was Absalom killed with these or was he possibly dislodged from the tree with them to be despatched on the ground? The description is unclear.

15. The murder of Absalom is ignominious; Joab and his *armour-bearers*, his close retinue, took no chances.

16. The tables are turned. Ahithophel had promised to kill David alone; but David the intended victim is safe. Absalom is dead and his death is decisive. So *the pursuit* is called off.

17. The immediate burial in a *pit in the forest* may be to avoid any examination of the body, or to reduce the probably elaborate ceremonial that David would have thought necessary. The last words of this verse are partly reminiscent of the cry to Israel to secede in 20: 1 (see note) and 1 Kings 12: 16.

18. We may suppose that the mention of the 'huge pile of

stones' raised over Absalom's body reminded a scribe of another monument associated traditionally with Absalom. This was a *pillar*, a term normally used for a sacred standing stone, known as *Absalom's Monument* (literally 'hand'; see note on 8: 3f.), the locality of which was evidently well known. *to this day:* this may indicate that the monument was still standing at the time of the scribal note, or may simply mean 'in perpetuity'. The explanation of the monument as a kind of substitute for a son conflicts with the evidently quite unconnected information of 14: 27; alternative traditions exist concerning Absalom. The *King's Vale* is possibly the Kidron valley (see plan, p. 55). A tomb which still stands in the Kidron valley and which is known by this name is of a much later period, Hellenistic or Roman; later tradition has here filled in a gap since the original monument could no longer be identified. *

DAVID AND ABSALOM

Ahimaaz son of Zadok said, 'Let me run and take the 19 news to the king that the LORD has avenged him and delivered him from his enemies.' But Joab replied, 'This 20 is no day for you to be the bearer of news. Another day you may have news to carry, but not today, because the king's son is dead.' Joab told a Cushite to go and report 21 to the king what he had seen. The Cushite bowed low before Joab and set off running. Ahimaaz pleaded again 22 with Joab, 'Come what may,' he said, 'let me run after the Cushite.' 'Why should you, my son?' asked Joab. 'You will get no reward for your news.' 'Come what 23 may,' he said, 'I will run.' 'Go, then', said Joab. So Ahimaaz ran by the road through the Plain of the Jordan and outstripped the Cushite.

David was sitting between the two gates when the 24

watchman went up to the roof of the gatehouse by the
25 wall and, looking out, saw a man running alone. The
watchman called to the king and told him. 'If he is
alone,' said the king, 'then he has news.' The man came
26 nearer and nearer. Then the watchman saw another man
running. He called down to the gate-keeper and said,
'Look, there is another man running alone.' The king
27 said, 'He too brings news.' The watchman said, 'I see
by the way he runs that the first runner is Ahimaaz son of
Zadok.' The king said, 'He is a good fellow and shall
28 earn the reward for good news.' Ahimaaz called out to
the king, 'All is well!' He bowed low before him and
said, 'Blessed be the LORD your God who has given into
your hands the men who rebelled against your majesty.'
29 The king asked, 'Is all well with the young man Absalom?' Ahimaaz answered, 'Sir, your servant Joab
sent me,*a* I saw a great commotion, but I did not know
30 what had happened.' The king told him to stand on one
31 side; so he turned aside and stood there. Then the Cushite
came in and said, 'Good news, your majesty! The LORD
has avenged you this day on all those who rebelled against
32 you.' The king said to the Cushite, 'Is all well with the
young man Absalom?' The Cushite answered, 'May all
the king's enemies and all rebels who would do you harm
33*b* be as that young man is.' The king was deeply moved
and went up to the roof-chamber over the gate and wept,
crying out as he went, 'O, my son! Absalom my son,
my son Absalom! If only I had died instead of you!
O Absalom, my son, my son.'

[*a*] Sir . . . sent me: *prob. rdg.; Heb.* At the sending of Joab the king's
servant and your servant.   [*b*] *19: 1 in Heb.*

Joab was told that the king was weeping and mourning **19**
for Absalom; and that day victory was turned to mourn- 2
ing for the whole army, because they heard how the
king grieved for his son; they stole into the city like men 3
ashamed to show their faces after a defeat in battle. The 4
king hid his face and cried aloud, 'My son Absalom; O
Absalom, my son, my son.' But Joab came into the king's 5
quarters and said to him, 'You have put to shame this
day all your servants, who have saved you and your sons
and daughters, your wives and your concubines. You 6
love those that hate you and hate those that love you;
you have made us feel, officers and men alike, that we are
nothing to you; for it is plain that if Absalom were still
alive and all of us dead, you would be content. Now go at 7
once and give your servants some encouragement; if you
refuse, I swear by the LORD that not a man will stay with
you tonight, and that would be a worse disaster than any
you have suffered since your earliest days.' Then the 8*a*
king rose and took his seat in the gate; and when the
army was told that the king was sitting in the gate, they
all appeared before him.

* Joab is well aware that David will react strongly to the
news of Absalom's death; hence the contriving of the way the
news is brought and hence too his vigorous action to recall
David to his responsibilities. The final scene of the rebellion
brings out to the full the tragic quality of the situation.

19. *take the news:* often, as here, the word means 'good
news'. *avenged him and delivered him:* the text has a single word
meaning 'vindicated'. The same word is used for the activity
of the Judges, who are vindicators, overthrowing enemies, re-
establishing their own people. The word also points to justice,

the establishing of right (cp. Isa. 1: 17: 'give the orphan his rights').

20. Joab's refusal to send Ahimaaz is made clear: that Absalom is dead is good news, but it will not appear so to David.

21. *a Cushite:* from Cush, south of Egypt, towards Ethiopia. It may be that Joab feared that David would take violent action against the messenger and so sent a foreigner (cp. David and the Amalekite who looked for a reward for good news in 1: 1–16).

23. In the end, Ahimaaz' insistence persuades Joab to let him go; he took a shorter or quicker route than the Cushite, through *the Plain of the Jordan*, the wide open valley.

24. *David was sitting between the two gates:* actually in the gate-house, between the inner and outer gates of the city, the place to which any incoming messenger must come. Cp. on 3: 27 for the recesses within the gateway. It is possible, however, that David was in a larger open space between an inner and an outer gate-house.

25. When David hears of a runner in sight, he makes a pronouncement: '*If he is alone...then he has* (good) *news.*' David's words are not simply a statement of fact or of hope; they are like a prophetic pronouncement, and by this David seeks to establish that the news is good. The point is repeated in verses 26 and 27. The irony is that the good news of Absalom's death is a word of tragedy to David himself.

26. *to the gate-keeper:* or better, with a very small change, 'into the gateway', to the king (cp. verse 25).

28f. Ahimaaz, in his words to David, shows himself most discreet. That Absalom is dead, he knows well (cp. verse 20); but he concentrates on the victorious campaign and declines to pronounce on something which he did not see personally. The Hebrew text is overloaded, incorporating alternative readings (cp. the N.E.B. footnote).

31f. The Cushite makes a similarly indirect statement of the victory. *avenged:* cp. note on verse 19. His comment on

Absalom is oblique, but without ambiguity. To wish a king prosperity in terms of the total overthrow of his enemies is a polite form of address.

33. The bringing of the news ends the first of the scenes here. We pass to David's distress, expressed here and in 19: 4 by the repetitive phrasing and the extreme statement *If only I had died instead of you!* The affection of David for his rebel son has become proverbial; it is a deep underlining of the tragedy. The repetitive wording suggests the use of the formal language of a lament or funeral dirge.

19: 1–3. The effect on the victorious army of the king *weeping and mourning for Absalom* is disastrous. The confidence of victory is transformed into the shame of defeat.

4. The repetition of David's distress here is a skilful literary touch.

5f. Joab is nothing if not courageous. He speaks forthrightly of David's ignoring of his servants' achievements. David has turned the whole victory upside down, weighing the life of Absalom as equal to that of his whole military force. There is a skilful reversal here of the army's claim in 18: 3.

7. But Joab does not stop at firm words; he issues a direct threat of new rebellion, and one greater than any disaster that David has suffered. It is implied that Joab himself will, as successful commander, lead the whole people away from David. Examples of military usurpers were to be familiar in the history of the northern kingdom, the most famous being Omri (cp. 1 Kings 16: 15–17).

8*a*. So David *took his seat in the gate:* as at the opening of the battle he gave blessing and strength to his men, so now, by his presence, he offers his acknowledgement of what they have done. ✳

Various events of David's reign

✳ The N.E.B. has a new heading at this point, but in fact the story of Absalom's rebellion really continues to the end of chapter 19, and chapter 20 contains an account of another rebellion, that of Sheba. The heading *Various events of David's reign* really belongs at the beginning of chapter 20. ✳

THE RESTORATION OF DAVID

8*b*, 9 MEANWHILE THE ISRAELITES had all scattered to their homes. Throughout all the tribes of Israel people were discussing it among themselves and saying, 'The king has saved us from our enemies and freed us from the power of the Philistines, and now he has fled 10 the country because of Absalom. But Absalom, whom we anointed king, has fallen in battle; so now why have we no plans for bringing the king back?'

11 What all Israel was saying came to the king's ears.[a] So he sent word to Zadok and Abiathar the priests: 'Ask the elders of Judah why they should be the last to 12 bring the king back to his palace. Tell them, "You are my brothers, my flesh and my blood; why are you last 13 to bring me back?" And tell Amasa, "You are my own flesh and blood. You shall be my commander-in-chief, so help me God, for the rest of your life in place of 14 Joab."' David's message won all hearts in Judah, and they sent to the king, urging him to return with all his men.

[a] What . . . ears: *prob. rdg.; Heb. has these words after* back to his palace *and adds* to his palace.

So the king came back to the Jordan; and the men of 15
Judah came to Gilgal to meet him and escort him across
the river.

✻ The narratives in 19: 8*b*–43 which complete the story of
Absalom's rebellion centre on the theme of loyalty and submission to David, restored to his throne, the true anointed
king of all Israel. There is at the same time a neat tying up of
some of the loose ends of the previous material, and some
points of anticipation of the sequels.

8*b*. The words echo the final sentence of 18: 17 (cp. note)
and these verses (8*b*–15) together with verses 40*b*–43 are concerned with the problem of the relationship between Judah,
the southern kingdom, and Israel, the northern. The true
purport of the interchanges is not entirely clear, but it is
evident that relations between north and south are strained,
and we may observe that a number of points look towards the
division of the kingdom in 1 Kings 12. We have here in
reality a reflection on the meaning of that later event rather
than merely a comment on David.

9. *were discussing it:* the meaning is not certain, but 'quarrelling' may be nearer. A résumé of David's reign picks out
David as deliverer and David as fugitive.

10. With the death of Absalom, only the restoration of
David is possible. *why have we no plans. . . ?:* literally 'why are
you silent about restoring the king?'

11f. The N.E.B. footnote indicates some disorder in the
text, probably due to an omitted phrase being written in the
margin and copied in at the wrong point (cp. on 1 Sam. 9: 9
for another kind of wrong insertion). In fact there appears to
be some duplication in these verses; the last phrases of verses
11 and 12 are duplicates. The point of these verses appears to
be a warning to Judah not to lose their position of special
relation to David; they are *my brothers, my flesh and my blood.*

13. The theme of verses 11f. is continued in verse 14. This

verse is parenthetic, noting the replacement of Joab by Amasa. Amasa appears as Absalom's *commander-in-chief* in 17: 25; he was a cousin of Joab. We may suppose this appointment to be due to David's anger with Joab for the death of Absalom, but such an explanation nowhere appears in the text and it is difficult to reconcile it with Joab's forceful action described in 19: 5-7. It is conceivable that David was attempting the conciliation of Absalom's supporters by the action; but the risk of offending his own men would surely be much more serious. Much more likely is the view that this verse is out of place; the note is entered here partly because of the verbal link *my own flesh and blood* with verse 12 and also to provide an anticipation of the murder of Amasa by Joab in 20: 4-13. But just how the various incidents are to be ordered remains a puzzle. Perhaps the compiler was endeavouring to reconcile elements of tradition which were in fact contradictory.

14. The king's encouraging message leads to immediate action by Judah, which, as the text actually says, behaved 'as one man'. The contrast between this speedy and loyal action of Judah and the suggestion of dilatoriness in Israel (verse 10), the other area under David's control, is again a pointer to that great disloyalty to the Davidic dynasty which is to be described in 1 Kings 12 at the disruption of the united kingdom. Another echo is to be found in verses 40b-43.

15. This verse continues the action of Judah; the new paragraph in the text should begin with verse 16. *Gilgal:* its location is uncertain, but near the Jordan and not far from Jericho. The sequel to this verse is in verses 40b-43. *

SHIMEI, MEPHIBOSHETH AND BARZILLAI

16 Shimei son of Gera the Benjamite from Bahurim hastened down among the men of Judah to meet King David
17 with a thousand men from Benjamin; Ziba was there too, the servant of Saul's family, with his fifteen sons and

twenty servants. They rushed into the Jordan under the
king's eyes and crossed to and fro conveying his household 18
in order to win his favour. Shimei son of Gera, when he
had crossed the river, fell down before the king and said 19
to him, 'I beg your majesty not to remember how dis-
gracefully your servant behaved when your majesty left
Jerusalem; do not hold it against me or take it to heart.
For I humbly acknowledge that I did wrong, and today 20
I am the first of all the house of Joseph to come down to
meet your majesty.' But Abishai son of Zeruiah objected, 21
'Ought not Shimei to be put to death because he cursed
the LORD's anointed prince?' David answered, 'What 22
right have you, you sons of Zeruiah, to oppose me
today? Why should any man be put to death this day in
Israel? I know now that I am king of Israel.' Then the 23
king said to Shimei, 'You shall not die', and confirmed
it with an oath.

Saul's grandson Mephibosheth also went down to 24
meet the king. He had not dressed his feet,*a* combed his
beard or washed his clothes, from the day the king went
out until he returned victorious. When he came from*b* 25
Jerusalem to meet the king, David said to him, 'Why
did you not go with me, Mephibosheth?' He answered, 26
'Sir, my servant deceived me; I did intend to harness my
ass and ride with the king (for I am lame), but his stories 27
set your majesty against me. Your majesty is like the
angel of God; you must do what you think right. My 28
father's whole family, one and all, deserved to die at
your majesty's hands, but you gave me, your servant,
my place at your table. What further favour can I expect

[a] *Josephus has* head.   [b] *So some Sept. MSS.; Heb.* to.

29 of the king?' The king answered, 'You have said enough.
My decision is that you and Ziba are to share the estate.'
30 Mephibosheth said, 'Let him have it all, now that your
majesty has come home victorious.'

31   Barzillai the Gileadite too had come down from
Rogelim, and he went as far as the Jordan with the king to
32 send him on his way. Now Barzillai was very old, eighty
years of age; it was he who had provided for the king
while he was at Mahanaim, for he was a man of high
33 standing. The king said to Barzillai, 'Cross over with me
and I will provide for your old age*a* in my household in
34 Jerusalem.' Barzillai answered, 'Your servant is far too
35 old to go up with your majesty to Jerusalem. I am already
eighty; and I cannot tell good from bad. I cannot taste
what I eat or drink; I cannot hear the voices of men and
women singing. Why should I be a burden any longer
36 on your majesty? Your servant will attend the king for a
short way across the Jordan; and why should the king
37 reward me so handsomely? Let me go back and end my
days in my own city near the grave of my father and
mother. Here is my son*b* Kimham; let him cross over
with your majesty, and do for him what you think best.'
38 The king answered, 'Kimham shall cross with me and I
will do for him whatever you think best; and I will do
for you whatever you ask.'

39   All the people crossed the Jordan while the king
waited.*c* The king then kissed Barzillai and gave him his
40*a* blessing. Barzillai went back to his own home; the king
crossed over to Gilgal, Kimham with him.

[*a*] your old age: *so Sept.; Heb.* for you.
[*b*] my son: *so Sept.; Heb. om.*   [*c*] *So Luc. Sept.; Heb.* crossed.

* David takes action to deal with both the loyal and the disloyal in a tidying-up operation. We may note the neat patterning of the material by which the first two are dealt with in the reverse order of their previous appearance in chapter 16.

16. Shimei's cursing of David was related in 16: 5–13. His reappearance with a large contingent from Benjamin represents an act of loyalty and submission. Saul's own tribe is here fully acknowledging David. We may note that while the Benjamite area often appears later to have been in dispute between the two kingdoms, a strong tradition claimed it for Judah (cp. the prophecy of Ahijah in 1 Kings 11: 29–39 which allots ten tribes to Jeroboam, first king of Israel, and one (i.e. Benjamin) to the Davidic line, in addition, of course, to Judah). For the Chronicler, the true Israel consisted of Judah and Benjamin (cp. 2 Chron. 11: 12). Thus a Davidic incident is used to bring out a wider point, relevant to later history.

17. The eappearance of *Ziba...the servant of Saul's family* echoes the earlier narratives of chapter 9 and 16: 1–4 and prepares the way for verses 24–30. It actually interrupts the Shimei narrative here, which continues with the words 'They rushed into the Jordan' though it is not in fact clear whether this originally referred to Shimei and his men or to the 'men of Judah' of verse 15. *They rushed into the Jordan:* a very uncertain, though traditional, rendering.

18. *and crossed to and fro;* equally an obscure phrase, perhaps the result of double copying. The N.E.B. takes it to mean that they kept crossing the river and escorting David and his men over. The Septuagint suggests a very appropriate alternative, based on an almost identical text: 'they worked manfully' (so the Jerusalem Bible). *when he had crossed the river:* the N.E.B. makes this refer to Shimei, but in the text it more naturally refers to David. Shimei waits on the western bank to greet David; or perhaps we should see the text as meaning that once David had crossed the river,

Shimei and his men came back to the western bank and Shimei prostrated himself to David there.

19f. Shimei's humble apology is interpreted by him as representing *the first of all the house of Joseph:* here the expression is evidently used to denote the northern kingdom, though in fact the Joseph tribes are Ephraim and Manasseh (cp. Gen. 48: 1). Is there here again a pointer forward to an ultimate restoration of the north to Davidic rule?

21. A death sentence would be appropriate for the cursing of *the LORD's anointed prince:* an attack on a divinely chosen ruler is an act of such impiety as to deserve this (cp. Exod. 22: 28).

22. The moment of restoration, when David is able to state confidently *I know now that I am king of Israel* is to be a moment of magnanimity, not marred by the putting to death of any man. Is this perhaps a reflection of a normal 'accession' procedure? (cp. Saul's attitude as presented in 1 Sam. 11: 12f.). *to oppose me today:* literally 'to be to me a *satan*', an adversary. The figure of a human adversary, using this term, is found again in 1 Kings 11: 14 of an enemy divinely raised up to oppose Solomon (cp. also on 1 Sam. 29: 4). In later writings (Job 1–2; Zech. 3: 1f. and 1 Chron. 21: 1 – cp. note on 24: 1 here), a 'Satan' is an officer of the divine court, a kind of prosecutor in the heavenly assembly. It is only later still that Satan becomes a name for an evil being opposed to God, but we can begin to trace the development in these Old Testament passages.

23. David's solemn oath assuring Shimei of his life was carefully observed. Yet the curse remained spoken and at the end of his life David is represented as handing on this legacy to his son Solomon. The latter, by a skilful stratagem, contrived to bring Shimei to a death which was a just judgement upon himself, avoiding any blood guilt on the royal house (1 Kings 2: 8f., 36–46). So Shimei may be seen both as a symbol of an opponent who offers his loyalty and as one who must in the end reap the reward of his opposition to the king whom God has chosen.

24. *Mephibosheth:* cp. chapter 9 and 16: 1–4. *He had not dressed his feet:* this presumably suggests the washing and anointing of the feet (cp. Luke 7: 38). Josephus (cp. the N.E.B footnote) has 'head'; some Greek texts have 'hands'. Thus the precise point is not clear, but we may see this, alongside the care of *his beard* (more strictly 'moustache') and his clothes, as a sign of mourning during the period of the absence of David the true king. The description is clearly intended to suggest the rightness of his attitude. But David is not apparently persuaded. We may recall the story of the Gibeonites who pretended to have come on a long journey from a distant land by bringing mouldy bread and wearing worn clothing to deceive Joshua successfully into making a treaty with them (Josh. 9: 3–27). Can we be sure that Mephibosheth was not being similarly astute?

25. *When he came from Jerusalem:* but the text has 'to Jerusalem', and we may wonder whether, in view of verse 26, this scene really belongs at David's arrival in his palace which Mephibosheth 'enters' (*came* most naturally means 'came in' not 'came to a place'); it has then been transposed, like the reference to Ziba in verse 17, to add to the scene at the Jordan.

26. The implication is that Ziba disobeyed orders or disappeared to take advantage of the situation. We must compare Ziba's own version in 16: 3, but we can no more decide between the two stories than David could.

27. *like the angel of God:* cp. note on 14: 17. A superhuman insight is attributed to David. Mephibosheth's attitude in this verse and in the next two may be understood equally as a true expression of loyalty or as an endeavour to gain favour and forgiveness in a delicate situation.

28. *What further favour can I expect. . . ?:* the word rendered 'favour' could be translated 'legal right' (as in Neh. 2: 20 where the N.E.B. has 'claim'); we might render Mephibosheth's words: 'What legal right have I left? All I can do is appeal (cry out) to the king.' A strong word meaning 'to cry

out in distress' is used here, often found in the Psalms where appeal is made to God (e.g. Ps. 22: 5). Some Septuagint texts render 'and he cried out again to the king'. The N.E.B. *expect* is much too weak a rendering. On the deserved fate of Saul's family, cp. also 21: 1–14.

29f. David modifies his decision of 16: 4, refusing to adjudicate between Ziba and Mephibosheth; for the latter's attitude cp. on verse 27.

31. The text of this verse is in considerable disorder, as a result of what appears to be accidental repetition of *the Jordan*. It has been tacitly corrected in the N.E.B. rendering.

32. This verse, with its brief reference back to the narrative of 17: 27–9, adds to the earlier information a note of Barzillai's age and status.

33. *I will provide:* an echo of verse 32. Barzillai provided for David; now David will provide for him.

34f. Barzillai's response is a poignant description of old age (cp. the vivid metaphors of Eccles. 12: 1–8 and the commentary in *Ruth, Esther, Ecclesiastes* etc. in this series, pp. 151–3). *I cannot tell good from bad:* probably, as in Isa. 7: 15, meaning 'what I like from what I dislike', and amplified by the parallel expression *I cannot taste what I eat or drink. the voices of men and women singing:* on occasions of festivity especially, such as would now take place, music would be appropriate. Sennacherib's records (about 800 B.C.) refer to tribute from Judah as including 'male and female musicians' (cp. *A.N.E.T.* (see p. 240), p. 288).

37. *in my own city near the grave of my father and mother:* a man prefers to be where he belongs, particularly as death approaches, so that he can be buried with his fathers.

38. The courtesy of Barzillai's offer of his son Kimham in his place, and his desire that the king should act as he thinks best (verse 37), are echoed by David's willingness to do whatever Barzillai wishes. This is an elegant example of courtly conversation.

39. If the N.E.B. is right in accepting the alternative *waited*

(cp. footnote), then we have here a concluding echo of the formal movements described in chapter 15 (cp. notes on verses 18 and 23).

40*a*. Finally the king and Kimham cross the Jordan.

We may observe that the narrator has skilfully reversed the theme of the flight of David into a theme of his return, weaving into the narrative units of material originally separate but now subordinated to the main point (cp. further the comment after verses 40*b*–43). ✶

RIVALRY OF ISRAEL AND JUDAH

All the people of Judah escorted the king over the river, 40*b* and so did half the people of Israel.

The men of Israel came to the king in a body and said, 41 'Why should our brothers of Judah have got possession of the king's person by joining King David's own men and then escorting him and his household across the Jordan?' The men of Judah replied, 'Because his majesty 42 is our near kinsman. Why should you resent it? Have we eaten at the king's expense? Have we received any gifts?' The men of Israel answered, 'We have ten times your 43 interest in the king and, what is more, we are senior[a] to you; why do you disparage us? Were we not the first to speak of bringing the king back?' The men of Judah used language even fiercer than the men of Israel.

✶ This strange and not fully intelligible passage is now employed as a link between David's return (verse 40) and the next narrative of rebellion in chapter 20. The northern tribes, ten in number (cp. on verses 8*b*–15 and notes on verses 16 and 19f.), claim a greater 'interest in the king' and also that they are 'senior'. Judah in fact does not stand among the tribes of

[a] senior: *so Sept.; Heb.* in David.

Israel as anything like the eldest (cp. Gen. 29: 29 – 30: 24, and the tribal sayings of Gen. 49 and Deut. 33). We may probably see here a reflection of the later problem of Judah's status. Davidic kingship was acknowledged by all Israel; but the Davidic line remained with Judah. The north was to claim its own kingship and to regard that as the true succession. By contrast Judah, the junior, claimed the higher status.

40b. We now pick up the theme which was left at verse 15, with an unexpected addition of *half the people of Israel*. Are we to suppose that the other half opposed the reacceptance of David (cp. the quarrelling in 19: 9)?

42. *any gifts*: special favours from the king.

43. *The men of Judah used language even fiercer...*: or possibly, 'what Judah said was too strong for what Israel said', i.e. the claim of Judah prevailed.

At a number of points we have noted the defective state of the text in this whole chapter. In particular, the problems are connected with the theme of 'crossing the Jordan'. But even if some overloading has now confused the matter, it remains evident that a main element here is that of bringing back the Davidic king by escorting him across the Jordan. Is this more than an inevitable narrative telling of his return from his fugitive position beyond the Jordan? We may note that a frequent theme of Deuteronomy is 'when you have crossed the Jordan', then you must obey God's will; the opening chapters of Joshua centre almost entirely on this and related points. For the Deuteronomic historians, a new entry to the land and a new life could mark a hope for the future in the period of the exile. We may perhaps see in this narrative as it now stands, telling of David's return to Jerusalem, a foreshadowing of the coming return – a return to well-being, peace (*shālōm*), the word which in this passage is used of David's victorious entry (cp. verses 24 and 30 where 'victorious' is literally 'in peace'). It is by such oblique hints that the writer suggests to his readers what the story, already no doubt familiar to them, now means for themselves. *

THE REBELLION OF SHEBA

There happened to be a man there, a scoundrel named **20**
Sheba son of Bichri, a man of Benjamin. He blew the
trumpet and cried out:

> What share have we in David?
> We have no lot in the son of Jesse.
> Away to your homes, O Israel.

The men of Israel all left David, to follow Sheba son of 2
Bichri, but the men of Judah stood by their king and
followed him from the Jordan to Jerusalem.

When David came home to Jerusalem he took the ten 3
concubines whom he had left in charge of the palace
and put them under guard; he maintained them but did
not have intercourse with them. They were kept in con-
finement to the day of their death, widowed in the
prime of life.

The king said to Amasa, 'Call up the men of Judah and 4
appear before me again in three days' time.' So Amasa 5
went to call up the men of Judah, but it took longer than
the time fixed by the king. David said to Abishai, 'Sheba 6
son of Bichri will give us more trouble than Absalom;
take the royal bodyguard and follow him closely. If he
has occupied some fortified cities, he may escape us.'
Abishai was followed by Joab[a] with the Kerethite and 7
Pelethite guards and all the fighting men; they left
Jerusalem in pursuit of Sheba son of Bichri. When they 8
reached the great stone in Gibeon, Amasa came towards
them. Joab was wearing his tunic and over it a belt

[a] Abishai . . . Joab: *prob. rdg.; Heb.* Some men of Joab followed him.

supporting a sword in its scabbard. He came forward,
9 concealing his treachery, and said to Amasa, 'I hope you
are well, my brother', and with his right hand he grasped
10 Amasa's beard to kiss him. Amasa was not on his guard
against the sword in Joab's hand. Joab struck him with it
in the belly and his entrails poured out to the ground;
he did not strike a second blow, for Amasa was dead.
Joab and his brother Abishai went on in pursuit of Sheba
11 son of Bichri. One of Joab's young men stood over
Amasa and called out, 'Follow Joab, all who are for
12 Joab and for David!' Amasa's body lay soaked in blood
in the middle of the road, and when the man saw how
all the people stopped, he rolled him off the road into the
field and threw a cloak over him; for everyone who came
13 by saw the body and stopped. When he had been dragged
from the road, they all went on after Joab in pursuit of
Sheba son of Bichri.

14   Sheba passed through all the tribes of Israel until he
came to Abel–beth–maacah,*a* and all the clan of Bichri*b*
15 rallied to him and followed him into the city. Joab's
forces came up and besieged him in Abel–beth–maacah,
raised a siege–ramp against it and began undermining the
16 wall to bring it down. Then a wise woman stood on the
rampart*c* and called from the city, 'Listen, listen! Tell
17 Joab to step forward and let me speak with him.' So he
came forward and the woman said, 'Are you Joab?'
He answered, 'I am.' 'Listen to what I have to say, sir',
18 she went on, to which he replied, 'I am listening.' 'In

[a] *Prob. rdg., cp. verse 15;* Heb. Abel and Beth-maacah.
[b] *Prob. rdg.;* Heb. Beri.
[c] stood . . . rampart: *transposed from verse 15.*

the old days', she said, 'there was a saying, "Go to Abel
for the answer", and that settled the matter. My city is 19
known to be one of the most peaceable and loyal[a] in
Israel; she is like a watchful mother in Israel, and you are
seeking to kill her. Would you destroy the LORD's own
possession?' Joab answered, 'God forbid, far be it from 20
me to ruin or destroy! That is not our aim; but a man 21
from the hill-country of Ephraim named Sheba son of
Bichri has raised a revolt against King David; surrender
this one man, and I will retire from the city.' The woman
said to Joab, 'His head shall be thrown to you over the
wall.' Then the woman withdrew, and her wisdom won 22
over the assembled people; they cut off Sheba's head and
threw it to Joab. Then he sounded the trumpet and the
whole army left the city and dispersed to their homes,
while Joab went back to the king in Jerusalem.

* A new and quite separate incident, not necessarily chronologically linked with Absalom's revolt, is placed side by side
with it and partly integrated. It provides a further example of
the overcoming of opposition to the Davidic line. Some
points of contact with the secession of the northern tribes after
Solomon's death (1 Kings 12) suggest that the compiler must
have seen this narrative too as an anticipation of that later
event (cp. on 18: 17; 19: 8b–15). The story of Amasa and his
murder by Joab (verses 4–13) is not very clearly integrated
with the rebellion theme, and we may wonder whether it
originally belonged to some other occasion. It provides yet
another example of both the ruthlessness and the loyalty of
Joab and his brother Abishai.

1. The implication of the opening words, *There happened*

[a] My city . . . loyal: *prob. rdg.; Heb.* I am the requited ones of the loyal
ones.

to be a man there, and the N.E.B.'s rendering of the last words of verse 2, 'followed him from the Jordan to Jerusalem' (cp. note on that verse), imply that the rebellion took place immediately as a result of the contention between Israel and Judah in 19: 41–3. *scoundrel:* literally 'man of *belī'al*', cp. notes on 16: 7 and 22: 5f. *of Benjamin:* the same tribe as Saul and Shimei (19: 16, where the loyalty of Benjamin is affirmed). May this rebellion perhaps be another aspect of Benjamite antagonism to David as having usurped Saul's position? *He blew the trumpet* (ram's horn): a summons to war, though curiously the poetic fragment that follows calls on Israel to go home. The poem is in fact also found in 1 Kings 12: 16 (and cp. note on 18: 17 above) at the division of the kingdom, where it properly expresses secession rather than armed rebellion. The repudiation of David and the Davidic line is characteristic of the attitude of the northern tribes at the division. In this passage and in 1 Kings 12: 16 (2 Chron. 10: 16), it is alleged by Jewish rabbinic tradition that the word for 'tents' (*'ohālīm*), here translated *homes*, has been altered from that for 'gods' (*'elōhīm*). The basis of this was the view that the northern tribes were apostates, worshipping other gods, a view partly to be associated with the popular belief that the Samaritans were descended from such apostates and from alien settlers (cp. 2 Kings 17), though such a view is clearly contradicted by the very evident conservatism of Samaritan religious belief and practice, and in fact the Samaritan community only came into existence at the end of the Old Testament period. The rabbinic tradition represents an example of interpretation directed towards the upholding of a truly orthodox line of faith.

2. The loyalty of Judah is again reminiscent of the events described in 1 Kings 12. *followed him:* no word for this is found in the Hebrew, but the N.E.B.'s paraphrase may well be right since the compiler clearly wished to suggest an immediate secession of the north from a loyal Judah restoring David to his kingly position.

3. A parenthetic note – appropriate to the supposition that David had only now reached Jerusalem – explains what happened to *the ten concubines* (cp. 15: 16; 16: 21f.). The action of Absalom in claiming them as his may be regarded as defiling them. The text suggests sympathy for these unfortunate pawns in the political game, now regarded as in a 'widowhood of living', i.e. cut off from life, or possibly 'of a lifetime', treated as if widows of the dead Absalom. The precise sense is not clear, and the N.E.B.'s *prime of life* is a paraphrase.

4. Amasa appears as commander (cp. 19: 13), asked to gather *the men of Judah* for battle, i.e. not the royal bodyguard, but the general levy.

6. The rather odd behaviour of David in entrusting the command to Amasa but giving special duties to Abishai, brother of Joab, is explained by the delay; yet it must be clear that such division of military authority is dangerous. A possibility, though not in any way clear in the text, is that Amasa was taking advantage of his position and of the duty entrusted to him to engage in rebellious activity on his own, to continue Absalom's revolt (cp. on verses 11–13). *some fortified cities:* this anticipates what is subsequently described in verse 14. *escape us:* the Hebrew is obscure. The Septuagint suggests 'becloud our eyes', i.e. 'give us anxiety'.

7. The appearance of Joab, the man whom Amasa had replaced, is ominous, though the text is not entirely clear as it stands. *Kerethite and Pelethite:* cp. on 8: 16–18.

8. *the great stone:* possibly an altar; cp. 1 Sam. 14: 33 for such a stone, possibly at Gibeah. *Gibeon* (see map, p. 29): a noted holy place; cp. 1 Kings 3: 4. *concealing his treachery:* the N.E.B. depends on a small emendation of the text, though it is not clear that the rendering given is really admissible. Literally, the text has 'and it fell', possibly 'and it (the sword) came out and fell', but in verse 10 it is in Joab's hand. The whole description of Joab is very confused in the Hebrew.

9f. Joab's treachery in regard to Amasa is comparable to his murder of Abner (3: 27).

11–13. Action is taken to ensure that the soldiers follow Joab and are not distracted by the murder of Amasa. The appeal for loyalty to Joab and David (verse 11) could suggest that Amasa's followers were tempted to rebel. For the battle-cry cp. 10: 12 and Judg. 7: 20.

14. *Abel-beth-maacah:* cp. map, p. 12. The statement of this verse suggests a much smaller incident, in which Sheba is supported only by his own clan. Possibly a local incident has provided the basis for the rebellion narrative here developed into a full-scale secession of the north.

15. Siege methods may be traced both in the Old Testament and generally in the ancient Near East. A very full portrayal of the siege of Lachish by the Assyrian ruler Sennacherib is in the British Museum in London (cp. *Old Testament Illustrations* in this series, pp. 80–3).

16. *a wise woman:* cp. the narrative of chapter 14. As there, the woman appears as one skilled in the use of words to persuade a sound course of action. *stood on the rampart:* cp. the N.E.B. footnote; the words were accidently misplaced, possibly having been inadvertently omitted, added in the margin and then copied into the wrong line of the text. If they are kept in verse 15, the sense would have to be 'it (the siege-ramp) stood against the rampart'.

18. *"Go to Abel for the answer", and that settled the matter:* the precise meaning of the text is not in fact clear. It may be that we have here a proverbial saying (cp. 1 Sam. 10: 11f.; 19: 24) of which the original sense is no longer known, and that it is here provided with a narrative context.

19. This verse too is far from clear. The Hebrew (cp. the N.E.B. footnote) seems to suggest that the wise woman speaks on behalf of the city, and the words might be slightly modified to read: 'I (the city) am among the most peaceable and loyal in Israel.' In the next clause, the phrase *a watchful mother* is an ingenious suggestion, but the actual text seems preferable: 'a city and mother', i.e. 'a city which is as a mother'. The significance of this is made plain in the question

Would you destroy the LORD's own possession? – actually 'put to death', again seeing the city personified as 'mother in Israel'. Here the point of the argument becomes evident. Israel as a community which belongs to God is a totality which ought not to be destroyed or depleted. The loss of a tribe would mean the undermining of this totality (cp. the narrative of Judg. 19–21, especially 21: 3, which stresses the risk of Benjamin ceasing to exist as a tribe). The laws of Israel included means to protect the inheritance of a family (cp. the story of Naboth's vineyard in 1 Kings 21 for an example of the strong sense of family land). So to destroy a city is to leave the community less than it ought ideally to be. Later writers used this theme for a wider theological purpose (cp. Ezek. 47–8 for an ideal conception of land and people, and Rev. 7: 4–8 for the idea of the perfect number of the heavenly community). The story of Sheba is thus made an occasion for a comment on the true wholeness of Israel, and this may be seen to underline the disaster of loss and secession.

A different theological theme appears here to be drawn out by the Greek translators, and this is followed by some modern ones (e.g. the Jerusalem Bible). This gives the sense: 'Let them ask in Abel and Dan whether that (true tradition) had ever come to an end which Israel's faithful ones had laid down', i.e. these cities claim to be guardians of the true religious traditions.

21. Sheba curiously appears here as from *the hill-country of Ephraim*. Joab claims that all he needs is to ensure Sheba's death; his belief, which proves justified, is that all further rebellion will then collapse.

22. We are not told the precise manner in which the wise woman *won over the assembled people*; no doubt she used similarly persuasive words. Rebellion against David is thus at an end. ✴

DAVID'S OFFICIALS

23^a Joab was in command of the army,^b and Benaiah son of
Jehoiada commanded the Kerethite and Pelethite guards.
24 Adoram was in charge of the forced levy, and Jehoshaphat
25 son of Ahilud was secretary of state. Sheva was adjutant-
26 general, and Zadok and Abiathar were priests; Ira the
Jairite was David's priest.

* This list is to be compared with 8: 16–18; cp. the notes
there and the reference also to 1 Kings 4: 1–6. Again here, the
list may be set out in tabular form as the N.E.B. does for
1 Kings 4. The order of the officials differs somewhat. Most of
the names are the same; *Sheva* appears for Seraiah. Additional
is *Adoram . . . in charge of the forced levy*: this is the forced labour
corps which becomes more prominent in the Solomon narratives and a matter for contention at the division of the kingdom. Probably Adoram is the same person as Adoniram in
1 Kings 4: 6, but whether he really survived to be stoned to
death as is stated in 1 Kings 12: 18 must be less certain, since
the lengths of reign given for David and Solomon (forty years
each) are conventional rather than historically precise. In
verse 26 the statement *Ira the Jairite was David's priest* replaces
the reference to David's sons as priests in 8: 18, but the nature
of Ira's function is quite unknown. *

APPENDICES TO THE BOOK

* Chapters 21–4 of 2 Samuel form a complex conclusion to
the book. We may observe that the theme of the throne,
legitimacy and succession, which has been a prominent feature
in the preceding narratives, reappears clearly in 1 Kings 1–2,
chapters which really provide the climax and conclusion to

[a] *Verses 23–6: cp. 8: 16–18; 1 Kings 4: 2–6; 1 Chron. 18: 15–17.*
[b] *Prob. rdg., cp. 8: 16; Heb. adds Israel.*

the David story. The intervening chapters contain several different elements and a clear literary structure appears. In considering this, we must note that some of this material is also used by the Chronicler, but whereas here the various elements appear simply as separate items, he has woven them closely into his presentation. Following on his version of the Ammonite war (1 Chron. 19: 1 – 20: 3), which contains only the first and last parts of 2 Sam. 10–12, he presents part of 21: 15–22 in 1 Chron. 20: 4–8. The narrative of chapter 24 is found in a significantly modified form in 1 Chron. 21: 1 – 22: 1, closely integrated into the theme of the choice of the temple site. The lists of David's heroes and their exploits in 23: 8–39 appear in a somewhat fuller form in 1 Chron. 11: 10–41 (with an additional section of the same list in verses 42–7), used there as part of a much larger presentation of the supporters of David as he takes up his place as king of all Israel at Jerusalem (1 Chron. 11: 10 – 12: 40). Chapter 22 appears in the Psalms, as Ps. 18.

The structure of chapters 21–4 suggests that the various elements were brought together in three stages. The two narratives of 21: 1–14 and 24 have close similarities (cp. e.g. the links between 21: 1 and 24: 1); between these have been inserted the exploits and lists of David's heroes (21: 15–22 and 23: 8–39), clearly originally part of one complex; between these again have been inserted two poems (chapter 22 and 23: 1–7, the 'Last words of David'). The effect of this structuring is to produce a chiastic pattern, that is, one which may be represented diagrammatically as *a*, *b*, *c*, *c*¹, *b*¹, *a*¹; but it is difficult to see how this could have been intended from the first. ✶

THE FAMINE

In David's reign there was a famine that lasted year after **21** year for three years. So David consulted the LORD, and he answered, 'Blood-guilt rests on Saul and on his family

2 because he put the Gibeonites to death.' (The Gibeonites were not of Israelite descent; they were a remnant of Amorite stock whom the Israelites had sworn that they would spare. Saul, however, had sought to exterminate them in his zeal for Israel and Judah.) King David sum-
3 moned the Gibeonites, therefore, and said to them, 'What can be done for you? How can I make expiation, so that you may have cause to bless the LORD's own
4 people?' The Gibeonites answered, 'Our feud with Saul and his family cannot be settled in silver and gold, and there is no one man in Israel whose death would content us.' 'Then what do you want me to do for you?' asked
5 David. They answered, 'Let us make an end of the man who caused our undoing and ruined us, so that he shall never again have his place within the borders of Israel.
6 Hand over to us seven of that man's sons, and we will hurl them down to their death before*a* the LORD in Gibeah of Saul, the LORD's chosen king.' The king agreed to
7 hand them over, but he spared Mephibosheth son of Jonathan, son of Saul, because of the oath that had been taken in the LORD's name by David and Saul's son
8 Jonathan. The king then took the two sons whom Rizpah daughter of Aiah had borne to Saul, Armoni and Mephibosheth, and the five sons whom Merab,*b* Saul's daughter,
9 had borne to Adriel son of Barzillai of Meholah. He handed them over to the Gibeonites, and they flung them down from the mountain before the LORD; the seven of them fell together. They were put to death in the first days of harvest at the beginning of the barley
10 harvest. Rizpah daughter of Aiah took sackcloth and

[a] *Or* for.   [b] *So some MSS.; others* Michal.

spread it out as a bed for herself on the rock, from the beginning of harvest until the rains came and fell from heaven upon the bodies. She allowed no bird to set upon them by day nor any wild beast by night. When 11 David was told what Rizpah daughter of Aiah the concubine of Saul had done, he went and took the bones of 12 Saul and his son Jonathan from the citizens of Jabeshgilead, who had stolen them from the public square at Beth-shan, where the Philistines had hung them on the day they defeated Saul at Gilboa. He removed the 13 bones of Saul and Jonathan from there and gathered up the bones of the men who had been hurled to death. They buried the bones of Saul and his son Jonathan in the 14 territory of Benjamin at Zela, in the grave of his father Kish. Everything was done as the king ordered, and thereafter the LORD was willing to accept prayers offered for the country.

＊ This is a difficult narrative to understand; it is probable that it contains more than one element, and evident that underlying it are relics of a kind of thinking which is strange to a modern reader. Indeed some of its features suggest the memory of very ancient beliefs concerning the relation between the giving of rain and ritual acts. In attempting to trace these earlier elements, we must also observe the aim of the narrator in the present context. Its placing here allows it to be understood both as a further judgement on the family of Saul and as an indication of David's piety towards that family in arranging proper burial.

1. *a famine:* it is clear from verse 10 that this was due to lack of rain (cp. the Elijah narrative in 1 Kings 17–18). *three years:* cp. 'three years...months...days' in 24: 13. Such a

disaster was seen as a divine judgement and the reason for it is sought from God himself. The interrelationship between man and his conduct and the world in which he lives is strongly felt in Old Testament thought. Man's failure in obedience in Gen. 3 brings a judgement that 'accursed shall be the ground on your account' (verse 17); the prophets often express judgement in terms of natural disaster (e.g. Hag. 1: 10f. where drought and famine are attributed to the failure to restore the temple after the exile). We should not state the matter in such simple terms, though we have become acutely aware in recent years of the disasters which can follow from a misuse of natural resources, and such a misuse may well be associated with a wrong style of life.

The divine word to David proclaims *Blood-guilt...on Saul and on his family*, and links this to an incident of which we have no record, a slaughter of Gibeonites. We may reasonably assume that the ancient readers were aware of the incident; it could be connected with the brief and obscure reference in 4: 2f. (see note). It could provide another illustration of Saul's unfitness to be king (cp. also 1 Sam. 22, the slaughter of the priests of Nob).

2. Most of this verse is designed to remind the reader of the background to the situation. The story of the Gibeonites and of how they tricked Joshua into making a treaty with them is told in Josh. 9. It is clear that the real point of that story lies in its conclusion that the Gibeonites became temple servants 'to this day' (Josh. 9: 27), that is, in perpetuity; and the story sets out to explain how this could have come about, since they were *not of Israelite descent*, but *a remnant of Amorite stock*. This is one of the terms used for the previous inhabitants of the land, though in ancient records it may refer to the Semitic people of whom Hammurabi (eighteenth century B.C.) was the most famous ruler. The treaty between Israel and the Gibeonites protected the latter: *Saul...had sought to exterminate them* – again an allusion to the unrecorded incident – *in his zeal for Israel and Judah*, a remarkable statement suggesting

that the glossator saw Saul as one to whom the preservation of the purity of people and religion was of primary importance. In fact, such a claim fits well with some few other hints that we have about Saul. His zeal, misguided but well-intentioned, in 1 Sam. 13 and 15, where he disobeys a divine command in a good cause; his oath imposed on the army in 1 Sam. 14 which nearly led to Jonathan's death; his removal of necromancers from the community noted in 1 Sam. 28: 3 – all these suggest an ardently religious ruler, whose ardour was not always sufficiently controlled by sense. But even if his motive was good – the removal of an alien influence which must not contaminate the religion of Israel – the infringement of a treaty could not pass uncondemned. The breaking of treaties in the ancient Near East might be understood as a cause of natural disaster, by plague or famine or other misfortune. Thus a broken treaty between the Egyptians and the Hittites in the late fourteenth century B.C. was held to have led to a plague lasting twenty years in the Hittite lands (cp. *A.N.E.T.* (see p. 240), p. 395). Some action must be taken to deal with the offence and its consequences.

3. David offers complete freedom of penalty to the Gibeonites; as the offended party, they can select who is to die for the offence. *make expiation:* the technical term, often used in religious laws, apparently denoting the 'covering' or 'wiping away' of the offence (cp. Exod. 32: 30 'to secure pardon'). *the LORD's own people:* literally 'the LORD's inheritance' or 'possession', as the same words are rendered in 20: 19. If the offence is removed, the Gibeonites will bless the people of God to which they belong by adoption.

4f. *no one man in Israel:* the rejection of any monetary compensation is followed by the rejection of any single Israelite victim. Only Saul is guilty, therefore only Saul's family can pay, and this by the total exclusion of the family of Saul from the community. A similar penalty is imposed on Achan and his family for the infringement of an absolute command in

Josh. 7. *never again have his place:* 'not be established' or 'not have status'.

6. *seven of that man's sons:* in fact not the whole family, but a clearly symbolic representative number, which will declare the family condemned. *hurl them down to their death:* the meaning of the Hebrew word rendered 'hurl' is uncertain. The hanging up of the bodies or their exposure or dismemberment may be intended. *before the LORD:* the text is correctly so rendered in verse 9, but here the N.E.B. footnote preserves the sense, for the victims are 'for God' in the sense that they are to expiate the sin which has occasioned famine for the whole people. *Gibeah of Saul:* see map, p. 29, and cp. 1 Sam. 10: 26. *the LORD's chosen king:* a remarkable phrase in this context, reflecting once again the tragedy of Saul the chosen who became Saul the rejected. It has been suggested that we might read the very similar 'on the LORD's mountain', i.e. in a notable holy place, perhaps with 'Gibeon' for 'Gibeah' (cp. on verse 9).

7. This verse should be in parenthesis: (*but he spared... Saul's son Jonathan*) since it is clearly an explanatory note to point the reader to the narrative of chapter 9 and its sequels. The annotator may have been reminded of the point by the occurrence of the name of another 'Mephibosheth' in verse 8; in any case the two narratives, which are not linked and which cannot be chronologically aligned, invite some sort of harmonizing comment.

8. Rizpah was a concubine, a lesser wife (cp. verse 11 and 3: 7). But her loyalty to Saul and his family is noteworthy. The names are confusing in this verse. For *Mephibosheth* some texts have 'Merab' possibly abbreviated from Meribbaal (cp. on 4: 4); for *Merab* some have 'Michal' (cp. the N.E.B. footnote). Merab for the latter accords with 1 Sam. 18: 19 where her marriage is noted. Michal is the more difficult reading, but may be due to a scribal slip. We cannot clearly identify the persons involved.

9. *flung them down:* cp. on verse 6. *from the mountain:* but the

text has 'on the mountain'. The phrase here strongly suggests that the execution was carried out as a ritual in a holy place. *fell together:* i.e. died together.

9f. The dating of the event points to a second feature in the narrative. The date given (cp. Ruth 1: 22) would be about April. Rain coming so exceptionally late in the season would be seen as a special act of divine favour. There is no reason to suppose that Rizpah was guarding the bodies for six months till the time of the early (autumn) rains. Rizpah guards the bodies from vultures and other birds of prey, and from wild beasts. This may be interpreted as an act of piety, to preserve the bodies for burial, but it may also be linked to a ritual associated with rain-giving and the growing of the crops. There appears here, in relation to the Saul theme, another and more primitive element.

11f. David's reaction to the news of what Rizpah has done is to ensure proper burial for Saul and Jonathan. There is a reference back to the story in 1 Sam. 31: 11–13 (cp. also on 2: 4b–7). The use here of the word *stolen* probably simply means that it was done secretly; but it could be that there is here evidence of an alternative tradition, of a kind implied in 1 Chron. 10: 11f., that the action of the men of Jabesh-gilead brought about the burial of Saul and Jonathan in an alien place.

13. The removal of *the bones of Saul and Jonathan* is here amplified with a reference to those of the seven men of verses 6–10, but both the preceding verse and verse 14 strongly suggest that the original story here concerned only Saul and Jonathan, and that this act of piety by David which would link well with 2: 4b–7 has been subsequently combined with the other narrative.

14. Burial in the family grave is proper; it is reminiscent too of the stress on proper burial for the kings of Judah (cp. e.g. 1 Kings 14: 31) and in some instances for the kings of Israel (cp. e.g. 1 Kings 16: 28). Some Greek texts here add a phrase to include also in this burial the bodies of the seven

victims (cp. on verse 13). *Zela:* unknown, but possibly not a place-name at all. The last part of the verse unites this motif with the main narrative and suggests a state of continual well-being for the community. *thereafter:* in the text, this comes at the end of the verse, and it has been suggested that it really introduced chapter 9 as a sequel showing David's further piety towards the memory of Jonathan. The story is now linked with chapter 24, which cites another instance of disaster. ✳

INCIDENTS OF THE PHILISTINE WARS

15 Once again war broke out between the Philistines and Israel. David and his men went down to the battle, but
16 as he fought with the Philistines he fell exhausted. Then Benob, one of the race of the Rephaim, whose bronze spear weighed three hundred shekels*a* and who wore a belt of honour,*b* took David prisoner and was about to
17 kill him. But Abishai son of Zeruiah came to David's help, struck the Philistine down and killed him. Then David's officers took an oath that he should never again go out with them to war, for fear that the lamp of Israel might be extinguished.

18*c* Some time later war with the Philistines broke out again in Gob: it was then that Sibbechai of Hushah
19 killed Saph, a descendant of the Rephaim. In another war with the Philistines in Gob, Elhanan son of Jair*d* of Bethlehem killed Goliath of Gath, whose spear had a shaft
20 like a weaver's beam. In yet another war in Gath there appeared a giant with six fingers on each hand and six

[a] shekels: *prob. rdg.; Heb.* weight.
[b] *Lit.* a new belt.
[c] *Verses 18–22: cp.* 1 Chron. 20: 4–7.
[d] Jair: *prob. rdg., cp.* 1 Chron. 20: 5; *Heb.* Jaare-oregim.

toes on each foot, twenty-four in all. He too was des- cended from the Rephaim; and, when he defied Israel, 21 Jonathan son of David's brother Shimeai killed him. These four giants were the descendants of the Rephaim 22 in Gath, and they all fell at the hands of David and his men.

＊ A group of notes of individual heroic conflicts is gathered here, presented in a very stylized manner, and summarized in verse 22. The Chronicler (1 Chron. 20: 4-7) included only part of this material, omitting the story of David's near death and rescue, possibly because it appeared to him to reflect on David's military prowess. The material is closely related to 23: 8-39.

15. *Once again war broke out...*: similar vague formulae appear in verses 18, 19 and 20. No clue is given to the chrono- logy; the incidents suggest a much longer conflict than is related in 5: 17-25.

16. *the race of the Rephaim:* the phrase used in this passage always in fact has the name in the form 'Raphah' (with the definite article: *hārāphāh*). This is usually thought to be a reference to the mysterious Rephaim, who appear in the Old Testament variously. They are said to be former and indeed often giant inhabitants of Palestine (thus Og king of Bashan in Deut. 3: 11, whose sarcophagus was enormous according to that verse; probably it was a great natural stone which had become associated with an ancient hero. Cp. also Deut. 2: 10-12 and 20-3, two pieces of ancient tradition which asso- ciate various other names, especially Anakim, with the Rephaim). The Rephaim are also described as the inhabitants of the realm of the dead, possibly 'weak ones', though this is only one possible sense. Here the tradition associates them with a whole line of giants, descended from a single individual named Raphah. But an interesting alternative suggestion notes that the phrase is not the normal 'sons of Raphah' which would

suggest descendants, but a phrase which could denote members of a particular group, and hence a warrior corps. The corps would be designated either with reference to a particular weapon (*hārāphāh* being understood to mean 'scimitar' or the like, though this is not by any means certain) or in reference to the deity who is patron of the group, described as 'the vigorous one'. From the accounts here, Gath (see map, p. 29) would seem to be the locality to which the group belonged. Evidence is provided by 23: 8–39 of special warrior groups associated with David. *was about to:* or 'thought to', 'had it in mind to'.

17. *Abishai:* brother of Joab (cp. e.g. 10: 10 and 16: 9–12), evidently a warrior, though, like Joab, also a trouble to David. The rescue of David from near death provoked strong reaction. David's officers swore that he would *never again go out...* *to war* – a proper function of the king (cp. 1 Sam. 8: 20) – *for fear that the lamp of Israel might be extinguished.* In this very significant phrase it is made clear that the life of the people is tied up in the life of the king (cp. note on 18: 3). Here we gain an insight into the nature of Hebrew kingship, with the indication of the king as one who brings well-being and blessing, and is in some sense the mediator of God's power to his people. The idea of a continually burning lamp as symbol may be connected with such a lamp in the shrine, both at Jerusalem and elsewhere (cp. on 1 Sam. 3: 3, and Exod. 27: 21 and Lev. 24: 1–3 for the regulating of the lamp in priestly law. For a fuller comment on kingship, cp. the note on 1 Sam. 11 in the commentary on 1 Samuel, pp. 92–4 and in the concluding comments to this volume, pp. 237f.).

18. *Gob:* an unknown place. *descendant of the Rephaim:* cp. on verse 16.

19. *Goliath of Gath:* this giant appears as the challenger of Israel killed by David in 1 Sam. 17, where he is named in verse 5 (cp. note on this verse). But here he is said to have been killed by someone other than David; the full title of this person is somewhat confused (cp. the N.E.B. footnote) because

the word for 'weaver' (*'ōregīm* – actually a plural in the text) has been accidentally written in the middle of the name. The Chronicler avoided the conflict with the Goliath story, which he actually does not relate, by adding 'Lahmi brother of' before 'Goliath' (1 Chron. 20: 5). We may recognize the probability that some details of one hero story have been transferred to David, though another explanation has been given, namely that Elhanan was David's real name, and David was his throne name (cp. note on 12: 25). But the father's name, Jair, does not fit. Another possibility is that the giant in 1 Sam. 17 was originally unnamed.

20. The giant mentioned here is also a monster in having excess fingers and toes. *Rephaim:* cp. note on verse 16.

21. *when he defied Israel:* this is a marked theme of the David story in 1 Sam. 17, where the same word 'defy' is used in verses 10, 25 and 45. *Shimeai:* the name appears as Shammah in 1 Sam. 16: 9 and is variously spelled in the text here and in 1 Chron. 20.

22. A summary shows that there has been a grouping of four tales, which have in common that all the giants are associated with Gath.

The sequel to this group of hero incidents is to be found in the hero lists and exploits of 23: 8–39, which also provides stories of the Philistine wars. ✳

A PSALM OF VICTORY

✳ At this point, the compiler has introduced two poems. The first is clearly a psalm and appears also as Ps. 18 in the Psalter. The second also has clear links with psalmody, though it has other features as well. In 1 Samuel, a psalm is introduced in 2: 1–10, described as the prayer of Hannah, but in reality a psalm like many in the Psalter. In that instance (see the commentary in this series), the placing of the psalm comments both on the immediate situation of Hannah at Samuel's dedication, and also on the wider position of Israel, as moves towards the monarchy begin. The poems placed here in 2 Samuel serve a similar purpose. Just as the Song of Moses (Deut. 32), a great hymn to God's dealings with Israel, is followed by the Blessing of Moses (Deut. 33), a kind of testament to the tribes, so here a psalm of victory is followed by the 'last words of David' (23: 1). The two poems stand at the end of David's life, though separated from the narrative of 1 Kings 1–2 by further additional material in 23: 8–39 and chapter 24.

The psalm in this chapter comments in some degree on the position of David, looking back on his victories, and was perhaps thought to follow well after the decision that David should never again risk his life and the well-being of his people in war (21: 17; cp. on 22: 29). It also comments on the dynasty which stemmed from David, and reflects on Israel and the meaning of its life. Since this psalm appears as Ps. 18, reference may also be made to the commentary on that psalm in this series. It will be seen that different interpretations of the content and wording of the psalm are possible. A close comparison of the two texts shows small but important differences, though the overall effect is the same. The existence of two texts of the same passage may in some points of difficulty help us to find a likely correct text; but we should not suppose that it is possible to reconstruct the 'original' psalm. It is better to recognize that the two forms exist side by side, reflecting different stages and contexts of transmission and interpretation. ✳

GOD THE DELIVERER

22 These are the words of the song David sang to the LORD on the day when the LORD delivered him from the power of all his enemies and from the power of Saul:

2[a] The LORD is my stronghold, my fortress and my champion,

[a] *Verses 2–51: cp. Ps. 18: 2–50.*

my God, my rock where I find safety;   3
my shield, my mountain fastness, my strong tower,
my refuge, my deliverer, who saves me from violence.
I will call on the LORD to whom all praise is due,   4
and I shall be delivered from my enemies.

When the waves of death swept round me,   5
and torrents of destruction overtook me,
the bonds of Sheol tightened about me,   6
the snares of death were set to catch me;
then in anguish of heart I cried to the LORD,   7
I called for help to my God;
he heard me from his temple,
and my cry rang in his ears.

The earth heaved and quaked,   8
heaven's foundations shook;
they heaved, because he was angry.

Smoke rose from his nostrils,   9
devouring fire came out of his mouth,
glowing coals and searing heat.

He swept the skies aside as he descended,   10
thick darkness lay under his feet.

He rode on a cherub, he flew through the air;   11
he swooped[a] on the wings of the wind.

He curtained himself in darkness   12
and made dense vapour his canopy.

Thick clouds came out of the radiance before him;   13
glowing coals burned brightly.

The LORD thundered from the heavens   14
and the voice of the Most High spoke out.

He loosed his arrows, he sped them far and wide,   15

[a] *Prob. rdg., cp. Ps. 18: 10; Heb.* was seen.

his lightning shafts, and sent them echoing.

16 The channels of the sea-bed were revealed,
    the foundations of earth laid bare
    at the LORD's rebuke,
    at the blast of the breath of his nostrils.

17 He reached down from the height and took me,
    he drew me out of mighty waters,

18 he rescued me from my enemies, strong as they were,
    from my foes when they grew too powerful for me.

19 They confronted me in the hour of my peril,
    but the LORD was my buttress.

20 He brought me out into an open place,
    he rescued me because he delighted in me.

21 The LORD rewarded me as my righteousness deserved;
    my hands were clean, and he requited me.

22 For I have followed the ways of the LORD
    and have not turned wickedly from my God;

23 all his laws are before my eyes,
    I have not failed to follow his decrees.

24 In his sight I was blameless
    and kept myself from wilful sin:

25 the LORD requited me as my righteousness deserved
    and my purity in his eyes.

✽ 1. This verse provides the title for the psalm. The N.E.B.
has deliberately omitted the titles in the Psalter (see the discussion in the Psalms commentaries); but the policy is not a
good one, since in some respects these titles form part of early
psalm interpretation. We have seen how certain psalms may
have been understood as associated with particular moments
in David's life (cp. e.g. on 7: 4); this psalm is understood as a
general reflection on God's delivery of David *from the power*

of all his enemies and from the power of Saul. The same title appears at the head of Ps. 18. Such an interpretation provides a clue to the way in which, at one stage of its use, the psalm was understood. References to 'stronghold', 'refuge' and the like (cp. verses 2, 3 and 47) may have suggested David's period as a fugitive from Saul (cp. 1 Sam. 21–31). We may also wonder whether the commentator who added this interpretative note did so partly because he saw a subtle word-play on the language of verse 6. The reference to Sheol, the realm of the dead, might well evoke the name of Saul (the letters of the Hebrew words are identical and such word-play was much loved by Hebrew writers), David's arch-enemy and rival for royal power. We shall see that the much more general themes of deliverance and victory in the psalm are given a specific reference in this title. The psalm thus becomes a kind of summary of David's reign, a reflection on its meaning for other men, even ordinary Israelite worshippers.

2–7. The psalm opens with the expression of confidence in divine deliverance.

2. Ps. 18 has an additional line at the beginning of this verse: 'I love thee, O LORD my strength', an initial confession of faith. *my champion:* or 'my deliverer'.

3. The psalmist piles up words to express divine power and protection. *my mountain fastness:* an ingenious translation, but the parallel with *shield* may suggest the more literal 'horn of salvation', i.e. my royal saving power. The horn is a frequent symbol of royal power (cp. 1 Sam. 2: 10 'raise high the head of his anointed prince', literally 'the horn of his anointed'). The last line of this verse is not found in Ps. 18.

5f. The metaphors of these verses refer first to the hostile waters associated with *death*, and belonging to the region of *destruction*, for which the term used is actually *belī'al* which, as we have seen (cp. on 16: 7), denotes the realm of alien power, associated here with death and *Sheol*. In the second pair of lines, the theme is that of the hostile power of Sheol or death which holds men prisoner. The forces ranged against the power of God have, as it were, taken control of the psalmist. Whatever his distress, it may be expressed in such language; and the worshipper can appropriate this to his own condition.

7. *in anguish of heart:* the expression, which appears in a similar form in David's prayer in 24: 14, 'in a desperate plight', suggests restriction. Deliverance may then be expressed in terms of 'an open place' (cp. verses 20 and 37). God is understood as hearing *from his temple*, the earthly counterpart of his heavenly dwelling-place (cp. on 7: 14-16 and see 1 Kings 8: 30 where prayer towards the temple is heard by God in heaven).

8-16. A series of pictures shows God as supreme, displaying his power and anger as he rides to battle (cp. Judg. 5: 4f., 20f. for another such description. The account of the theophany at Sinai (Exod. 19) has also many points of resemblance).

8. The march of God in anger causes upheavals in the earth: the psalmist understands natural phenomena as expressive of the action of God (cp. Ps. 64). *heaven's foundations:* Ps. 18: 7 has 'mountains'. The earth and heavens are sometimes understood as built upon pillars (cp. Job 38: 6), which can be shaken by earthquake. *earth* might here be understood to mean 'the underworld, Sheol'.

9. *glowing coals and searing heat:* suggestive of the fire associated with the divine presence (cp. Ezek. 1: 4, 27). These and similar words appear again in verse 13, producing an echo effect. Hebrew poetry is often made effective by such repetition, sometimes in the form of a refrain, but more often by the occurrence of similar words or phrases more than once within a psalm (cp. also verses 20 and 37; and comments on the lament in 1: 17-27).

10f. God is depicted as riding *on a cherub*, the winged lion creature which often appears as a guardian, and is associated with his enthronement in the temple (cp. 1 Kings 6: 23-8). *swooped:* like a vulture on its prey (Deut. 28: 49), as in Ps. 18: 10; the Hebrew here (cp. the N.E.B. footnote) has 'was seen', i.e. 'revealed himself', a less good parallel but still an appropriate sense.

12f. The theme of God concealed in darkness is expressive of the sense of the mystery which surrounds him (cp. 1 Kings 8: 12: 'O LORD who hast...chosen to dwell in thick darkness'). The contrast of dark clouds and *radiance* uses imagery associated with a storm, taken further in the next verses.

14. Thunder as the voice of God is another favourite expression: it is used for God speaking from Jerusalem in Joel 3: 16 and Amos 1: 2, both passages probably quoting a familiar liturgical saying.

15. *arrows* as God's weapons are frequently associated with *lightning* (cp. Zech. 9: 14).

16. With this verse we return to the opening theme of this section in verse 8; the whole earth is exposed, the waters withdraw as if in awe at God's presence.

17–25. The two themes handled so far are drawn together. God's revealing of his power is expressed in his deliverance of the psalmist.

17. Deliverance is by God acting *from the height*, that is, from heaven; he rescues from the forces of evil, described as *mighty waters*. *he drew me out:* the same term as is used to explain the name of Moses – 'I drew him out of the water' (Exod. 2: 10).

18f. The *enemies* of the psalmist are not specified: in verse 1 they are interpreted as enemies of David, but clearly the worshipper can see in such language the expression of his own needs in all the dangers of life. *my peril:* perhaps 'my terror'. *buttress:* or 'support'.

20. *an open place:* cp. on verse 7. This contrasts with the restriction of distress. The metaphor derives from the insecurity of a narrow defile contrasted with the security of a wide open area. *because he delighted in me:* here and in the succeeding lines to verse 25 the psalmist bases his confidence in God's deliverance on his right response to the divine command. Thus there are linked together two ideas: God's

supreme power to deliver (so especially in verses 8–16), and man's willingness to conform to the divine law (so here).

21. *my hands were clean:* another example of echoing words and ideas is to be seen here and in verse 25 where 'my purity' could equally be rendered 'my cleanness'.

22f. The theme of obedience to the law is most fully developed in the reiterated statements of Ps. 119, where a wide range of terms is used to express the completeness of obedience. ✳

GOD THE GIVER OF VICTORY

26 With the loyal thou showest thyself loyal
   and with the blameless man blameless.
27 With the savage man thou showest thyself savage,
   and*ª* tortuous with the perverse.
28 Thou deliverest humble folk,
   thou lookest with contempt upon the proud.
29 Thou, LORD, art my lamp,
   and the LORD will lighten my darkness.
30 With thy help I leap over a bank,
   by God's aid I spring over a wall.

31 The way of God is perfect,
   the LORD's word has stood the test;
   he is the shield of all who take refuge in him.
32 What god is there but the LORD?
   What rock but our God? –
33 the God who girds me*ᵇ* with strength
   and makes my way blameless,*ᶜ*

[a] With the savage ... savage, and: *or* With the pure thou showest thyself pure, but ...
[b] who girds me: *prob. rdg., cp. Ps. 18: 32; Heb.* my refuge *or* my strength.
[c] and makes ... blameless: *prob. rdg., cp. Ps. 18: 32; Heb. unintelligible.*

who makes me swift as a hind   34
and sets me secure on the*a* mountains;
who trains my hands for battle,   35
and my arms aim an arrow tipped with bronze.

Thou hast given me the shield of thy salvation,   36
in thy providence thou makest me great.
Thou givest me room for my steps,   37
my feet have not faltered.
I pursue my enemies and destroy them,   38
I do not return until I have made an end of them.
I make an end of them, I strike them down;   39
they rise no more, they fall beneath my feet.
Thou dost arm me with strength for the battle   40
and dost subdue my foes before me.
Thou settest*b* my foot on my enemies' necks,   41
and I bring to nothing those that hate me.
They cry out*c* and there is no one to help them,   42
they cry to the LORD and he does not answer.
I will pound them fine as dust on the ground,   43
like mud in the streets will I trample them.*d*
Thou dost deliver me from the clamour of the people,*e* 44
and makest*f* me master of the nations.
A people I never knew shall be my subjects.
Foreigners shall come cringing to me;   45
as soon as they hear tell of me, they shall obey me.

[a] *So Sept.; Heb.* my.
[b] *Prob. rdg., cp. Ps. 18: 40; Heb. unintelligible.*
[c] cry out: *prob. rdg., cp. Ps. 18: 41; Heb.* look.
[d] *Prob. rdg., cp. Ps. 18: 42; Heb. adds* will I stamp them down.
[e] the clamour of the people: *so Sept. and Ps. 18: 43; Heb. obscure.*
[f] *So Luc. Sept. and Ps. 18: 43; Heb.* keepest.

46 Foreigners shall be brought captive to me,
and come limping from their strongholds.

47 The LORD lives, blessed is my rock,
high above all is God my rock and safe refuge.

48 O God, who grantest me vengeance,
who dost subdue peoples under me,

49 who dost snatch me from my foes and set me over my
enemies,
thou dost deliver me from violent men.

50 Therefore, LORD, I will praise thee among the nations
and sing psalms to thy name,

51 to one who gives his king great victories
and in all his acts keeps faith with his anointed king,
with David and his descendants for ever.

* There is no break in the psalmist's thought, the theme of the law and of obedience leads on into reflection upon its nature and meaning and hence to renewed confidence in victory.

26–30. A first reflective passage considers in more general terms the nature of God's dealings with men.

26f. In a series of sayings, the relationship of God with man is described, bringing out the twofold nature – loyalty and judgement – in which he responds to men's ways. *the blameless man:* more literally 'the acceptable warrior', an allusion to the general theme of victory in the psalm. *the savage man:* an uncertain rendering, but one which provides a better parallel to the next clause than the more usual 'the pure' (cp. the N.E.B. footnote). We then have two clauses expressing God's loyalty to those who are faithful and two stating God's judgement on the wicked. *tortuous:* or possibly 'astute'.

28. The same contrast is to be found here as in the preceding verses. *humble folk:* or better 'a humble people', i.e. Israel

having a right attitude to God. In that case *the proud*, or 'those who set themselves up', may be Israel when it fails to show a proper regard for God. For this theme, cp. also the fuller expression in 1 Sam. 2: 1-8.

29. *my lamp:* possibly recalling the theme of the Davidic king as 'the lamp of Israel' (21: 17), the expression of the people's well-being, though the image may be more general than this.

30. *leap over a bank...spring over a wall:* these may be military metaphors, expressive of the skill of the bold soldier in attack (cp. Jonathan in 1 Sam. 14: 6-15 where verse 6 stresses the divine giving of power).

31-5. The surety of God's word and the uniqueness of his being underlie the confidence that he will give strength to his worshipper.

31f. From confidence that *The way of God is perfect*, his *word* reliable, the thought moves to his protective power and hence to his sole claim to be God, to be the *rock*. The theme of divine incomparability – none like God in heaven and earth (cp. 7: 22) – is an important one in Old Testament thought, particularly elaborated in the writings of the Second Isaiah (Isa. 40-55).

33. The second clause is uncertain: we might expect another statement of the strengthening of the psalmist.

34. *the mountains:* the text has 'my mountains' (cp. the N.E.B. footnote). The word is not in fact the normal one for mountains, and perhaps should be understood as 'my high places', possibly an allusion to the king as ruler in the worship of his people.

35. *arrow tipped with bronze:* the text actually refers to a 'bronze bow', presumably one decorated with bronze, or possibly one used only for ceremonial purposes (cp. on 8: 5-8 and 'the shields of gold that Solomon had made' (cp. 1 Kings 10: 16) which were replaced by Rehoboam with 'bronze shields' (1 Kings 14: 26f.)).

36-46. These verses now develop the theme just set out,

namely God's giving of military power to the worshipper, clearly understood to be the king himself.

36. *in thy providence:* the meaning is very uncertain, literally perhaps 'in thy answering me', i.e. in God's promise of victory. Ps. 18: 35 has literally 'thy humility', but this hardly seems right. It is in fact very difficult to know which of several Hebrew words is here being used. The Septuagint has 'thy disciplining of me'; this might point to the theme of the humiliation of the king, a theme more fully developed in Ps. 89: 38–51 where it is seen in the context of confidence in God's power and of his covenant with David. (Cp. also comments on chapters 15 and 16.)

37. *givest me room:* for the theme cp. verse 20.

38. *destroy them:* the variant in Ps. 18: 37 'overtake them' may well be preferred, since this gives the natural sequence of pursuit, overtaking and destruction.

40f. Total subjection of the enemies is emphasized here.

42. While the military metaphors which precede and follow are not lost to sight, the more general theme of the 'enemies of God' is here drawn out. No deliverance can be found from the power of God; the enemies of God may appeal to him, but he will not respond. Thus the psalm has meaning for a wider range of situations than that of battle.

43. *trample them:* the Hebrew has a second verb 'stamp them down'. This may be an alternative reading, preserved alongside the first; or both verbs may be original, giving emphasis: 'I will trample them, yes, stamp them down.'

44f. *the clamour of the people:* the N.E.B. footnote wrongly derives this meaning from Ps. 18: 43 which in fact has exactly the same text as here. The Hebrew text may be rendered: 'from the contentions, the legal attacks of my people', or better 'of the peoples', parallel to the plural *nations*. This pictures the nations engaged in an attempt to discredit Israel's king in a law court; but God makes him supreme over them. For a similar theme, that of a conspiracy of the nations, cp. Ps. 2: 1f. The extension of the king's rule to other nations is a related theme, also to be found in Ps. 2. This is part of a view of the king as the regent of God whose rule must eventually extend over all nations (cp. Ps. 72: 8–11).

46. *be brought captive:* clearly an appropriate sense for the context, though alternatives are 'decay' or 'be dismayed'. *come limping:* or perhaps 'come trembling'.

47–51. The final verses break out into a reassertion of confidence in God, echoing the opening of the psalm and offering worship for God's enduring faithfulness.

47. The link back to the beginning of the psalm is clear. *The LORD lives:* comparison may be made with the Canaanite literature from Ras Shamra (cp. *The Making of the Old Testament*, pp. 25–9, in this series). There it is similarly affirmed

> 'See Aleyn Ba'al (Ba'al the powerful) lives;
> See the prince, the lord of the earth, exists.'

Such a statement is in contrast to passages where Ba'al is lamented as dead. The psalmist makes the affirmation that Israel's God is alive, but it is in the confidence that God does not die; so too we may compare the prophetic affirmation that he is 'my God, the holy, the immortal' (literally 'thou shalt not die'; Hab. 1: 12). He is the living, saving God.

48f. These verses echo again the theme of victory and deliverance, already expressed in similar terms (cp. especially verses 17–20, 40–6).

51. The culminating thought is that of God's protection and empowering of *his anointed king*, that is to say *David and his descendants*, the whole royal dynasty. There is an echo of the covenant with David set out in chapter 7. The psalm thus reaches its climax in confidence in the choice of David and his successors.

The emphasis in this psalm is clearly upon God's giving of victory over his enemies to the Davidic king: as such it provides a comment on the achievements of David, and comes fittingly almost at the end of the narratives. But military achievement was not in the long run to be the lasting value of David's reign. In 587 B.C. Davidic kingship came to an end, and later hopes of restoration were not realized. Stress came to be laid rather on David as the originator of worship and psalmody, and so as the truly pious worshipper whose life and trials could mirror those of anyone who cries to God in a moment of need. The victory of God is understood to be 'not against human foes, but against cosmic powers' (Eph. 6: 12), the forces of evil described in mythological terms as belonging to the realm of darkness, or in terms of human experience of the inadequacies and failures of human life. So the story of David becomes a pattern for the understanding of God's victorious purpose. ✶

THE LAST WORDS OF DAVID

23 These are the last words of David:

The very word of David son of Jesse,
the very word of the man whom the High God raised up,
the anointed prince of the God of Jacob,
and the singer of Israel's psalms:
2 the spirit of the LORD has spoken through me,
and his word is on my lips.
3 The God of Israel spoke,
the Rock of Israel spoke of me:
'He who rules men in justice,
who rules in the fear of God,
4 is like the light of morning at sunrise,
a morning that is cloudless after rain
and makes the grass sparkle from the earth.'

5 Surely, surely my house is true to God;
for he has made a pact with me for all time,

its terms spelled out and faithfully kept,
my whole salvation, all my*[a]* delight.
But the ungodly put forth no shoots,   6
they are all like briars tossed aside;
none dare put out his hand to pick them up,
none touch them but*[b]* with tool of iron or of wood;   7
they are fit only for burning in the fire.*[c]*

* This poem is set out as if it were the final message of David
to his descendants. We may contrast it with the other 'last
words' to be found in 1 Kings 2: 1–9, a testament to Solomon,
exhorting his obedience and imposing on him specific duties
regarding certain persons involved with David. The poem
here is of a quite different order. It is much more like the last
words of blessing pronounced by Jacob on his sons, as representatives of the tribes (Gen. 49), and even more like that of
Moses (Deut. 33). It is a poem expressive of a certain view of
David's status and of the position to be occupied by his
successors in the dynasty.

1. *The very word:* the term used is particularly associated
with prophetic utterance. It is evident that David is here
understood as a prophetic figure, not unlike Balaam (Num.
22–4, e.g. 24: 3, where the same Hebrew word describes his
utterances), pronouncing both on his status and on the future
of dynasty and people.

The description of David opens with three parallel expressions, stressing his status: his family, *son of Jesse* (cp. 1 Sam. 16:
1–13 and Ruth 4: 18–22); his exaltation by *the High God*, the
supreme deity; and his position as *anointed prince* (the term in
Hebrew being *māshīaḥ*, anglicized as Messiah, of which the
Greek rendering gives us the title Christ). Three further
parallel phrases may be seen, being the last line of this verse

[a] *Prob. rdg.; Heb. om.*   [b] but: *prob. rdg.; Heb.* he shall be filled.
[c] *Prob. rdg.; Heb. adds* in sitting.

and the two lines of the next; these draw out his function as spokesman of God, and first as *the singer of Israel's psalms*, an indication of the position which David came to occupy as the traditional originator of the psalms. David's reputation as a musician (cp. 1 Sam. 16: 14–23) and as a composer of laments (2 Sam. 1: 17–27; 3: 33f.), had grown into the view of him as psalmist and as organizer of temple worship and song (so 1 Chron. 15–16). But there are uncertainties of interpretation in the text here. The rendering *singer of Israel's psalms* depends on a particular interpretation of the first word, which may very probably mean 'favourite' or 'beloved', i.e. David as the one most praised in the songs of Israel. Yet another interpretation, which fits this line closely with the three which precede, understands it to mean 'beloved of the guardian (strong one) of Israel', i.e. God, an expression for him which appears in other psalm passages (e.g. Isa. 12: 2) where the N.E.B. renders it 'defence'. It is not easy to decide between the alternatives. We may observe that a psalter from Qumran has a passage in which this poem (of which only the very last words survive there) is immediately followed by an interesting account of the way David's writings and functions were understood in roughly the New Testament age. We can see that the theme of David the prophet is developed, as also is that of David as the great composer of psalms (cp. p. 14 for Josephus' use of this theme). It is worth quoting the Qumran text in full because of the light it sheds on these developments:

'David, the son of Jesse, was wise, and a light like the light of the sun; skilled and understanding, and perfect in all his ways before God and men. The LORD gave him a spirit of understanding and of light. He wrote 3600 psalms; and songs to be sung before the altar with the perpetual sacrifices every day, for every day of the year, 364; and for the offering of the sabbaths, 52 songs; and for the offering of the new moons and of the festal days and of the Day of Atonement, 30 songs. So all the songs which he spoke amounted to 446, together with songs to be played over those stricken, 4. So the total was 4050. All these he spoke in the prophecy which was given him by the presence of the Most High.'

This passage, linked as it is to the poem which we find here in 2 Samuel, suggests that the writer understood this first verse to speak of David as singer. The list of David's compositions is clearly designed to exceed that attributed to Solomon in 1 Kings 4: 32 (3000 proverbs plus 1005 songs).

2. The theme of David as spokesman of God is developed here in the association of David with the prophetic word, inspired by *the spirit of the LORD*. Here, in wording similar to that of the Qumran passage already quoted, we may see how psalmody is being understood not simply as the poetry of worship, but as prophetic words, representing a source of revelation of the will of God for later generations. This concept of David as prophet is to be found also in the New Testament (e.g. Acts 2: 29f.) and this is part of a process by which the words of the Old Testament as a whole came to be so understood, as prophetic of the future. This is too limited a view of their meaning, but it has been deeply influential in the development of later religious thinking both Jewish and Christian.

3f. There is a shift here from the idea of David as spokesman of God to that of God's permanent favour to him. *the Rock:* a frequent symbol of the protection and enduring power of God (cp. Ps. 19: 14). The Davidic king is here described in terms of *justice* (cp. Isa. 11: 3f. for a poetic expression of this ideal in fuller form): the true king is the upholder of law and right. Justice is paralleled by *the fear of God*, a proper regard for the status of God, for true religion as a right attitude to God. This just rule is associated with the picture of the king as mediator of divine blessing in life and fertility: he is like *the light of morning* after the darkness and its dangers; he is associated with *rain* and with the growth of the crops. Such a collocation of ideas is often found in royal psalms, as clearly in Ps. 72 where the king as upholder of justice (especially verses 1–4, 12–14) is associated with the king as giver of life (especially verses 6, 16).

5. What David is, his *house*, his dynasty, is also. The theme of the eternal covenant (here the word is rendered *pact*) is a common one seen already in chapter 7. Its fullest expression is in the related Ps. 89, especially in verses 3f. and 19–37.

6f. The last phrase of verse 5 in the Hebrew is rightly in the N.E.B. attached to this verse, rendered *put forth no shoots. the ungodly:* a free rendering of the term transliterated as *belī'al*, the figure associated with chaos and evil (cp. on 16: 7 and 22: 5f.). In a vivid series of pictures, the fate of the opponents of God, which are by implication those of his chosen king, is depicted: no growth; thrown away *like briars*; *fit only for burning.* The contrast between the true royal house and the blessings which it brings (verses 3–5) and all alien powers is sharply drawn. The final word 'in sitting' (cp. the N.E.B. footnote) is probably an accidental copying from verse 8 and does not belong here. ✳

DAVID'S HEROES

8[a] These are the names of David's heroes. First came Ishbosheth the Hachmonite,[b] chief of the three;[c] it was he who brandished his spear[d] over eight hundred dead, 9 all slain at one time. Next to him was Eleazar son of Dodo the Ahohite,[e] one of the heroic three. He was with David at Pas-dammim where the Philistines[f] had gathered for

[a] *Verses 8–39: cp. 1 Chron. 11: 10–41.*
[b] *Prob. rdg.; Heb.* Josheb-basshebeth a Tahchemonite.
[c] *So Luc. Sept.; Heb.* third.
[d] who . . . spear: *prob. rdg., cp. 1 Chron. 11: 11; Heb.* unintelligible.
[e] the Ahohite: *prob. rdg., cp. 1 Chron. 11: 12; Heb.* son of Ahohi.
[f] He was . . . Philistines: *prob. rdg., cp. 1 Chron. 11: 13; Heb.* With David when they taunted them among the Philistines.

battle. When the Israelites fell back, he stood his ground 10 and rained blows on the Philistines until, from sheer weariness, his hand stuck fast to his sword; and so the LORD brought about a great victory that day. Afterwards the people rallied behind him, but it was only to strip the dead. Next to him was Shammah son of Agee a 11 Hararite. The Philistines had gathered at Lehi, where there was a field with a fine crop of lentils; and, when the Philistines put the people to flight, he stood his ground 12 in the field, saved it*a* and defeated them. So the LORD again brought about a great victory.

Three of the thirty went down towards the beginning 13 of harvest to join David at the cave of Adullam, while a band of Philistines was encamped in the Vale of Rephaim. At that time David was in the stronghold and a Philistine 14 garrison held Bethlehem. One day a longing came over 15 David, and he exclaimed, 'If only I could have a drink of water from the well*b* by the gate of Bethlehem!' At this 16 the heroic three made their way through the Philistine lines and drew water from the well by the gate of Bethlehem and brought it to David. But David refused to drink it; he poured it out to the LORD and said, 'God 17 forbid that I should do such a thing! Can I drink*c* the blood of these men who risked their lives for it?' So he would not drink it. Such were the exploits of the heroic three.

Abishai the brother of Joab son of Zeruiah was chief 18 of the thirty.*d* He once brandished his spear over three

[*a*] saved it: *or* cleared it of the Philistines.　　　[*b*] *Or* cistern.
[*c*] I drink: *prob. rdg., cp. 1 Chron. 11: 19; Heb. om.*
[*d*] *So Pesh.; Heb.* three.

hundred dead, and he was famous among the thirty.[a]
19 Some think he even surpassed the rest of the thirty[b] in
reputation, and he became their captain, but he did not
20 rival the three. Benaiah son of Jehoiada, from Kabzeel,
was a hero of many exploits. It was he who smote the
two champions of Moab, and who went down into a
21 pit and killed a lion on a snowy day. It was he who also
killed the Egyptian, a man of striking appearance armed
with a spear: he went to meet him with a club, snatched
the spear out of the Egyptian's hand and killed him with
22 his own weapon. Such were the exploits of Benaiah son
23 of Jehoiada, famous among the heroic thirty.[b] He was
more famous than the rest of the thirty, but he did not
rival the three. David appointed him to his household.

24 Asahel the brother of Joab was one of the thirty, and
25 Elhanan son of Dodo from[c] Bethlehem; Shammah from
26 Harod, and Elika from Harod; Helez from Beth-pelet,[d]
27 and Ira son of Ikkesh from Tekoa; Abiezer from Ana-
28 thoth, and Mebunnai from Hushah; Zalmon the Aho-
29 hite, and Maharai from Netophah; Heled[e] son of Baanah
from Netophah, and Ittai son of Ribai from Gibeah of
30 Benjamin; Benaiah from Pirathon, and Hiddai from the
31 ravines of Gaash; Abi-albon from Beth-arabah,[f] and
32 Azmoth from Bahurim;[g] Eliahba from Shaalbon, and
33 Hashem the Gizonite; Jonathan son of[h] Shammah the

[a] So Pesh.; Heb. three.   [b] Prob. rdg.; Heb. three.
[c] from: so some MSS.; others om.
[d] Prob. rdg., cp. Josh. 15: 27; Heb. from Pelet.
[e] So many MSS.; others Heleb.
[f] Prob. rdg., cp. Josh. 18: 22; Heb. from Arabah.
[g] Prob. rdg., cp. 1 Chron. 11: 33; Heb. from Barhum.
[h] Hashem . . . son of: prob. rdg., cp. 1 Chron. 11: 34; Heb. the sons of
Jashen, Jonathan.

Hararite, and Ahiam son of Sharar the Hararite;[a] Eli- 34
phelet son of Ahasbai son of the Maacathite, and Eliam
son of Ahithophel the Gilonite; Hezrai from Carmel, and 35
Paarai the Arbite; Igal son of Nathan from Zobah, and 36
Bani the Gadite; Zelek the Ammonite, and Naharai from 37
Beeroth, armour-bearer to Joab son of Zeruiah; Ira the 38
Ithrite, Gareb the Ithrite, and Uriah the Hittite: there 39
were thirty-seven in all.

* This passage appears in a somewhat fuller form in 1 Chron.
11: 10–41, where verses 42–7 add a further section of the same
list. It is closely linked to 21: 15–22, and contains some further
incidents from the Philistine wars, as well as the list of 'the
thirty' in verses 24–39. As will be seen from the N.E.B. footnotes, there are many problems of text and translation, as was
also the case in chapter 21. The Chronicles text sometimes
helps in the tentative reconstruction.

8. *These are the names . . . :* the heading to the whole passage.
Verses 8–12 deal with the exploits of a small group, *the three.*
The text of the latter part of this verse is quite unintelligible;
the N.E.B. follows the Chronicles text, though that could
itself be the result of an early attempt at guessing the meaning.

9. *Pas-dammim:* cp. 1 Chron. 11: 13 for this emendation of
an obscure text. Presumably the same as Ephes-dammim in the
Vale of Elah in 1 Sam. 17: 1 (cp. map, p. 29, for the general
locality).

10. The story as related in 1 Chron. 11: 13f. has very different elements in it, linked to what appears here in verse 11.
It may be that the Chronicles text has accidentally omitted a
section. We may note the theme, here and in verse 12, of the
giving of victory by God through the agency of the hero (cp.
on 8: 6, 14*b*).

11. It is clear from this verse that the conflicts with the

[a] *Prob. rdg., cp. 1 Chron. 11: 35; Heb.* Ararite.

Philistines were often simply border raids, designed to get the crops (cp. the Midianite raids in Judg. 6: 1-11). *Lehi:* cp. the story of Samson in Judg. 15: 9-19, which relates a story of the origin of the name (Lehi meaning 'jaw-bone') and of the spring there. Since Lehi is there part of Judah, we may see the Philistines here attempting to get the lentil crop for themselves, and the heroic act is in origin the driving away of the raiders. It becomes in its present form a great single action against the enemies of Israel, like the corresponding heroic act of Samson.

13f. The second passage, verses 13-17, is linked to the preceding one by the number *three*, here three heroes who are from among *the thirty* (cp. verses 18-39). It relates a single heroic act. The text is in fact by no means so clear as the translation implies. *the cave of Adullam:* centre of David's period as an outlaw; cp. on 1 Sam. 22: 1 (see map, p. 29). The cave is here, as there, identified as a *stronghold. Vale of Rephaim:* cp. on 5: 18 and also the discussion of 21: 16. Clearly the situation, with *a Philistine garrison* at *Bethlehem*, belongs to the time before David's accession to the throne. We should see it as an example of the conflicts in which David appears to have been involved during Saul's reign.

15. *the well:* or 'cistern' (cp. the N.E.B. footnote). We may picture David and his men in the desert area where water is scarce; water from the Bethlehem well would be a particular pleasure and relief.

16. *the heroic three;* more literally 'the three warriors'. *he poured it out to the LORD:* to be understood as a libation, comparable to the pouring of wine alluded to in Hos. 9: 4, and described more fully in Ecclus. 50: 15. As the comment in verse 17 explains, water purchased at the risk of men's lives ('the blood of these men') could not be used properly for a secular purpose, but belongs to God as does the blood of a sacrificial victim. The story gives a vivid picture of a heroic exploit; it also draws out the themes of David's piety and of the loyalty existing between him and his men.

18. Here the writer turns to the *thirty*, giving first some details of exploits and then a list of names. *Abishai:* cp. e.g. 3: 30 and 16: 9. He and Joab together appear both as great warriors and as men of violence and passion. The Hebrew text in fact associates him with the three, but this does not appear to be correct.

19. *Some think:* the text appears to be defective. In 1 Chron. 11: 21 the comment is simply 'He held higher rank'; cp. verse 23 for a comparable expression.

20. *Benaiah:* in 1 Kings 2: 35 he is appointed as commander of the army in place of the dead Joab who had been involved in the attempt at putting Adonijah on the throne. *the two champions:* the word so rendered (*'arīēl*) closely resembles that for *lion* (*'arī*). Its meaning is uncertain, possibly 'lions of God', i.e. warriors; but there is evidently a word-play here. An alternative is simply to understand it as meaning 'very large and fierce lions' (i.e. more than normally so, and hence thought to be in some way supernatural, belonging to the divine realm. Cp. Gen. 1: 2 'mighty wind' (N.E.B.) for the more common rendering 'wind of God'). Yet another though less suitable meaning would be 'altars' (cp. Ezek. 43: 15 'altar-hearth'), but this hardly fits the context. *on a snowy day:* when it could be tracked easily.

21. *the Egyptian* may well have been a mercenary soldier with the Philistines: the incident has some similarities to the story told of David and the giant in 1 Sam. 17.

23. *David appointed him to his household:* or perhaps better (cp. note on 1 Sam. 22: 14) 'to his bodyguard'. This detail, not related elsewhere, paves the way for Benaiah to become Joab's successor; he has already held high office under David.

24. The remainder of the chapter lists other warriors, presumably all members of *the thirty*. For *Asahel*, cp. 2: 18–23. *Elhanan:* cp. also on 21: 19. *Dodo* could be rendered 'his uncle'. We may recall that Joab and his brothers were cousins of David.

26. *Tekoa:* home of Amos (cp. Amos 1: 1; map, p. 29).

27. *Anathoth:* home of Jeremiah (cp. Jer. 1: 1; map, p. 29), and the place to which Abiathar the priest went after his deposition by Solomon (1 Kings 2: 26).

30. *Benaiah:* presumably not the same man as was mentioned in verse 20.

34. *Ahithophel:* cp. on 11: 3 and the note on p. 162).

35. *Carmel:* in the south (cp. map, p. 29); cp. on 1 Sam. 15: 12.

37. *Ammonite:* a foreigner in David's service (cp. on verse 39).

39. *Uriah the Hittite:* cp. on 11: 3; possibly also a foreigner in David's service, though we note that his name suggests one whose family had become fully part of Israel. The total *thirty-seven* is odd: presumably it is designed to cover the whole section, but the number of names does not exactly fit, possibly because of some textual error.

We may note that the Chronicler's text uses this material as part of a larger section stressing the loyalty of men to David. Here it is isolated. ✻

THE CENSUS AND PLAGUE

24 1[a] Once again the Israelites felt the LORD's anger, when he incited David against them and gave him orders that
2 Israel and Judah should be counted. So he instructed Joab and the officers of the army[b] with him to go round all the tribes of Israel, from Dan to Beersheba, and make a record of the people and report the number to him.
3 Joab answered, 'Even if the LORD your God should increase the people a hundredfold and your majesty should live to see it, what pleasure would that give your

[a] *Verses 1–25: cp. 1 Chron. 21: 1–27.*
[b] Joab . . . army: *prob. rdg., cp. 1 Chron. 21: 2; Heb.* Joab the officer of the army.

majesty?' But Joab and the officers were overruled by the 4
king and they left his presence in order to count the
people. They crossed the Jordan and began at Aroer and 5
the level land of the gorge, proceeding towards Gad*a*
and Jazer. They came to Gilead and to the land of the 6
Hittites, to Kadesh,*b* and then to Dan and Iyyon*c* and so
round*d* towards Sidon. They went as far as the walled 7
city of Tyre and all the towns of the Hivites and Canaanites, and then went on to the Negeb of Judah at Beersheba. They covered the whole country and arrived back 8
at Jerusalem after nine months and twenty days. Joab 9
reported to the king the total number of people: the
number of able-bodied men, capable of bearing arms,
was eight hundred thousand in Israel and five hundred
thousand in Judah.

After he had counted the people David's conscience*e* 10
smote him, and he said to the LORD, 'I have done a very
wicked thing: I pray thee, LORD, remove thy servant's
guilt, for I have been very foolish.' He rose next morning, 11
and meanwhile the command of the LORD had come to
the prophet Gad, David's seer, to go and speak to David: 12
'This is the word of the LORD: I have three things in
store for you; choose one and I will bring it upon you.'
So Gad came to David and repeated this to him and said, 13
'Is it to be three*f* years of famine in your land, or three
months of flight with the enemy at your heels, or three

[a] began at . . . Gad: *prob. rdg.; Heb.* encamped in Aroer on the right
of the level land of the gorge Gad.
[b] of the Hittites, to Kadesh: *so Luc. Sept.; Heb.* of Tahtim, Hodshi.
[c] *Prob. rdg., cp. 1 Kings 15: 20; Heb.* Yaan.
[d] *So Sept., Heb. obscure.*   [e] *Lit.* heart.
[f] *So Sept., cp. 1 Chron. 21: 12; Heb.* seven.

days of pestilence in your land? Consider carefully what
14 answer I am to take back to him who sent me.' Thereupon
David said to Gad, 'I am in a desperate plight; let us fall
into the hands of the LORD, for his mercy is great;
15 and let me not fall into the hands of men.' So the LORD
sent a pestilence throughout Israel from morning till the
hour of dinner, and from Dan to Beersheba seventy
16 thousand of the people died. Then the angel stretched
out his arm towards Jerusalem to destroy it; but the LORD
repented of the evil and said to the angel who was destroying the people, 'Enough! Stay your hand.' At that
moment the angel of the LORD was standing by the
threshing-floor of Araunah the Jebusite.
17   When David saw the angel who was striking down the
people, he said to the LORD, 'It is I who have done wrong,
the sin is mine; but these poor sheep, what have they
done? Let thy hand fall upon me and upon my family.'
18 That same day Gad came to David and said to him,
'Go and set up an altar to the LORD on the threshing-
19 floor of Araunah the Jebusite.' David did what Gad
told him to do, and went up as the LORD had commanded.
20 When Araunah looked down and saw the king and his
servants coming over towards him, he went out, pros-
21 trated himself low before the king and said, 'Why has
your majesty come to visit his servant?' David answered,
'To buy the threshing-floor from you to build an altar
to the LORD, so that the plague which has attacked the
22 people may be stopped.' Araunah answered David,
'I beg your majesty to take it and sacrifice what you
think fit. I have here the oxen for a whole-offering, and
their harness and the threshing-sledges for the fuel.'

Araunah[a] gave it all to the king for his own use and said 23
to him, 'May the LORD your God accept you.' But the 24
king said to Araunah, 'No, I will buy it from you; I
will not offer to the LORD my God whole-offerings that
have cost me nothing.' So David bought the threshing-
floor and the oxen for fifty shekels of silver. He built an 25
altar to the LORD there and offered whole-offerings and
shared-offerings. Then the LORD yielded to his prayer
for the land; and the plague in Israel stopped.

* This chapter is closely linked in theme with 21: 1–14 (cp.
p. 193). Both stories concern natural disasters which are interpreted as divine judgement for human sin; both tell how
divine favour is invoked. This latter story leads up to the
acquisition of a threshing-floor on which a great sacrifice is
offered. Nothing further is said of its significance. The later
form of the narrative, however, in 1 Chron. 21: 1 – 22: 1,
which differs in some important points, culminates in the
identifying of the threshing-floor as the designated site of the
Jerusalem temple, and thus integrates this story into the whole
sequence of narratives. It may be that the compiler who placed
the story here at the end of 2 Samuel, just before the accession
of Solomon which leads on into the temple building, believed
this to be the real significance of what he was relating. But he
does not make this explicit, and we should not assume that the
identification was made at an early date. The tendency to
identify and hence to explain is often strong in biblical
narratives.

1. *Once again:* a clear link to 21: 1–4. *he incited David:* the
responsibility for the wrong action is attributed directly to
God (cp. 1 Kings 22: 21f. where a 'spirit' from the heavenly
court undertakes to be a 'lying spirit' and to lead all the prophets astray). In 1 Chron. 21: 1 'Satan' or 'an adversary', a

[a] *Prob. rdg., Heb. adds* the king.

member of the heavenly court (cp. on 19: 22), is substituted, thereby shifting the responsibility and avoiding some part of the theological difficulty posed by making God act himself. We may see this story as depicting a testing of David and of Israel; the narrator leaves it to his readers to appreciate the problems of divine–human relationships and their description. *and gave him orders:* both here and in verse 2 'to go round', the N.E.B. has turned the vivid direct speech of the Hebrew into this indirect form. It would be more impressive as 'Go and count Israel and Judah' and 'Go round all the tribes of Israel.' *Israel and Judah* are treated as two separate entities (cp. verse 9).

2. *the officers of the army:* as also in verse 4. The Hebrew text accidentally omits the words (cp. the N.E.B. footnote). *Dan to Beersheba:* a common way of stating the limits of the land (cp. on 3: 9f.).

3. Joab protests against what David proposed; he is apparently aware of the impropriety of such an action. '*Even if...*': an alternative sense would be: 'May the LORD your God increase...and may you see it. But why does your majesty take pleasure in this thing (i.e. this improper act)?' (cp. 1 Chron. 21: 3). It is not clear why a census is here regarded as wrong, since an enumeration of the people appears as divinely commanded in Num. 1. Evidently to some it appeared improper, perhaps because it was felt that the increase of population must be regarded as a divine gift; it may be that some primitive ideas underlie the reluctance to enumerate. From verse 9 it can be seen that the purpose of the census was a military one, and from this we might deduce that the narrator saw here a theme often found in the prophets (e.g. Isa. 31: 1) concerning wrong trust in military power. God, the reader is often reminded, can save by few or many (cp. 1 Sam. 14: 6).

5–7. These verses give a rough idea of the extent of the kingdom by listing the main boundaries, though not every detail is clear. *and the level land of the gorge:* cp. the N.E.B. footnote, though the text could mean 'they encamped south of the city'. *the land of the Hittites:* if this is correct, it must refer to the small kingdoms north of Israel, areas once under Hittite control and remaining so named after the collapse of the Hittite Empire around 1200 B.C. Assyrian texts speak of the western (Syro-Palestinian) area as 'Hatti-land'. *Kadesh:* also uncertain, but perhaps the important town on the Orontes river (see map, p. 85). *all the towns of the Hivites and Canaanites:* a general description of the coastal areas of Phoenicia and southwards, not under Israelite control but marking the border.

8. The length of time must allow for stays in local centres to get details of the manpower in each area.

9. *able-bodied men, capable of bearing arms:* the purpose of the census is linked to military service. We may compare the criticism of kingship in 1 Sam. 8: 11 for taking men for military duties. The separate enumeration of Israel and Judah indicates their separate administrative and military organization.

10. The piety of David in recognizing his fault is somewhat unexpected. We should have expected the narrative to continue with the direct statement of divine judgement as in 1 Chron. 21: 7. Perhaps the narrator, or a later commentator, has sought to moderate the degree of David's responsibility. The prayer of David is conventional and appears not to be taken into account in what follows.

11. *He rose next morning:* David is envisaged as praying all night, presumably in the shrine (cp. 12: 16). *and meanwhile:* the N.E.B. thus correlates the statements. More naturally we may begin a new sentence: 'Now the word of the LORD came...' *the prophet Gad, David's seer:* mentioned also in 1 Sam. 22: 5 where he warns David of impending danger. In 1 Chron. 29: 29 a later tradition associates him with other prophetic figures as recording the events of David's reign. Clearly his activity as a prophet, closely associated with David, as a kind of court religious adviser, is similar to that ascribed in other narratives to Nathan (cp. chapter 12 and 1 Kings 1). The text uses two different words for prophet; cp. 1 Sam. 9: 9 where, however, the word for 'seer' is not the

one used here. Here we see the prophet as the one who delivers a message of judgement from God; this function is often to be found with the great prophets of the eighth century B.C. onwards – Amos, Hosea, Isaiah and their successors to the time of exile. Prophets as advisers to kings are found in other parts of the ancient Near East from very early times.

12. *three things in store:* literally 'I am imposing three things.' David is offered a choice of judgements, set out in full in verse 13.

13. *three years of famine:* since the other judgements are in terms of *three months* and *three days,* this correction of the Hebrew text is right. The text has 'seven' (cp. the N.E.B. footnote), which may have been influenced by, for example, the story of seven years' famine in Egypt (Gen. 41). The number three also provides a precise correspondence with the 'three years' of famine in 21: 1. The presentation of the three judgements is in a poetic style: we are presumably to regard them as equivalent in their severity. There is also a skilful point in the way that David is now forced to take the responsibility for making the right choice for his people. *him who sent me:* the prophet is one who is 'sent' by God, a messenger on his behalf to carry his word to his people.

14. David's response is an expression of his right attitude to God, whom he knows as more merciful than man. It is evident from the sequel that he has shown discernment in making the right choice, since the full rigour of judgement is withdrawn. Of the three judgements, only the second, warfare, is the result of human agency; both famine and pestilence would qualify for David's choice. The Septuagint explicitly makes David choose the third judgement. But the point is clear nevertheless. The language of this verse is strongly reminiscent of some psalm passages (cp. 22: 7 = Ps. 18: 6; Ps. 51: 1). The narrator has used appropriate liturgical language, traditionally associated with David, to express David's own thoughts.

15. *till the hour of dinner:* i.e. the midday meal (so the Septuagint) but such a meaning for the Hebrew word is very

improbable; it could mean 'the appointed time', i.e. the time decreed by God for bringing the disaster to an end, but this would more naturally denote the end of the three days. Another possibility is to see a reference to an appointed religious moment, an hour of sacrifice, suggesting that a moment of worship evoked a merciful response from God. The moment of the withdrawal of judgement would then coincide with the moment at which prayer was regularly offered, perhaps the evening act of worship. *seventy thousand:* numbers with seven and seventy are most often conventional rather than literal; this means 'a very great number'.

16. *the angel:* the agent of divine destruction, described in the next clause as 'the destroying angel' (cp. Exod. 12: 23 for such a destroyer in Egypt, 2 Kings 19: 35 at the overthrow of the Assyrians, and Ezek. 9: 1 for the application of the theme to total judgement on Jerusalem). *stretched out his arm:* 1 Chron. 21: 16 pictures the angel with drawn sword between earth and heaven, and this element appears in a Qumran text of Samuel. A total destruction of Jerusalem is here anticipated but withdrawn. Such special protection of Jerusalem provides a link with ideas of God's special care for his city and of its inviolability while so under his hand (cp. Isa. 37: 33–5; Ps. 46: 5). The narrator is perhaps reminding his readers that the final disaster to the city did not come without previous warnings (cp. also 2 Kings 19: 32–5). *standing by the threshing-floor of Araunah the Jebusite:* apparently incidentally the final and crucial stage of the narrative is introduced. In fact we are told that God has already halted the judgement; the final stage links his compassion with the offering of worship in a newly-established holy place, and thus serves to authenticate that place. On Araunah, cp. verse 23. He appears only in this narrative: his name in 1 Chron. 21: 15 is given as Ornan.

17. *It is I who have done wrong, the sin is mine:* the text offers a more poetic parallel: 'It is I who have sinned: even I who have acted wrongly.' As often, Hebrew prose acquires a rhythmic structure in moments of emotion. *these poor sheep:*

a Qumran manuscript has appropriately in the preceding phrase 'even I, the shepherd, have done wrong'. *me and . . . my family:* the sentiment fits the description of David well, but it is not easy to see how it relates to the preceding narrative. Perhaps we have here a clue to the originally separate nature of this last section of the chapter.

18. *set up an altar:* no blame is suggested for David's setting up an altar in a place other than the shrine at Jerusalem; this suggests that an identification is already implied with the temple site, though it does not necessarily follow that the identification is correct. *the threshing-floor:* as an exposed level place, naturally outside the city and appearing in 1 Kings 22: 10 as a place of public assembly (the N.E.B. here paraphrases as 'the entrance to the gate'). It would clearly make a good place for public worship, and perhaps religious rituals were already associated with such places since harvesting had its religious significance (cp. worship at the wine-press in Judg. 9: 27).

19. Again, as in verse 17, the N.E.B. misses the parallelism of the phrases: 'David went up at God's command: just as the LORD had ordered him.'

20f. The purchase of *the threshing-floor* and the building of *an altar* are here clearly designed to bring an end to *the plague* – a quite different word from that rendered 'pestilence' in verses 13 and 15.

22. Araunah's piety is exemplified by his response: he will give all that is needed. *their harness and the threshing-sledges:* the order is reversed from that of the text. For a similar sacrificial action cp. 1 Sam. 6: 14. Threshing-sledges are made of wooden boards with sharp stones on the under side; they are drawn over the grain by the oxen.

23. The text (cp. the N.E.B. footnote) is puzzling. Most commentators, followed by the N.E.B., omit 'the king' with *Araunah*: it is true that it may simply result from a double writing of the next word *to the king* which refers to David. But could the text be right? In that case, Araunah is here named as

the Jebusite king. The point could possibly be further confirmed by the fact that in verse 16 the name 'Araunah' has the
definite article, i.e. 'the Araunah'. Could this be a title, rather
than a name? Its derivation from a Hittite or Hurrian word
meaning 'lord' has been proposed. This would put a different
complexion on this story. We should then have a portrayal of
the Jebusite ruler of Jerusalem submitting to David, and David
as new ruler taking over the threshing-floor, perhaps already a
holy place, as his own. Does the narrative possibly conceal an
attempt at explaining how an ancient holy place of the former
inhabitants of the city became, as tradition was to have it, the
site of the new temple? This would be an example, of which
there are others (cp. Bethel in Gen. 28: 10–22), of a 'sanctuary
legend', telling how a holy place came to be so revered, and in
particular how an older holy place became one associated with
Israel's religion. But these are only possibilities, hinted at by
various odd features in the text.

24. David's piety answers that of Araunah: he cannot
accept a gift, but must pay the price: '*I will not offer to the
LORD* that which has *cost me nothing*': worship is the expression of a man's giving of his own to God.

25. *Then the LORD yielded:* the final sentence sums up the
story. The new place of worship and the sacrifices bring about
the withdrawal of divine anger.

The narrative of this chapter is at first sight coherent, but
examination of its detail suggests the possibility that three
originally separate elements have been combined and partly
though not wholly integrated. The census, plague and holy-
place themes are really in some measure distinct. In the final
form, the story may well have been designed to make im-
plicitly the point that in 1 Chron. 21: 1 – 22: 1 is made
explicitly: out of disaster, God brings good. David's folly led
to the new and lasting holy place, just as his sin with Bathsheba
brought the birth of Solomon (cp. the notes on chapter 12).

Such a view of the chapter would explain the inconsisten-
cies. The census, apparently so displeasing to God, is so only

because it has now been linked to the story of the pestilence. The pestilence could originally have been the sequel to some other act of disobedience; its fullest effects are withdrawn in a spontaneous act of divine mercy. The story of the threshing-floor is linked then to another disaster, a 'plague', and it is only with the offering of worship on the designated site that this is withdrawn. But the whole makes an impressive conclusion to the book, both as a reminder of David's relationship to God and as a pointer to the establishment of the temple in 1 Kings. ✻

✻ ✻ ✻ ✻ ✻ ✻ ✻ ✻ ✻ ✻ ✻ ✻ ✻

THE MESSAGE OF THE BOOK

The story does not stop here. It has already been observed that to read either the first or the second book of Samuel by itself is to read only an instalment of a much longer work (Deuteronomy to 2 Kings). The break between the two books, at the death of Saul (1 Sam. 31), is convenient; but it cuts into the continuous narrative. The fact that in 2 Samuel the last chapters (21–4) form an appendix to what precedes, makes the break here equally convenient; with 1 Kings 1 we may be said to resume the series of stories told in the chapters leading up to 2 Sam. 20. But in reality there is no break. As we have seen (p. 3), the Greek translation calls the four books, Samuel and Kings, the books of Kingdoms or Reigns. Some of the Greek texts make the break not after 24: 25 but at the death of David in 1 Kings 2: 11; yet others indicate a division at the end of 1 Kings 2, starting the new book with 'Thus Solomon's royal power was securely established' (2: 46b). We must not let the divisions familiar to us in the English translations obscure the need to read on.

When we consider the content of 2 Samuel, we see how right this is. In the brief notes at the end of the commentary in this series on 1 Samuel (pp. 230f.), it is pointed out that that book shows the moves forward, towards a true priesthood, a true holy temple, a true monarchy. Each of these is taken further by 2 Samuel. The theme of the priesthood is much less evident, but we have seen how, without explanation, a new priest, Zadok, appears on the scene (8: 17 and 15: 24); it is he who will take over from Abiathar in 1 Kings 2: 26f. (cp. 1: 32–40). He is the head of the priestly line which comes to be regarded as the one legitimate priesthood of Jerusalem (cp. e.g. 1 Chron. 6: 1–15). The theme of the true shrine is subtly developed. David captures Jerusalem (chapter 5) and the way is open for the taking in of the Ark, symbol of God's presence with his people (chapter 6). David's wish to build a temple is rejected, but the presentation of this theme in chapter 7 draws out the assurance that it will be built, though by his son (Solomon, not yet named, but to be born at 12: 24f.). The story of chapter 24, not explicitly linked to the site of the temple, though later (1 Chron. 22: 1) given that link, is so placed as to point the reader forward to what he knows Solomon will do. The way is open for the culmination of this development. True monarchy, foreshadowed in 1 Samuel, is now plainly established in the figure of David; and the long, almost unbroken, line of his descendants down to the beginning of the sixth century B.C., roughly a 400-year period, testifies to the validity of that kingship. Whatever may have to be said by way of criticism of the monarchy, and there is much of this in 1 and 2 Kings, the institution itself and David, the founder of the dynasty, are seen as divinely chosen and supported. Yet, right from the start, there are reminders that kingship is at the same time a human institution, an imperfect expression of God's will for his people. Kings may rise and fall, as was true of the family of Saul; the opening chapters of 2 Samuel (1–4) remind us of this, and subsequent allusions point to the complete rejection of Saul's line (cp. on chapter 6 and the stories of Mephibosheth and Shimei). But David too is under judgement. The contrasting pictures of his successes and failures underline this. He is the chosen king, brought to a climax of power and victory over all his enemies; and he is the one who sins and falls under judgement. It is in the Absalom story that the two aspects are mostly closely interwoven, for here the judgement on David pronounced in 12: 10–14 is fully brought about; yet the fugitive king, rejected by his favourite son and by many of his people, still meets with loyalty and through this darkest hour comes again to his full royal status.

But this is not just a series of stories told about the period of David. More than once in the comments on the text it has been suggested that the writer or compiler has in mind an audience for whom the temple is destroyed and Davidic kingship has come to an end. What meaning do these assurances of divine choice and divine blessing have for those in exile or in a devastated homeland in the sixth century B.C., the time when the whole Deuteronomic History reached its virtually final form (cp. p. 4)? The assurance lies in the story of what God has done. He gave Israel a land; the land has been lost, but implicit in the story is the promise of a renewed entry for a people obedient to the law (this is especially underlined in Deuteronomy and Joshua). He made Israel a united people under a true king and with a true place of worship. The unity is broken, the people is scattered, king and temple gone; but implicit in the telling of the story is the belief that the promises of God are firm. Men's failure may frustrate his purpose, but it cannot alter his nature. The experience of their history, for those who endeavoured to draw out its meaning, was a way towards the fuller understanding of that nature and purpose. The storyteller becomes the teacher and the theological interpreter; he tells a good story and his artistry is fascinating. But if the reader stops at the story and does not ask about the meaning, then he is hearing only part of what it is all about.

Already in these two books of Samuel and still more in the narratives of the books of Kings, the storyteller underlines this theological purpose by portraying within the story those with whom he particularly associated interpretation, the prophetic figures, from Samuel to Gad and Nathan; these are to be followed by others, named and unnamed. Remarkably, except for one passage in 2 Kings 18–20 where Isaiah is portrayed, the great prophets of Israel do not appear in the story as these books present it to us. But our reading of these books and our understanding of their significance depend upon an awareness of the prophets' interpretation of the experience of their people; the Deuteronomic writers owed much to prophetic thought. We must read the prophets alongside this narrative interpretation; the narratives provide us with something of the background and of the context of prophetic teaching; they also provide us with an exemplification in story form of the consequences of disobedience and of obedience to the divine will as this is declared supremely clearly by the prophets, though also by the lawgivers and the psalmists and the wise in ancient Israel. The story becomes a vehicle of truth, to be evaluated and assimilated, and long outlasting the particular moments described or the particular audiences to which it was once directed.

A NOTE ON FURTHER READING

A fuller commentary on 2 Samuel may be found in H. W. Hertzberg, *I and II Samuel* (S.C.M. Old Testament Library, 1964), based largely on the R.S.V.; shorter but useful commentaries are by W. McKane (S.C.M. Torch series, 1963; paperback 1967), J. Mauchline (New Century Bible, Oliphants, 1971) and R. D. Gehrke (Concordia Commentary, St Louis, 1968). Background material for the period may be found in the first two volumes of the New Clarendon Bible (Oxford University Press, 1966 and 1971) and in B. W. Anderson, *The Living World of the Old Testament* (Longmans, 2nd ed. 1967). The reader who is interested in institutions will find much that is of importance discussed in R. de Vaux, *Ancient Israel* (Darton, Longman and Todd, 1961) and in articles in the Bible dictionaries and one-volume commentaries. From these, he may be guided further into the wealth of other literature concerned with history, archaeology, religion and theology which has a bearing on questions raised by the study of this book of the Old Testament.

Reference is made in the text to the collection of documents published as *Ancient Near Eastern Texts relating to the Old Testament*, ed. J. B. Pritchard (Princeton University Press, 3rd ed. 1969), abbreviated as *A.N.E.T.* The companion volume, *The Ancient Near East in Pictures relating to the Old Testament*, ed. J. B. Pritchard (Princeton University Press, 2nd ed. 1969), will also be found useful.

INDEX